The Twentieth-Century World of Henry James

Flatiron Building, Broadway and Fifth Avenue, built in 1903. Photograph from 1905. *Courtesy the Museum of the City of New York*

The Twentieth-Century World of
Henry James

CHANGES IN HIS WORK AFTER 1900

Adeline R. Tintner

 LOUISIANA STATE UNIVERSITY PRESS

BATON ROUGE   MM

First printing
09 08 07 06 05 04 03 02 01 00
5 4 3 2 1

Designer: Erin Kirk New
Typeface: New Caledonia
Typesetter: Coghill Composition Co., Inc.
Printer and binder: Thomson-Shore, Inc.

Parts of some of the chapters in this book originally appeared in a somewhat different form as articles in the following publications as noted. The author is grateful to their editors for permission to use this material. Portions of Chapter 1 appeared as "Landmarks of 'The Terrible Town': The New York Scene in Henry James's Last Stories," in Volume 2 of *Prospects* (Burt Franklin, 1976), ed. Jack Saltzman, and "An Interlude in Hell: James's 'A Round of Visits' and *Paradise Lost*," *Notes on Modern American Literature*, 5 (Spring 1981). Portions of Chapter 2 appeared as "The House of Atreus and Madame de Bellegarde's Crime," *Notes and Queries*, 20 (March 1973), "Sir Sidney Colvin in *The Golden Bowl*: Mr. Crichton Identified," *Colby Library Quarterly*, Series 10 (September 1974), and "A Source for Prince Amerigo in *The Golden Bowl*," *Notes on Modern American Literature*, 2 (Summer 1978). Portions of Chapter 3 appeared as " 'In the Dusky, Crowded, Heterogeneous Back-Shop of the Mind': The Iconography of *The Portrait of a Lady*," *Henry James Review*, 7 (Winter–Spring 1986) and "Autobiography as Fiction: The Usurping Consciousness as Hero of James's Memoirs," *Twentieth Century Literature*, 23 (1977): 239–68. A portion of Chapter 4 appeared as " 'The Great Condition': Henry James and Bergsonian Time," *Studies in Short Fiction*, 21 (Spring 1984). Portions of Chapter 5 appeared as "A Gay *Sacred Fount*: The Reader as Detective," *Twentieth Century Literature*, 41 (1995): 224–41, and "A Bibliographical and Biographical Note: Henry James's Markings in Zola's *La Débâcle*," *Henry James Review*, 17 (1996): 204–207. A portion of Chapter 6 appeared as "Some Notes for a Study of the Gissing Phase in Henry James's Fiction," *Gissing Newsletter* Vol. 16, no 3 (1980). A portion of Chapter 8 appeared as "Henry James and the First World War: The Release from Repression," in *Literature and War: Papers of the 1984 Monterey Institute of International Studies Symposium*, ed. Elizabeth W. Trahan (Monterey Institute of International Studies, 1985).

Library of Congress Cataloging-in-Publication Data:

Tintner, Adeline R., 1912–
     The twentieth-century world of Henry James : changes in his work after 1900 / Adeline R. Tintner.
         p. cm.
     Includes bibliographical references and index.
     ISBN 0-8071-2534-2 (cloth : alk. paper) — ISBN 0-8071-2604-7 (pbk. : alk. paper)
     1. James, Henry, 1843–1916—Criticism and interpretation.   2. Literature and society—United States—History—20th century.   3. Literature and society—England—History—20th century.   4. Modernism (Literature)—United States. 5. Modernism (Literature)—England.   I. Title.

PS2124.T56   2000
813'.4—dc21   99-059203

The paper in this book meets the guidelines for permanence and durability of the Committee on Production Guidelines for Book Longevity of the Council on Library Resources. ⊗

Again for Henry Janowitz, the other H.J.

Contents

Acknowledgments

I wish to thank the entire staff of the New York Society Library in New York City, headed by Mark Piel, for providing the many titles used in this book nowhere else obtainable. I am once more in debt to Professor Donald D. Stone for his reading of this manuscript and for his thoughtful decisions about what should be revised and what should be retained or eliminated. I am grateful to Professor Pierre Coustillas, the "chairman of the board" of George Gissing studies, for encouraging me in my intertextual work on Gissing's and James's fiction, which he published over a period of a few years in his remarkable journal *The Gissing Newsletter*. Finally, I am grateful to the editorial staff at Louisiana State University, especially its executive editor, John Easterly, who has always gone out of his way to see to my needs. Christine Cowan has edited the manuscript with remarkable lucidity and has clarified many an opaque statement. Michael Griffith has once more checked details and quotations with his customary dependability. Linda Webster has provided me as usual with a fine index, and Elizabeth Armour has made superior hard copy, as she has done with all my books. In spite of all this aid, I am responsible for any errors that may have slipped in.

Illustrations

Abbreviations

I–XII	*The Complete Tales of Henry James,* ed. Leon Edel (12 vols.; Philadelphia, 1961–64)
AM	Henry James, *The Ambassadors* (New York, 1964)
AN	Henry James, *The Art of the Novel* (New York, 1934)
AS	Henry James, *The American Scene,* ed. Leon Edel (Bloomington, Ind., 1969)
AU	Henry James, *Autobiography* (1956; rpr. Princeton, 1983)
BG	Edith Wharton, *A Backward Glance* (New York, 1934)
BL	*The Bazar Letters,* ed. Leon Edel and Lyall H. Powers (New York, 1958)
BS	*The Twenty-five Best Plays of the Modern American Theater,* ed. John Gessner (New York, 1952)
CH	Ron Chernow, *The House of Morgan* (New York, 1990)
CN	*The Complete Notebooks of Henry James,* ed. Leon Edel and Lyall H. Powers (New York, 1987)
CP	*The Complete Plays of Henry James,* ed. Leon Edel (Philadelphia, 1949)
CQ	Leon Edel, *Henry James: The Conquest of London* (Philadelphia, 1962)
DB	Connie Willis, *Doomsday Book* (New York, 1992)
DF	Rhoda Broughton, *Dear Faustina* (New York, 1895)
DFS	Patricia Lorrimer Lundberg, "Dialogic Fiction of the Supernatural," ELT, XLI, No. 4 (1998), 389–407
EL	Henry James, *English Literature: Essays* (New York, 1984)

GB   Lucas Malet, *The Gateless Barrier* (New York, 1900)

HGW   *Henry James and H. G. Wells,* ed. Leon Edel and Gordon N.
            Ray (London, 1959)

HJC   *Henry James and Culture,* ed. Pierre A. Walker (Lincoln,
            1999)

HJL, IV   *Henry James Letters,* Vol. IV of 4 vols. (Cambridge, Mass.,
            1984)

IT   Henry James, *Collected Travel Writings: The Continent* (New
            York, 1993)

LA   Rupert Brooke, *Letters from America* (New York, 1916)

LD   Emile Zola, *La Débâcle* (Paris, 1892)

LE   Adeline R. Tintner, *Henry James and the Lust of the Eyes*
            (Baton Rouge, 1993)

LM   Simon Nowell-Smith, *The Legend of the Master* (New York,
            1948)

LU, II   *The Letters of Henry James,* ed. Percy Lubbock, Vol. II of 2
            vols. (New York, 1920)

MA   Leon Edel, *Henry James: The Master* (Philadelphia, 1974)

MY   Leon Edel, *Henry James: The Middle Years* (Philadelphia,
            1962)

NGS   George Gissing, *New Grub Street* (1891; rpr. New York,
            1926)

NN   Henry James, *Notes on Novelists* (New York, 1914)

NYE, I–   *The Novels and Tales of Henry James* (24 vols.; New York,
NYE, XXIV   1907–1909), known as the New York Edition

OC   Henry Newbolt, *The Old Country* (London, 1906)

P   Marcel Proust, *Remembrance of Things Past,* trans. C. K.
            Scott Moncrieff and Terence Kilmartin (3 vols.; New York,
            1981), Vol. I.

PL   John Milton, *Paradise Lost and Paradise Regained* (New
            York, 1968)

PO   Henry James, *The Portrait of a Lady* (1881; rpr. New York,
            1963)

PW   Adeline R. Tintner, *The Pop World of Henry James* (Ann
            Arbor, 1989)

PY	James Joyce, *A Portrait of the Artist as a Young Man* (New York, 1928)
RH	Henry James, *Roderick Hudson* (1875; rpr. London, 1969)
RM	*Selected Letters of Henry James to Edmund Gosse,* ed. Rayburn S. Moore (Baton Rouge, 1988)
RO	William Roughead, *Tales of the Criminous* (London, 1956)
RP	Henry James, *The Portrait of a Lady,* ed. Leon Edel (Boston, 1963), reprint of 1908 edition
SF	Henry James, *The Sacred Fount* (1901; rpr. New York, 1953)
SP	Henry James, *The Sense of the Past* (London, 1917)
TM, I– *TM,* II	Henry James, *The Tragic Muse* (2 vols.; rpr. New York, 1908)
TR	Leon Edel, *Henry James: The Treacherous Years* (Philadelphia, 1969)
TS	Thalia Schaffer, "Some Chapter of Some Other Story: Henry James, Lucas Malet, and The Real Past of *The Sense of the Past,*" *Henry James Review,* XVII, No. 2 (1996), 109–29.
UL	*Three Unpublished Letters and a Monologue by Henry James* (London, 1922)
VFP	*Victorian Fairy Painting* ed. Jane Martineau. Catalog of an exhibition at the Frick Collection, New York City, from October 13, 1998, to January 17, 1999.
WF	*The Whole Family* (New York, 1908)
WR	Henry James, *Within the Rim and Other Essays* (London, 1919)

The Twentieth-Century World of Henry James

Introduction

It is convenient at present to conclude a study of Henry James with the completed novels of the major phase and the revisions of the New York Edition (1907–1909). However, James lived on to write vigorously for a decade longer. Not only did he continue to create, but he did so in a manner that proclaimed him a writer who heralded the modernist period some time before such writers as James Joyce, Marcel Proust, and T. S. Eliot became the full-blown representatives of the first quarter of the twentieth century. The topics of this volume represent a personal selection of some of the modernist themes that preoccupied Henry James as he entered the new century and that, in turn, were to preoccupy many of the writers who came to maturity in the first half of the twentieth century. James is a writer who alluded to the "kodak," "flying-machine," and "the cinematograph" in three stories published in 1909.[1] He also is the man who, in one of these tales, referred to being "snap-shotted," who is the first serious creative writer to make the skyscraper submit to his detailed and pervasive analysis, and who was equally aware of the overwhelming technological development of the new century.[2] Indeed, his last three completed novels published in the first four years of the twentieth century had adumbrated some new emerging patterns of the novel.

The twentieth century came to life for James when he confronted it dur-

---

1. "Kodak," in XII, 249 ("The Velvet Glove," 1909); "flying-machine," in XII, 316 ("Mora Montravers," 1909); and "the cinematograph," in XII, 343 ("Crapy Cornelia," 1909).

2. "Snap-shotted," in XII, 339 ("Crapy Cornelia," 1909).

ing his long delayed visit to America in 1904 and 1905. When *The Golden Bowl* appeared in November, 1904, James was already in the New World. The new New York electrified him like the "electric button at his door" and the electric trolley car, inventions that invaded the stories of 1909 and 1910.[3] The city confronted him, overwhelmed him, and his favorite epithet for it was "the terrible town," while, at the same time, its horrors also held wonders for him. It foretold to him that the new century was to focus on finance, that the number of rich men was to increase and set the stage for the multiplication of the millionaires and billionaires who now populate America. He foresaw it all, as we see from the incomplete *Ivory Tower*, written in 1917, as well as from the seven stories he wrote after he returned to England in 1905. It is only now that *The American Scene* is being read as he had hoped it would have been read in 1907, for it took almost a century for the truths about his native country to be appreciated—truths he alone discovered in their embryonic stages. It was he also who responded to the growing interest in and the appreciation and collecting of art in this country (which has exploded in the 1990s), from its first appearance in the monied class to the nationwide religion of art—art-watching, art-collecting, and art-worshipping—all symptomatic of our life in America today. It appeared in an intense form in his last novel, *The Outcry*.

The romance of art, which occupied much of *The American Scene,* joins in James's mind the romance of finance, for in the twentieth century "downtown" changes from a long-neglected topic into a newly discovered donnée for the twentieth-century James. "Downtown" is no longer totally evil but also now curiously attractive, in spite of the horror it can cause for those who trust its agents, as we see not only in "A Round of Visits" but also in "The Bench of Desolation" and in *The Ivory Tower*. We see making money as a worthwhile activity, as well as an evil one, operating in "The Jolly Corner," "A Round of Visits," and *The Ivory Tower*. Having a genius for financial investment makes it possible for a destructive woman like Kate Cookham to become a benefactor in "The Bench of Desolation."

The impact of the New World on James's long-standing "lust of the eyes" makes him now for the first time aware of the glory of the Impressionist

3. "The electric button at his door" and an electric trolley-car, "a choked trolley-car that howled," in XII, 443, 442 ("A Round of Visits," 1910).

painters Claude Monet and Edgar Degas when he sees them grouped together by the unerring taste of a collector in a private house in Farmington, Connecticut, yet it is in Boston, far from the land of its origin and at the other end of the time spectrum, that he feels a fragment of Greek sculpture finally and fully reveal its beauty.

The trip to America seems to have revitalized his review of his whole oeuvre. The older James confronts the young James as in Max Beerbohm's witty cartoon. The older James corrects his omission of Pinturicchio as a great artistic experience for him while he was writing *Roderick Hudson* in 1874, by inserting the painter in his 1907 revision. Revising the book for the New York Edition, he drops a phrase here and there in *The American* to further his intentions. In his revision of *The Portrait of a Lady,* he refines Isabel Archer's aesthetic tastes to match his own.

James's intense interest in "the usurping consciousness" led to his discovery that autobiography also could be a form of experimental fiction, and in his *Notes of a Son and Brother* he defended *his* version of the truth. He also saw the limits of this approach and parodied it in his "Monologue for Ruth Draper."

We can see how James anticipated several of the chief ideas that would dominate modern literature, such as the concept of time in Proust's novel. These included James's intuition of the theories about time that Henri-Louis Bergson was formulating philosophically. James presented in a short story, "The Great Condition," the practical observations of time as duration and time as an abstraction. Close analysis of this tale reveals it as an imaginative reworking of the Bergsonian concept. Whatever his fragmentary knowledge of Proust may have been, James had begun his own attempt to recapture the past in his unfinished novel *The Sense of the Past,* which curiously parallels Henry Newbolt's *The Old Country.*

In addition, James showed a new concern with the deprivation of culture among the lower middle classes, a concern seemingly stimulated by his personal introduction to George Gissing at the turn of the century in 1901. It was a concern that would be part of the literature of the twentieth century in both the United States and Great Britain.

James's interest in sexuality seems, after the turn of the century, to be easier and looser than in the past, both in the text and in the subtext. Auto-eroticism appears to be suggested in "The Figure in the Carpet" through a subtextual vocabulary. With James energized perhaps by the example of his good friend Rhoda Broughton, whose *Dear Faustina* in 1897 was the first lesbian novel in English that we know about, as well as by his friendly relations with many of both closet and open homosexuals of the literary fraternity in England, there is a strong possibility that he wrote a hidden gay novel in *The Sacred Fount*. At least such an interpretation seems to explain the plot of that novel, which has eluded so many critics. Such revisions as that of "The Siege of London," an early story of 1883, revised for his New York Edition, show his much greater freedom in using sexual innuendo.

In addition to including these covert aspects, James, like many other writers of the period, some of whom were directly influenced by Sigmund Freud, wrote a series of stories from 1908 to 1910 (collected in *The Finer Grain*) about heroes and heroines plagued by deep-seated neuroses.

The concluding section of the volume deals with James and World War I. Whatever the "deeper psychology," as he named it in his study of Nathaniel Hawthorne, and his later freedom from repression, as he recognized his delight in the appearance of beautiful young men, his feeling of release was reinforced by the outbreak of World War I in 1914. Yet even before this date, an interest in crime, murder, and murder trials is revealed in his correspondence with the criminal historian William Roughead, begun just before the outbreak of war. James had, in such stories as "The Third Person" from 1900, shown a humorous handling of a crime story. But it was his active role in bringing comfort to young men wounded in the war that seemed to make up for his missing the Civil War in his youth. This new activity associated with World War I allowed him to identify with Walt Whitman, whom he had criticized harshly in his youth but who at the turn of the century he now considered one of the greatest of poets.

James at this time, in order to influence America to join the European allies, became a writer of propaganda. A man who had never before bothered with this genre of writing now engaged himself in it, for his last published works are devoted to an emotional tribute to the casualties of the war, including his beautiful preface to Rupert Brooke's posthumously published *Letters from America* in 1916. James's acceptance of the chairmanship of the American Volunteer Motor-Ambulance Corps, combined with his interview for the *New York Times Magazine,* which he actually wrote himself, made the end of his writing career devoted to an effort to stimulate American involvement in the war. So, when, in the midst of these activities, he was felled by a fatal stroke early in 1916, one might say that he died on the field of battle like his hero, Owen Wingrave.

Exploring these topics and avenues of James's last years shows us new depths and directions in his thought and makes us rethink his place.

1

James Enters the Twentieth Century in America, 1904–1905

Tales of "The Terrible Town": The Architecture of the New New York

James's twentieth-century work begins with his three major completed novels: *The Wings of the Dove* in 1902, *The Ambassadors* in 1903, and *The Golden Bowl* in 1904. In two of these his American characters finally turn their backs on Europe and return to America, Strether to digest it all and Verver to create a museum in his native American City. Even Milly Theale turns her back on Europe, for, dying, she "turns her face to the wall," with her back to the Europe where she has been betrayed. If his puppets had had enough of Europe, so had James himself, at least for a while, and in 1903, after the last novel of the major phase had been completed, his wish to return to the States for a visit became urgent. His real entry into the twentieth century was his revisit to America.

To understand the twentieth century of Henry James, we need to appreciate the overpowering effect that America had on him when he returned in 1904 after a twenty-year absence, the trip that produced *The American Scene* in 1907; for the great shock that gave its reverberations to James's final work was his rediscovery of his native country. In particular, the effects of the new New York, which James called the "terrible town" (*AS*, 72), are recorded in his New York stories ("The Jolly Corner," "Julia Bride," "Crapy Cornelia," and "A Round of Visits") written between 1906 and 1909, as well as "The Married Son," James's chapter in the composite novel *The Whole*

Family, published in 1908. We must remember that he saw his life work as comprising a New York Edition.

The stories attest to the impact that the new building structures (skyscrapers, museums, hotels, and apartment houses), the landscape architecture (such as Central Park), and even its zoo (represented through the imagery of an amazing variety of animals) had on James's imagination in the new century. *The American Scene* showed that he was aghast and overpowered by the emergence of the new skyscrapers. He saw in them the solid expression of the new American drive that he found so alien and yet so compelling.

"Terrible" as the city was in its most extreme forms of architectural energy and in its extremes of temperature, James felt its attraction. In January, 1905, he wrote to Jessie Allen from Washington, D.C., that he had been spending a month "in the horrific, the unspeakable, extraordinary, yet partly interesting, amusing, and above all fantastically *bristling* New York" (*HJL,* IV, 338). His feelings about New York were intensely ambivalent, and in *The American Scene* he invents a small dialogue between himself and the city to account for the presence of the contradiction in his feelings:

> "It's all very well," the voice of the air seemed to say . . . "it's all very well to 'criticise,' but you distinctly take an interest and are the victim of your interest, be the grounds of your perversity what they will. You can't escape from it, and don't you see that this, precisely, is what *makes* an adventure for you (an adventure, I admit, as with some strident, battered, questionable beauty, truly some 'bold bad' charmer), of almost any odd stroll, or waste half-hour, or other promiscuous passage, that results for you in an impression? There is always your bad habit of receiving through almost any accident of vision more impressions than you know what to do with. . . . You *care* for the terrible town, yea even for the 'horrible,' as I have overheard you call it, or at least think it, when you supposed no one would know. . . . What makes the general relation of your adventure with it is that, at bottom, you are all the while wondering, in presence of the aspects of its genius and its shame, what elements or parts, if any, would be worth its saving, worth carrying off for the fresh embodiment and the better life, and which of them would have, on the other hand, to face the notoriety of going *first* by the board." (*AS,* 108)

The important words in this passage are "its genius and its shame," the combination of vitality and horror that James knew had some "elements" that "would be worth saving, worth carrying off" for the purposes of art, or, as he put it, "for the fresh embodiment and the better life." His sorting out of the retrievable aspects of the great city is evidenced in the New York stories, and the way he uses those aspects creatively shows that he did "*care for the terrible town.*"

In the stories written after his American trip, architecture was used to symbolize the variances within and the solid information about New York society; instead of using paintings as he had before, he used buildings. "Glory" comes from architectural structures; he saw it in the Union building at Harvard and in the Boston Public Library. But it was the new New York buildings that overwhelmed him: the Metropolitan Museum, the opera house, the luxury hotel, the "apartment" houses (the homes of the rich and of the newly arrived immigrants). He intensely disliked the new structures with their alarming visual effect, the society they serviced, and the abominable effect ("its bold, bad promiscuousness") they appeared to have on American mores. But at the same time he was fascinated by it all. In fact, architecture so strongly influenced James's imagination and was so representative of certain basic drives for power in his nature that in his famous death-bed dictation he directed the construction of new apartments for the Louvre, which he signed "Napoleone" (*MA,* 552).

James's work in the years following his return to England shows how American architecture was deeply enmeshed in his thinking and writing of *The American Scene* and in his revisions for the New York Edition, the multi-volume collection of novels for the most part about Americans in Europe. The frontispiece for each volume of the New York Edition, selected from a group of photographs all by Alvin Langdon Coburn, depicted details from buildings. In addition, the row house, the portal to the Metropolitan Museum, and a group of New England houses were represented in a rather large proportion of the pictures used to illustrate the fiction selected, even though most of the stories situated in America had been eliminated from the New York Edition.

The first New York story was "The Jolly Corner," whose composition kept James awake one night in August, 1906, six weeks after a visit from Hamlin Garland. He wrote it, "striking while the iron is hot," as he told his agent (*MA,* 313), and a week or so later he followed it with "Julia Bride." He had just sent his publisher the various parts of *The American Scene.* He was revising *The American* for the New York Edition, and he would soon write chapter 7 of *The Whole Family,* "The Married Son," which, with "The Jolly Corner" and "Julia Bride," represented his efforts at translating his impressions of the cityscape into literature. The following year was spent in continuing to revise the New York Edition, and it was not until late 1908 and early 1909 that he finally got around to writing the stories that would comprise *The Finer Grain,* two of which, "Crapy Cornelia" and "A Round of Visits," again represent the flowering into literature of his New York impressions.

The four New York stories and "The Married Son" concentrate on the New York architectural scene, which had changed so radically since 1884, when James had last been in America. "The Jolly Corner" could be called a skyscraper story. "Julia Bride" is a museum story, since the first half is laid in the Metropolitan Museum, whose new façade and monumental stairway had just been opened to the public. "The Married Son" involves Central Park, a run-down row house, and the Art Students' League, lodged in the Fine Arts building on Fifty-seventh streeth. "Crapy Cornelia" also touches on Central Park (as does "Julia Bride") and concentrates on a contrast between the interior domestic decor of two New York women, one of the old New York and one of the new. "A Round of Visits" is a hotel story in which the dominance of the luxury hotel, its effect on society (its dictation of styles, of interior decoration, of subjects for conversation, of shifting standards of behavior), and its reflection of the mobility of the new society are ruthlessly pursued. The new studio apartment house designed for artists or bachelors appears in this tale, where Newton Winch's apartment enjoys a "high studio light" and with its "high north-light of the March afternoon" has its "vulgar appeal of fifty overdone decorative effects" (XII, 444–45).

In "The Jolly Corner," the old family house will soon be sacrificed to make way for the skyscraper. However, the old home is what the story is really about. In "Crapy Cornelia," once the age of the skyscraper is instituted, the home is gone; protagonist White-Mason has only "rooms," and Central Park is his virtual home, as Julia Bride's home is really the Metropolitan Museum and the park. There is no real home left in "A Round of Visits"; the hotel has taken over the city and its soul. Even Mrs. Ash, who has transported her "things" to New York, lives in an environment that the hero, Mark Monteith, finds "alien." It is a tale of woe, pain, and anguish. Betrayal, adultery, embezzlement, and death are housed in an engineering complex formed by the hotel, the studio apartment, and noisy trolley cars—a complex that dominates the story. Architecture creates taste and controls conversation (a young woman expresses herself "exclusively in hotel terms"). There is a crescendo of horror in all the stories, ending in a horror story itself, "A Round of Visits."

Of all these stories "The Jolly Corner" best reflects the full impact of James's reaction to the architectural changes in New York. He had written that the skyscrapers "are the element that looms largest for me through a particular impression . . . of 'downtown' seen and felt from the inside" (AS, 80). "Feeling," he said, was a bad word, since what he was trying to describe was a "relation to matters of magnitude and mystery that [he] could bring neither to measure nor to penetrate, hovering about them only in magnanimous wonder, staring at them as at a world of immovably-closed doors behind which immense 'material' lurked, material for the artist, the painter of life, as we say, who shouldn't have begun so early and so fatally to fall away from possible initiations" (AS, 80).

This statement can be a clue to a new reading of "The Jolly Corner." It contains the subjects and theme of the basic iconic form. The alter ego in the story exists in the figure of "material for the artist, the painter of life," which, like the ghost on the top story of Spencer Brydon's house, had hidden behind a door so shut that it was "immovably-closed" to Brydon. He travels through the old empty house of his childhood and of his forefathers to stalk his alter ego and, when confronted by it, realizes that the old house must be demolished and that a skyscraper, a "tall" building of flats, must be erected in its place. Why does he do this? His woman friend, Alice Staverton, who has waited for him to marry her, feeds his obsession and assures him that "he would have discovered his genius in time really to start some new variety of awful architectural hare and run it till it burrowed in a goldmine" (XII, 197).

"He was to remember these words," James writes, "for the small silver ring they had sounded over the queerest and deepest of his own lately most disguised and most muffled vibrations" (XII, 197). The view taken by Miss Staverton was derived from Brydon's expertise in managing his other piece of property, which he had renovated into a "tall" building of flats and the proceeds from which, along with the recently expired lease on his one-

family structure, had supported his life in Europe. One reason not to con-
fuse Brydon with James is that James himself lamented the demolition of
the brownstone family house, even deplored its becoming a boarding house.
Brydon, however, discovers he is really hard pressed by his fears of the alter
ego dispossessing him, though he "tried to think of something noble, as that
his property was really grand" and "this nobleness took the form too of the
clear delight with which he was finally to sacrifice it. They might come in
now, the builders, the destroyers—they might come as soon as they would"
(XII, 223).

The story line is clear. Brydon discovers that it is not too late for him to
become the financial giant that he might have been. Alice Staverton has not
only encouraged him to do so but is responsible for suggesting that his obsession about finding out "what fantastic, yet perfectly possible, development of my own nature I mayn't have missed" (XII, 204) might indicate a
genius for building. She suggests, "you'd have had power" (XII, 205), and
when Brydon accuses her of preferring him as the "billionaire" (XII, 205)
he might have been, she hedges. She doesn't permit him to view his life as
being over, and she is responsible for the entire adventure by suggesting that
he might have invented the skyscraper. It was this that made him conjure up
as a "quaint analogy," after he opened "a door into a room shuttered and
void," the discovery of a figure that faced him "through the dusk" (XII,
198). The analogy becomes reality to Brydon during his nocturnal excursion
through the family house. The inventor or even the exploiter of the skyscraper was a figure that gained immeasurable financial power from "the
white towers, all new and crude and commercial," James wrote in *The
American Scene* (*AS*, 81). Such towers are "consecrated by no uses save the
commercial at any cost" and "are simply the most piercing notes in that
concert of the expensively provisional into which your supreme sense of
New York resolves itself. They never begin to speak to you . . . with the
authority of things of permanence or even of things of long duration. One
story is good only till another is told, and sky-scrapers are the last word of
economic ingenuity only till another word be written" (*AS*, 77). The property owner must respond to the economic necessity in New York of architectural evanescence and built-in obsolescence as being in the very nature of
the role of any building, office, or residence. "I build you up but to tear you
down, for if I were to let sentiment and sincerity once take root . . . what

would become of *us,* who have our hands on the whipstock, please?" (*AS,* 112), the spirit of New York says.

The "towers of marble" are, above all, "payers of dividends," and Spencer Brydon proceeds to become the man he despised. The conversion of his house into a rent-paying, flat-bearing, "tall" building like his other converted house will satisfy both his deepest longings to belong to his property-owning class of New Yorkers and Alice Staverton's desire to have a powerful husband. Such, James is implying, is what happens to a New York property owner, for the nature of New York real estate of the twentieth century is that it *must* be converted into tall, rent-paying structures, made possible by the inventions of the steel frame, the elevator, and plate glass. Aesthetically, James regretted the demolition of the old houses; morally, he regretted the loss of behavioral standards and of personal intercourse in the new city dominated by the skyscraper, the visible sign of the almighty dollar, yet he was fascinated by the power behind the American scene.

In *The American Scene,* James describes the clubs of New York as "doorless apertures, vainly festooned, which decline to tell him where he is" (*AS,* 168), which, though not too inappropriate in a club, unfortunately also are found in private houses where the "custom rages like a conspiracy for nipping the interior in the bud" (*AS,* 167) (Figures 1 and 2). This results in "the enlargement of every opening . . . the substitution . . . of resounding voids for enclosing walls, for practicable doors, for controllable windows, for all the rest of the essence of the room-character" (*AS,* 167).

He preserves the old house in "The Jolly Corner" by the itemization of those features that were disappearing in contemporary New York architecture, in the club, office building, or apartment hotel. His trip through the house is a loving itemization of his feelings for "the mere sight of the walls, mere shapes of the rooms, mere sound of the floors, mere feel, in his hand, of the old-silver plated knobs of the several mahogany doors" (XII, 201). Doors, especially, have become the visible and palpable symbol of the noble architectural feature of the building that will fall under the demolitioner's hammer. He applauds "the native architecture of the particular time, which could rejoice so in the multiplication of doors—the opposite extreme to the modern, the actual almost complete proscription of them" (XII, 217), and the dramatic climax of the vision of the alter ego in the house is silhouetted against "the painted panels of the last barrier to his escape" (XII, 224), the front door of the house.

It was just after writing this story that James selected the frontispieces for the New York Edition, and it is not surprising that out of the twenty-three photographs, James chose ten doors to symbolize the stories illustrated. In addition to doorways, in "The Jolly Corner" house, James lovingly catalogs the more intricate upper rooms, which "abounded in nooks and corners, in closets and passages" (XII, 212). He stresses "reaches of communication between rooms and by passages" (XII, 207), all such complications wiped out by the format of the new tall buildings, the studio apartments, the apartment hotels. As Brydon looks out of the window from the top story, he tries to find some message in the taller buildings that have grown up around his four-story house: "Had they ever spoken so little to any need of his spirit? Great builded voids, great crowded stillnesses put on, often, in the heart of cities, for the small hours, a sort of sinister mask, and it was of this large collective negation that Brydon presently became conscious" (XII, 220–21). But confronted by his fears of the now assuredly palpable alter ego, he turns his house over to the destroyers to become a "great builded void."

After Brydon collapses in the presence of his frightening double, he regains consciousness and tells Alice his experience. She, however, reports a dream of her own and encourages him to take on the positive aspects of the other side of his nature. That "compartment of his mind" that he had "never yet penetrated" had shown a "capacity for business and a sense for construction" (XII, 195), and by claiming that she, too, had seen the alter ego and had found him attractive, she encourages Brydon to emulate him as much as possible. The reader will remember that Brydon had decided earlier to bring in the house demolitioners. Now that he has missed discovering the skyscraper himself, he is going to become at least the owner and designer of a "tall" apartment house and will benefit by the multiple rents instead of the few he has been collecting. His passage through the old house changes him into a New York real estate operator.

It is customary to see this story as a piece of self-congratulation on the part of Brydon, who, regretting that he might have missed something by going abroad, is reassured that if he had stayed, he would have been an ugly, damaged, brutal billionaire, for which avoidance he and Alice Staverton are immensely grateful. In such an interpretation, the significance of Brydon's unequivocal decision to have the house demolished the day following his nighttime experience is missed. Alice pressures him by telling him that if he had stayed in New York, he would have "anticipated the inventor of the sky-scraper" (XII, 197), that therefore he would have had power, which would not have at all prevented her from liking him ("How should I not have liked you?" [XII, 205]), and she chides him for living off the rent of the other house he has built into flats so that he could afford the luxury of his family home, in which he has never lived and has no intention of living. He, how-ever, is unaware of her influence because he is so wrapped up in his selfish obsession with the question of what he would have become had he stayed.

James's other aim in the story seems to have been the creation of a literary memorial to a house destined for destruction. It was not his own natal house, which had already been demolished, but the East Eleventh Street house of his dear friend Mary Cadwalader Jones, where he stayed in New York during his trip in 1904 and 1905, with the exception of a week spent in the Park Avenue house of Edith Wharton and a week in the West Tenth Street house of Lawrence Godkin, the son of the editor of *The Nation* and an old friend. It is interesting how the features of the two Greenwich Village houses, which ironically have survived as New York landmark-designated buildings, contributed to the invented house of "The Jolly Corner." In a letter that James wrote to Mrs. Jones, we see the notion of being haunted by a house: "My New York of those dear East Eleventh Street 'first-floor-back' hours lives again for me as I write. . . . it's astonishing, it's prodigious, how I find my spirit gratefully haunting them always—or rather how insidi-ously *turning the tables* they, the mystic locality itself, *haunt and revisit my own departed identity*" (italics added).[1]

This reference to James's being haunted by the house indicates that 21 East Eleventh Street was the locus for the stalking of the alter ego ghost; James in this letter, by "insidiously turning the tables," reverses the roles of the haunter and the haunted. "People enough, first and last, had been in terror of apparitions, but who had ever before so turned the tables and become himself, in the apparitional world, an incalculable terror?" (XII, 211).

The fictitious "Jolly Corner" house does indeed resemble Mrs. Jones's

1. Millicent Bell, *Edith Wharton and Henry James* (New York, 1965), 52.

Eleventh Street house except for a few details, for in the story, Brydon's house is placed on the corner of the block, which runs westward to Sixth Avenue, "the 'jolly' one precisely, of the street now so generally dishonoured and disfigured in its westward reaches, and of the comparatively conservative Avenue" (XII, 198). The avenue still had pretensions, as Miss Staverton said, to "decency." It had four stories, as the Jones house does, though the mahogany doors inside are now gone.

The parts of the house where the main events of the story take place (the stairwell, the skylight, the hallway floor with its black-and-white marble squares) are still intact today in the Eleventh Street house. The shapes of the Jones's stairwell and skylight are described in the story: "Only the high skylight that formed the crown of the deep well created for him a medium in which he could advance" (XII, 222–23). "At the end of two flights [of stairs] . . . he recognised the influence of the lower windows . . . of the occasional gleam of street-lamps, of the glazed spaces of the vestibule. This was the bottom of the sea, which showed an illumination of its own and which he even saw paved—when at a given moment he drew up to sink a long look over the banisters—with the marble squares of his childhood" (XII, 223). His "ease increased with the sight of the old black-and-white slabs" (XII, 223).

These "large black-and-white squares that he remembered as the admiration of his childhood" (XII, 209) were not just an insignificant detail in this house, for even today they dominate the hallway. They were a convention of the time (they still exist in other houses on Tenth and Eleventh Streets east and west of Fifth Avenue) and probably also existed in James's destroyed family house. In the story they are symbolic of an education in taste. When he was a child, they "had then made in him [Brydon], as he now saw, for the growth of an early conception of style" (XII, 209).

The actual confrontation between Brydon and his double takes place in the vestibule. The "hinged halves of the inner door" that "had been thrown back" still exist in the house. But James substituted, from the Godkins' West Tenth Street house, the beautiful fan light with cast-iron tracery that still creates today "glazed spaces" of mysterious colors in the vestibule along with its side-lights: "Inasmuch as the side-lights and the high fan-tracery of the entrance were glimmering straight into the hall" (XII, 223). Brydon asks, "Wasn't he now in *most* immediate presence of some inconceivable occult activity?" (XII, 224). The "answer hung fire still and seemed to lose itself in the vague darkness to which the thin admitted dawn, glimmering archwise over the whole outer door, made a semicircular margin, a cool silvery nimbus that seemed to play a little as he looked—to shift and expand and contract" (XII, 224).

The ghost ego advances aggressively and Brydon wakes up hours later with his head on Alice's lap. "His long person" remained "stretched on his old black-and-white slabs. They were cold, these marble squares of his youth; but *he* somehow was not" (XII, 227). Brydon is going to become his alter ego.

In all these four New York stories James worked out an analogy paralleling the effects of the New York architecture, for the stories are both set within and made meaningful by those forms. In "The Jolly Corner," he joins the reality of the old house to the analogy of the adventure story based on the stories of his friend Robert Louis Stevenson. The house is, indeed, named "The Jolly Corner" because, like the Jolly Roger, "the black flag of piracy," it presides over the adventure.

The machinery of each story is a combination of the architectural reality plus the analogy taken from literature. In "Julia Bride," the heroine is a homeless waif likened to Nancy in *Oliver Twist* because of her petty thievery and her desire to barter and gain respectability through her "street" thievery—her bargaining for social sanctions that takes place, not under London Bridge or near Covent Garden, but in the Metropolitan Museum and in Central Park. Since she is as pretty as a picture, she is placed in the newly refashioned Metropolitan Museum, whose trustees were conducting a campaign of "acquisition," seeking only for the most expensive masterpieces of unimpeachable reputation. Julia is blemished, and so, in this new society where only the richest and the best-placed succeed, she fails. "Julia Bride" depicts a world in which the ability to marry for money and security is lost to a young woman reared in an atmosphere of divorce. Her only means of gaining what she lacks is by a campaign for guarantees, procurable only if her old friends will lie for her. However, although she fulfills the requests for favors from the men from whom she seeks help, they, in turn, fail her.

What facilitates the burden of James's tale is the enlarged Metropolitan

Museum, with its new façade (Figure 3), opened to the public on Fifth Avenue and Eighty-second Street in 1902 and seen for the first time in 1904 by James, who had remembered the museum from at least two earlier downtown installations. In "Julia Bride," the museum not only provides the world in which the plot unfolds but also acts as a concrete parallel for the quest of Julia and for her function in the economy of the city. As the story opens, the young woman and her fiancé are found at "the top of the [newly constructed] wide steps of the Museum, those that descend from the galleries of painting" (XII, 151). The retreat of the fiancé down the imperial flight of stairs encapsulates through an architectural structure the theme of the tale.

The frontispiece for the volume of the New York Edition that includes "Julia Bride" features not this entrance but the 1879 wing and portal. It is as if James and Coburn, who photographed this portion of the museum long after the other façade had been opened to the public, are saying that the earlier entrance represented the real museum and that the new front and wing represent those aspects of the museum that James had criticized in *The American Scene*. In fact, it is his comments in that book on the Metropolitan Museum as he found it in 1904 that act as a clue to our interpreting the meaning of this "museum" story. Its action and mood, its lesson and meaning are assisted by the ironical running commentary that the newly overhauled Metropolitan Museum is indeed the proper setting for the petty lying and moral thievery engaged in by a New York urchin.

Setting the story in the Metropolitan Museum was done for reasons other than the enjoyment of art. Julia does not look at the art nor are any specific paintings referred to in the story. Julia's view of the museum is summed up in one sentence: "She saw the great shining room, with its mockery of art and 'style' and security, all the things she was vainly after" (XII, 167) (Figure 4). James makes quite clear in *The American Scene* that the generally overhauled Metropolitan Museum has changed since he had frequented the "large eccentric house in West Fourteenth Street." Now it is "a palace of art, truly, that sits there on the edge of the Park" (*AS*, 191).

James had criticized in *The American Scene* the new ideals of the Metropolitan Museum, now governed by money and by a wish to acquire only the most expensive items. Julia's quest for little white lies to help her secure the richest and the most influential husband parallels the quest of the trustees of the Metropolitan Museum in 1904 for the most expensive and, therefore, the most desirable artifacts.

The values of the museum cannot be the values for Julia and her friends without becoming invidious, because they cannot be applied to personal interests. Julia, in fact, is an example of the application of the museum policy de-acquisitioning certain paintings, pretty though they be. She, like them, is "to be turned out into the cold world as the penalty of old error and the warrant for a clean slate" (AS, 193), and in her case it does draw "tears from the eyes." What happens to outdated pictures once considered valuable that on investigation turn out to have a shady past is that they are consigned as one of "the sacrifices" necessary for the museum's present policy. James's museum story could only be written after "The Jolly Corner" had shown that even a man in love with the old order succumbs to the pressures of the new New York, where "money" was "in the air." Julia's scramble for that money and power as a ledge to hang on to parallels the exclusive program for buying only guaranteeable works of art to which the new administration of the museum, run by the city's bankers, was committed.

In "Julia Bride," where again an architectural feature of the new New York lies in the foreground, we are aware of images and figures that derived from building as a trade and from building as a place of habitation—habitation both of the rich and of the somewhat fallen in fortune. In all five pieces of fiction dealing with New York, James makes very clear that there are places in New York where it is fashionable to live and places where it is not. Julia, the New York waif, lives with her multi-divorced mother in a "horrible flat which was so much too far up and too near the East Side" (XII, 176), a place similar to Mrs. Chataway's brownstone, also too far uptown and too far east, in chapter 7 of *The Whole Family,* written two or three months after "Julia Bride" and employing both a socially unacceptable residential area and Central Park as settings.

Building images abound in "Julia Bride": Mrs. Drack, Mr. Pitman's fiancée, is described with her "suspended weight and arrested mass" (XII, 172), terms used in the construction industry; "she had quickly broken ground" (XII, 178); and, finally, it was like a "dumpage of bricks at your door" (XII, 179). Having "all his cables cut" (XII, 187), an image applicable to the elevator, the electric trolley car, and the elevated train, is associated with all the mobile architectural forms invented during the age of the skyscraper and serving the skyscraper, thoroughly modern and thoroughly indicative of the New York scene.

However, the outstanding architectural figure used to show how Julia's past wrongdoings will prevent her from obtaining a respectable fiancé, is probably drawn from the Villard houses, one of the outstanding private residences in New York. Located on Madison Avenue and Fiftieth Street, they had been under construction during the 1880s, when James had returned briefly to New York at the time of the deaths of his parents, and were completed in 1888. Designed by the firm of McKim, Mead, and White, their distinguishing feature is that they consist of two houses joined together to look like a large castle built around a square front courtyard. The composite building appears as the embodiment of what marriage to Basil French represents to Julia. It was one thing to send a girl flowers, novels and chocolates.

> But [it was] something quite other to hold open for her . . . the gate, moving on such stiff silver hinges, of the grand square forecourt of the palace of wedlock. . . . Poor Julia could have blushed red . . . with the memory of the way the forecourt, as she now imagined it, had been dishonoured by her younger romps. She had tumbled over the wall with this, that and the other raw playmate, and had played "tag" and leap-frog, as she might say, from corner to corner. . . . She had already, again and again, any occasion offering, chattered and scuffled over ground provided, according to his idea, for walking the gravest of minuets. (XII, 160–61)

The extended metaphor seems to be based on the Villard buildings, which must have struck James's keen eye for architectural novelties in New York (Figure 5). If he did not mention it in *The American Scene,* he at least memorialized it in this story.

Central Park, the setting for Julia's last rendezvous in these stories, is closely associated with both the museum and the newly erected fashionable residences of the wealthy that had grown up during James's absence. The park served as the front lawn for the new residences and as a substitute drawing room for Julia to meet her former lover, who, she felt, might sully her experiences in the museum, sacred to visits with her intended fiancé. James himself visited the park whenever he could. If the visitor, he wrote, "doesn't here, in his thought, keep patting the Park on the back, he is guilty not alone of failure of natural tenderness, but of a real deviation from social morality," since it had "directly prescribed to it . . . to 'do' officially, on behalf of the city, the publicly amiable" (AS, 174). "To the Park . . . only . . . the aesthetic appetite has had to address itself" (AS, 175). What is more, it provides "in the most agreeable manner possible," when one turned in from the Plaza, a kind of "tour of the little globe" (AS, 177). This aspect of the park, this kind of substitution for Europe, accentuated by the statuary and the formal aspects of the gardens, the artificial lake, and the architecture of walls, gates, entrances, and even the zoo, was a pastoral extension of the costlier types of residences that all could enjoy in democratic fashion.

The European link was what enchanted Charles Edward, the son in chapter 7 of *The Whole Family* who comes to New York to find out why Harry Gower has been flirting with his Aunt Elizabeth and who finds that Harry has found a bench in the park, which is the only place "the stricken deer may weep—or even, for that matter, the hart ungalled play" (WF, 182). The park resurrects not only *Hamlet* (III, ii, 249–50) for Charles Edward but also *The Tempest* for White-Mason of "Crapy Cornelia," who also finds the park his only place for deciding with which woman he should spend the rest of his life. The park is a recurring feature in these three stories dominated by the new architecture and serves as "another part of the forest."

In *The Whole Family* chapter, commissioned with its restrictive conditions (James had to follow the plot line given in the foregoing chapter and had to create a story line that could be followed by the writer of the next chapter), James takes his protagonist to the Art Students' League in New York. On his New York trip James saw for the first time the new Fine Arts building, which even today houses the league and which, in 1902, had been opened to the public with a student body of over a thousand members. At the league, Charles Edward meets his future wife, Lorraine, and the image of his taking her away from what he called "the bear garden," in which she had been wandering as "a little bleating stray lamb" (WF, 168), a figure his mother had brought up earlier when referring to Peggy's going to a coeducational college, consolidates a metaphor that recurs in each of the five stories, that of animals in a menagerie. The zoo buildings at Sixty-sixth Street and Fifth Avenue had been in existence for many years, and James's references to every kind of animal from a lamb to a panther, from a pigeon to a tropical bird, suggest that he is assimilating the zoo as a building in the park and that he sees it as part of the architectural New York scene. In "Julia Bride" the heroine compares herself and her mother to "antelopes or zebras, or even some superior sort of performing, of dancing, bear" (XII, 159). "The Jolly Corner" hero stalks his ghost in the terms of the chase, and "by the tremendous force of analogy" (XII, 210), he fancies himself "in close quarters with the great bear of the Rockies" (XII, 210). Cornelia is compared to a "mangy lion" or "muzzled house-dog," planted by Mrs. Worthingham (XII, 342), and the hotel atmosphere of "A Round of Visits" is a veritable "jungle" or "some wondrous tropical forest, where vociferous, bright-eyed, and feathered creatures . . . were half smothered between undergrowths of velvet and tapestry" (XII, 431). The zoo, therefore, becomes part of the architectural actuality and part of the moral analogy.

Chapter 7 of *The Whole Family* brings in the architecture of New York through the park and its structures and the Art Students' League to suggest the atmosphere of Paris, to which Charles, a frustrated artist, will soon be headed. It also includes the run-down brownstone "boarding house" of the unrespectable Mrs. Chataway with its "high lopsided stoop of its very, very East Side setting" (*WF*, 177). The chapter throws an architectural network of socially graded structures across the width of Manhattan, running from east to west and settling down finally on a park bench.

In the next two years, 1906 through 1908, James finished the revisions for the New York Edition. Complaining that he yearned for creative work again, he turned out five stories later published as *The Finer Grain*. Two of the stories in this collection, "Crapy Cornelia" and "A Round of Visits," are the last of his New York stories. Written a year after he digested his "impression," these thoughtful and pessimistic tales are set in a city made up only of the new buildings.

"Crapy Cornelia" demonstrates a man's recognition in midlife that he must repudiate the bright, the shiny, the "glare" of the new money for the nostalgic past: the brilliant, young, rich widow for the dim spinster from his past, *their* past, of a vanished New York. The story is framed around the contrast between the "glaring" light of the new New York and the shaded world of the daguerreotype and of the old New York. Both worlds are personalized in the characters of Mrs. Worthingham, the newly rich exponent of the new New York, and Cornelia Rasch, the faded relic of a vanished society. The architectural note is expressed in the changes in interior furnishings that accompanied the changes in New York social roles. The interior of Mrs. Worthingham's house is furnished in eighteenth-century rococo: "The whole place seemed to reflect . . . the lustre of Mrs. Worthingham's own polished and prosperous little person" and "to surround the most animated of . . . Dresden china shepherdesses with exactly the right system of rococo curves and convolutions and other flourishes, a perfect bower of painted and gilded and moulded conceits" (XII, 340). She had an "iridescent surface" (XII, 342). Physically, she even resembles an architectural form: "Her outlook took form to him suddenly as a great square sunny sindow that hung in assured fashion over the immensity of life" (XII, 343). She is an example of the new rich and "the music of the future" (XII, 348), "if people were but rich enough and furnished enough and fed enough, exercised and sanitated and manicured . . . all they had to do for civility was to take the amused ironic view of those who might be less initiated" (XII, 348). Cornelia, in contrast, is compared to a piece of furniture that was made to be ignored, a hand-over from a past fashion in interior decoration: "This oddly unassertive little rotund figure whom one seemed no more obliged to address than if she had been a black satin ottoman 'treated' with buttons and gimp; a class of object as to which the policy of blindness was imperative" (XII, 345).

There is a determined contrast between the two habitations. Mrs. Worthingham's house was probably modeled on Edith Wharton's home at 884 Park Avenue. Built in the 1880s, it was a traditional double brownstone except for a shorter stoop, but it was decorated in the latest mode of interior design. Well-to-do New Yorkers were changing their interiors to make them more exotic. Chinese, Turkish, and French rooms were the fad. James must have had in mind the "*bonbonnière* of the last daintiness" (which is how he described Wharton's house) (*AS*, 472), because he wrote that Mrs. Worthingham's house was "a perfect bower of painted and gilded and moulded conceits."

Crapy Cornelia, however, lives in a new "small and quite cynically modern flat—the house had a grotesque name, 'The Gainsborough,' but at least wasn't an awful boarding-house, as he had feared, and she could receive him quite honourably, which was so much to the good" (XII, 355). The *New York Directory* of 1902 and 1903 lists an apartment house called "The

Gainsborough" at 112 Riverside Avenue, now Riverside Drive. Although similar houses still remain on Riverside Drive, "The Gainsborough" was demolished after World War II and replaced by a larger and taller apartment house, following the pattern of replacement that James described in *The American Scene*.

James was amused by the American tendency, exhibited by the energetic young builders of the apartment houses that arose between the late nineteenth century and 1929, to name their houses after celebrated places and people, including characters from novels. James's introduction to this peculiarity probably came from a letter William Dean Howells wrote him in 1902, telling him about a new apartment house in Manhattan called "The Henry James." James wrote back to Howells that his "most kind communication . . . has at once deeply agitated and wildly uplifted me." He speaks of the "intensity of hope, of the delirious dream that such a stroke may 'bring my books before the public,'" but he claims that "no power on earth can ever do that," that the house will fail and "it will presently have to close in order to reopen as the Mary Johnston or the K[ate] Wiggin or the James Lane Allen. Best of all as the Edith Wharton!" (*HJL*, IV, 222). "The Henry James" was situated on 113th Street and Amsterdam Avenue, in the area occupied by Columbia University, and was demolished during the late forties or early fifties, to be replaced by a tall apartment building. It fits in with James's theory of necessary replacement, even though a number of houses of the period still stand on both sides of the block between Amsterdam Avenue and Broadway.

The mention of "The Gainsborough" in the story is followed by a reminiscence by White-Mason (the bachelor who must choose between the two women, one modern and the other old fashioned) of the houses Cornelia's family used to own, highlighting the contrast between the old and the new structures.

> "Have you still your old 'family interest' in those two houses in Seventh Avenue?—one of which was next to a corner grocery, don't you know? and was occupied as to its lower part by a candy-shop where the proportion of the stock of suspectedly stale popcorn to that of rarer and stickier joys betrayed perhaps a modest capital on the part of your father's, your grandfather's or whoever's tenant? . . . I haven't been round there lately—we must go round together; but don't tell me the forms have utterly perished!" (XII, 355)

The mood of the scene also contrasts the old and the new: they discuss old-fashioned architecture while sitting within the confines of the new apartment house, which ironically shelters family mementos of past generations. In "Crapy Cornelia" the old property is merely a memory; it has all been destroyed.

In Cornelia's living room, White-Mason talks about how they used to fill their days "with the modern fever, but that were so different from *these* arrangements of pretended hourly Time that dash themselves forever to pieces as from the fiftieth floors of sky-scrapers" (XII, 357). (This image is hyperbolic. There were no fifty-story skyscrapers at the turn of the century in New York City.) As the passage indicates, "Crapy Cornelia" also abounds in images and figures of speech involving building and construction terms. White-Mason manages his life with an economy in which he moves "the melancholy limits, the significant signs, constantly a little further on, very much as property-marks or staked boundaries are sometimes stealthily shifted at night" (XII, 339). He entices Cornelia to talk of old memories: "So certainly should he find out that wherever he might touch her, with a gentle though firm pressure, he would, as the fond visitor of old houses taps and fingers a disfeatured, overpapered wall with the conviction of a wain-scot-edge beneath, recognize some small extrusion of history" (XII, 352). In this story, the images are based on types of architecture no longer standing.

In *The American Scene* James described walks through certain northward and eastward streets and avenues, which would take him to Edith Wharton's house at 884 Park Avenue and Seventy-eighth Street. The only way one could walk from there to "The Gainsborough" (at Eighty-fourth Street and Riverside Drive) would be to cross the park, and that is where White-Mason, who lived in "rooms" and was now looking for a home in either one of the two ladies' establishments, found himself twice, once before attempting to propose to Mrs. Worthingham and again when he left her house after *not* proposing and after having seen Cornelia, which changed all his plans.

The park becomes the background for revery in "Crapy Cornelia." It resurrects, through its pastoral quality unique in New York, the pastoral parts of Shakespeare, which James had been rereading from 1902 to 1907. *The Tempest* images, the echoes of Sonnet XXX in the sentence "his second brooding session till the sweet spring sunset had begun to gather" (XII, 350), and the Virgilian overtones of a dim trip to the underworld of his own consciousness and past history thrive beautifully for James's creative purposes in Central Park. The park allows the hero to make his choice for Cornelia Rasch's "massive little bundle of data" (XII, 352). White-Mason is induced by the presence of architectural "voids" to choose Cornelia with her household of memories.

By covertly suggesting the real locales of both characters' homes, James makes a trip around Manhattan through the two new elegant residential sections of the city, one of which extends the near-East Side abutting on Central Park and the other encompassing the Hudson. Cornelia's apartment, with its sweeping riparian setting, allows for Virgilian, underworld suggestions, with the river as the equivalent, in White-Mason's imagination, of what the waters of the Mediterranean had been for Aeneas, to "make over and recreate . . . our lost world" (XII, 357). The literary parallel in "Crapy Cornelia," drawn to invoke the shades of the past, is characteristically Virgil. The quotation from Book One of the *Aeneid*, line 118, "rari nantes in gurgite vasto," referring to the relics that floated on the waters in the wake of the shipwreck of Aeneas and his Trojan party, is pertinent to the "surviving representatives of a society once 'good' " who were able to hold their own with the new New Yorkers even "amid old shades once sacred" (XII, 349). So we see that the few members of old New York society meet in the underworld of memory in a modern apartment, where White-Mason is going to visit daily for the rest of his life, a few blocks away from the memorial to the Civil War soldiers and sailors. The mementoes of the 1860s are set in a park environment that memorializes the 1860s. In James, nothing is accidental.

"Crapy Cornelia" depicts a city bereft of its old landmarks, but it also shows how a modern apartment flat, when filled with the personal relics and reminders of a vanished society, can constitute an underworld of memory. But "A Round of Visits" portrays a totally transformed society. New York is devoid of its Old World aura, old values, old amenities. Mark Monteith, returning from Europe to investigate charges that his cousin Phil Bloodgood has swindled him out of his stock dividends, arrives in an unrecognizable city.

In this story, the luxury hotel is the architectural structure that incorporates the new character of the new society and satisfies all its yearnings and its capacity to spend its new wealth. James formed this view in a visit to the

Waldorf-Astoria when it was located on Thirty-fourth Street. In *The American Scene* he described "the portentous impression of one of the great caravansaries administered to me of a winter afternoon" (*AS*, 99), for "New York told me more of her story at once, then and there, than she was again and elsewhere to tell" (*AS*, 100). With the city "fairly shrieking it into one's ears," there was nothing to do "but to stare with all our eyes and miss as little as possible of the revelation" (*AS*, 100). It is because of the intensity of his impression that the quintessential New York story could be found in this hotel, and "A Round of Visits" becomes, by virtue of it, *the* New York story. Violence, harshness, the total disappearance of the old values and the old houses, and the appearance of the strange new skyscraper hotels and transient quarters are recurring New York themes in the story.

New York was almost as noisy then as it is now. The "shriek" is followed carefully throughout, in the "choked trolley-car that howled" (XII, 442), the "suffering shriek of another public vehicle" (XII, 442) and the chatter of the young woman he meets at the hotel luncheon (Figure 6). "Hotel terms" and "the names of those establishments" play "through her speech as the *leitmotif* might have recurrently flashed and romped through a piece of profane modern music" (XII, 435). The electric bell of Newton Winch's apartment is "a long sharp sound" that "shrill[s] in from the outer door, seeming of so high and peremptory a pitch" (XII, 458) that it gives Monteith a start. The sounds reach their ghastly heights when the suicide of Winch announces itself by "the infallible crack of a discharged pistol and, so nearly with it as to make all one violence, the sound of a great fall" (XII, 459).

The hotel provides security for a world only the skyscraper can administer to, a world complete in itself. The visitor, James wrote in *The American Scene*, "is transported to conditions of extraordinary complexity and brilliancy, operating—and with proportionate perfection—by laws of their own and expressing after their fashion a complete scheme of life. The air swarms, to intensity, with the *characteristic*. . . . It jumps out to meet his every glance, and this unanimity of its spring . . . is what I just now referred to as the essence of the loud New York story" (*AS*, 102).

In "A Round of Visits," all the characters are living in temporary dwellings, and all confront each other within the many interiors, both public and private, established in and by the hotel. The promiscuity and lack of privacy, the gregariousness of the New Yorker are all guaranteed by the hotel system, and in "A Round of Visits," the system so operates that the protagonist, in the midst of his postinfluenza depression, heightened by his unhappiness at being despoiled of his money, floats through the corridors. After meeting Mrs. Folliott, he is wafted along to a luncheon in one of the restaurants of the hotel and into the crowd's sociability. From there he is carried by the movement of the city to Mrs. Ash's apartment, after which he treks through the snow to Winch's bachelor studio apartment. Monteith's progress is a kind of repeated ascent and descent from one form of horror to the next. In fact, the word *horror* appears ten times in the story. Other recurring words are "loss," "pain," "ache," "blow," "dismay," "alien," "misery," "epidemic," "monstrous," "anguished," "jungle," and "terrible," each one occurring at least twice.

The story is divided into seven sections, which seem to have a kind of calendar significance. Most critics, noting the calendar stress in the first four pages of the story—the placing of the main action on a Sunday, the suggestion of cleansing by suicide, and the awareness of evil on the part of the self-conscious embezzler contrasted to the unawareness of suffering on the part of the innocent victim—tend to view this story as James's Christian tale. The action begins on a Wednesday in March, which could be Ash Wednesday. The sacrifice of Winch, offered as salvation for the other embezzlers, could be a symbol of Christ's self-sacrifice in order to redeem the sins of man. This is all very well except that James's fiction has always tended to be secular. The overtones are here, but they have been secularized. One fact strongly in favor of a secular interpretation of this calendar arrangement is the existence of that extraordinary book called the *New York Directory*, which, in its earlier issues, opened with an almanac and which, before the telephone, took the place of our current telephone book and Yellow Pages. It was the "bible" of every New Yorker. There is evidence to indicate that James was using the *Directory* as an ironic substitution for the Bible.

The first section of "A Round of Visits" represents a parallel to the almanac that had prefaced the *Directory* in the years of James's youth; the only echo of the old New York, it exists as a kind of ghost in the story. The next six sections all take place on Sunday. The plot moves from the illness of three of the characters to the suicide at the end, from embezzlement to adultery and divorce and back to embezzlement. Everything goes from bad to worse, from a blizzard and influenza, which keep Monteith confined

within the "caravanserai" (XII, 428), to confrontation with the alien architectural milieu that houses his old friend Mrs. Ash in impersonal, interior-
decorated confines. Although Mrs. Ash transported all her furniture from
Paris, there was something wrong in the way it was installed. The "things"
were "reconstituted, regrouped, wonderfully preserved," but everything
else "was different, and even vaguely alien." Every encounter Monteith has
is a disappointment.

Monteith's quest is for sympathy, and, like Julia Bride, he finds that *he*
is the one from whom sympathy is elicited. Finally, he does gain Winch's
sympathetic attention but only because the embezzler is killing time while
he waits to be arrested. Every disappointment is housed in an environment
and in a building that shrieks its strictly New York character. The hotel is at
the apex of the hierarchy.

"The great gaudy hotel—The Pocahontas, but carried out largely on 'Du
Barry' lines" (XII, 428), is based on the old Waldorf-Astoria, which was
located on Thirty-fourth Street and Fifth Avenue, and contains a whole new
world in itself (Figure 6). By the arrangement and decoration of its rooms,
it more or less dictates to its inhabitants how to think and how to talk. It is
an expression of the gregarious state "breaking down every barrier but two"
(one must be rich and one must be respectable) (*AS*, 103). Monteith, settled
in a lavish bedroom (Figure 7), is carried from one stage-set room to the
next, in what James calls in his travel book "halls and saloons in which art
and history, in masquerading dress, muffled almost to suffocation as in the
gold brocade of their pretended majesties and their conciliatory graces" (*AS*,
103). Monteith sees "the complete social scene in itself, on which types
might figure and passions rage and plots thicken and dramas develop, without reference to any other sphere, or perhaps even to anything at all outside" (XII, 431). He encounters Mrs. Folliott, the self-centered "terrible
little lady" (XII, 435) who had just come to the "terrible town" on the same
errand as Monteith, to investigate the embezzlement of her funds. She "sat
with him, under a spreading palm, in a wondrous rococo *salon*," an accurate
description of the main foyer in the Waldorf (XII, 432) (Figure 8). Monteith
would rather have listened to the waiter "dangling in the long vista that
showed the oriental *café* as a climax," a description of the Peacock Alley
corridor, imitated today in the present Waldorf on Park Avenue (XII, 433).
From the salon they moved on to lunch at what must be the Palm Garden,

dining there with three or four of Mrs. Folliott's crowd, "a new crowd, rather, for her, all great Sunday lunchers there" (XII, 434) and kept together because of their feeling for the hotel rather than for each other (Figure 9).

Section three takes Monteith out of the hotel into the outside world of the city, dominated by a group of architectural structures, "the long but still sketchy vista . . . of the northward Avenue, bright and bleak, fresh and harsh, rich and evident somehow, a perspective like a page of florid modern platitudes" (XII, 437). In this figure of speech he finally assesses in his fiction the houses of the new rich. On his walk uptown from Thirty-fourth Street and Fifth Avenue, he finally reaches Winch's apartment on Fiftieth Street, the same neighborhood where the other stories unfolded. Monteith realizes when he sees Winch's apartment that all the people he visits share the new wealth of New York: "Winch was in these days rich, as most people in New York seemed rich; as, in spite of Bob's depredations, Florence Ash was, as even Mrs Folliott was in spite of Phil Bloodgood's, as even Phil Bloodgood himself must have been for reasons too obvious; as in fine everyone had a secret for being, or for feeling, or for looking, everyone at least but Mark Monteith" (XII, 444).

Winch lived in a studio apartment, the chic place to live in at the turn of the century. As early as 1879 studio apartments were being designed, not only for artists, but for men who lived the bachelor life. A news item from the New York *Tribune* on August 8, 1879, tells us that "The Sherwood," John H. Sherwood's "new apartment house, is a most eligible one at Fifty-seventh Street and Sixth Avenue." Each "suite consists of a good-sized parlor with open fireplace and bedroom and closets. . . . Besides the convenience of an elevator which will run til midnight there is a back staircase for the servants."

Winch's apartment, however, is more contemporary. "The place," which had "a general air of other profusions and amplitudes, might have put him off a little by its several rather glaringly false accents, those of contemporary domestic 'art' striking a little wild" (XII, 444). Cornelia's modern apartment with her own idiosyncratic possessions has disappeared and the hotel, which now dominates all of New York life, dictates the elaborate furnishings of Winch's studio. "The scene was smaller, but the rich confused complexion of the Pocahontas, showing through Du Barry paint and patches, might have set the example—which had been followed with the costliest candour—so that clearly Winch was in these days rich, as most people in New York seemed rich" (XII, 444). The Louis XV craze, which dominated the bedrooms and the public rooms at the Waldorf, characterized the decor of the bachelor's flat.

Through "the quite splendidly vulgar appeal of fifty overdone decorative effects," Winch achieved style: "Were these the things New York did when you just gave her *all* her head, and that he himself then had perhaps too complacently missed?" (XII, 445). However, these "decorative effects" were but a masquerade, as the rooms in the hotel had been, designed to conceal the corrupt nature of Winch's career (Figure 10).

The hotel world James talks about in *The American Scene* has a different tone from the world of "A Round of Visits." The myriads of rich leisurely New Yorkers who find their shrine in the large hotel do not quite have the desperate tone of the lost characters who haunt James's story. The characters in the story are depressed and unlucky. Monteith is a spiritless man who cannot even feel strongly about Winch's suicide. All he can say is "I really think I must practically have caused it." Mrs. Ash, a woman who has social status in Paris but not in New York, is now without a husband and without her expatriate glamour. The hotel girls are simply ornaments of the hotel world and could not exist in another medium. Winch is a doomed embezzler, a stockbroker who cannot face infamy and therefore takes his own life when his crimes are discovered.

As building images peppered the other New York stories, so we find them again in "A Round of Visits," in which there are more varieties of New York buildings than in any of the other stories. The brownstone has been thoroughly demolished, but the hotel and the studio apartment buildings arch over the events of the story and affect the personalities and destinies of the characters. The hotel is described in terms of some rare architecture, thus representing the alien and exotic elements in New York life: the rooms are "rococo"; the "blocks and tiers and superpositions" are itemized; and it is called a "caravanserai," a term suggestive of an Eastern inn where caravans stopped. James also calls it a "labyrinth," a word used often both in this story and in *The American Scene* to characterize the luxury hotel. Since everything is "terrible" in this tale (from "the terrible little lady," Mrs. Folliott, to the terrible city itself, the terrible weather, the terrible influenza) and since the violence of the images prepares us for the violent suicide at the end, the ineffectuality of the poor hero reaches a point not equalled even by Herbert Dodd in "The Bench of Desolation."

The new architectural structures that set the stage in the New York stories (the skyscraper, the museum, the interior-decorated drawing rooms, the apartment house, the studio flat, and the hotel) are softened by the presence of the park, a true oasis in the "inverted comb." It is the one realm where construction and demolition cannot take place. Outside the "magic isle," "very much as the boa-constrictor winds round the group of the Laocoön" (AS, 89), the electronically driven trolley system spirals around the city in a serpentlike vise. In "A Round of Visits," the trolley's contribution to the noise of the city is major, as Monteith takes his wintry pilgrimage from hotel to house to studio apartment. "The hug of the serpent" is a subsidiary of the skyscraper, a must for the mobility of the "gregarious" population increased by the upward building. The elevator is a "hoisted and packed basket" in which freedom of will has been temporarily but necessarily suspended.

The conditions laid down by the laws of the skyscraper-hotel affect all of the characters in "A Round of Visits." Mrs. Ash has located Monteith through the hotel lists; she too has been affected by at least one plague fostered by the big city, divorce, and the hotel shelters her husband's mistress. Separation from her husband, combined with the character of New York, which does not foster individuality, makes it impossible to pull her transplanted salon together without "something alien" creeping in. The ladies of the Pocahontas at Sunday lunch are purely puppets of the skyscraper hotel. Their friendship depends on their liking to take lunch there and on their ability to "talk only in hotel terms." The hotel has by architectural design arranged for all the rituals and even the necessities of urban life.

Monteith is propelled by the momentum of encounters within "the labyrinth" of the hotel, the place where he met Mrs. Folliott, where Mrs. Ash found him, where he met Winch's sister-in-law, and, finally, where he came to be cajoled to visit Winch. The city, James is implying, in its extreme weather contrasts (outside polar and inside tropical) exerts an extremity of control over persons, destroying the will and actually delivering the innocent victims of unscrupulous "downtown" operators and manipulators over to slaughter. In some ways, James's New York has become Milton's hell.

An Interlude in Hell

Elements from the underworld haunt "A Round of Visits" and other stories of this period. Even "The Married Son" from *The Whole Family*, appearing two years before the *Finer Grain* tales, opens with the mother's fears expressed by the atmosphere of the "black forest of the 'facts of life,' " similar to Africans' "nocturnal terrors, the mysteries and monstrosities that make them seal themselves up in the huts as soon as it gets dark" (*WF*, 145). "The Jolly Corner" has the ghost of the man Brydon might have been. "Crapy Cornelia" is haunted by the specters of the old society, by the youth of the middle-aged "old" New Yorkers, and by the ghost of a vanished life. But when we get to "A Round of Visits," we are placed in "remarkable, unspeakable New York," the very realm of Satan himself. In 1900 "The Great Good Place" had reflected James's notion of a heaven; now, in 1909, "A Round of Visits" reflects his notion of hell. Heaven, or James's equivalent of such a place, had been situated in a dream and placed somewhere near London in Sussex, Kent, or Surrey. But James's hell is located in New York City at the time he visited it, in a world distinguished by betrayal, freezing weather, snow, influenza, and finally suicide. His model is John Milton's epic, *Paradise Lost*.

"A Round of Visits," published in 1910, gives us as close a picture of hell as James ever invented, and that hell is for James the reality of New York life. Its begetter, its symbol, and its habitation is the skyscraper.

James's tale, placed in "remarkable, unspeakable New York," describes the realm of Satan himself. The tapestry bergère with the "spectral subjects" unites the one episode of Mrs. Ash with the suicide episode of Newton Winch in his beautifully decorated, impersonal, hotel-inspired studio apartment. "Mark sat back in his chair . . . very much in fact as he had appeared an hour ago in the old tapestry *bergère*" (XII, 449). The reader is to remember that Mrs. Ash's similar chair had "delicious little spectral 'subjects' on the back and seat" (XII, 439–40), a reminder undoubtedly of the underworld element of both "rounds" in the story.

The literary parallel can be found in Book One of Milton's *Paradise Lost*. In *The American Scene* James identifies the Waldorf-Astoria with Satan's palace, Pandemonium. On a "winter afternoon" through "the endless labyrinth [a Miltonic word] of the Waldorf-Astoria was I happily to chance . . .

into enlightened contemplation of a pandemonium not less admirably ordered . . . than rarely intermitted [another Miltonic word]" (AS, 99). Curiously and significantly, Milton's Pandemonium had also arisen through the combined efforts of Mammon and that genius of engineering, Mulciber (Vulcan). In fact, James is not one to have missed the implication from Book One of *Paradise Lost* that these two rebel angels had, between them, in hell invented the skyscraper.

These "Spirits reprobate" seem to have discovered how to make a steel foundation from "the massy ore." By skimming its dregs and making "A various mould," they "fill'd each hollow nook," and "out of the earth a Fabric huge / Rose like an Exhalation" (*PL*, I, 710–11). In the same manner that the skyscrapers of the turn of the century in New York would boast of classical architectural motifs, so this huge building in Hell was "Built like a Temple, where Pilasters round / Were set, and Doric pillars overlaid / With Golden Architrave" (*PL*, I, 713–15). Its height Milton stresses: "Th'ascending pile / Stood fixed her stately highth" (*PL*, I, 722–23). One familiar with the skyscrapers of the twentieth century would see their myriad windows blazing with electric light (windows James describes in *The American Scene*), prefigured in the skyscrapers in Hell: "from the arched roof / Pendent by subtle Magic many a row / Of Starry Lamps and blazing Cressets fed / With Naphtha and Asphaltus yielded light / As from a sky" (*PL*, I, 724–30). Mulciber's "hand was known / In Heav'n by many a Tow'red structure high, / Where Scepter'd Angels held their residence" (*PL*, I, 732–34). Outlawed with Satan from heaven, he "was headlong sent / With his industrious crew to build in Hell" (*PL*, I, 750–51). "At Pandemonium, the High Capital / of Satan and his Peers" (*PL*, I, 756–57), the great hall was erected and James's skyscraper hotel is the modern equivalent.

Monteith the hero is propelled by the momentum of encounters within "the labyrinth" of the hotel. The Miltonic word *labyrinth* is used often both in this story and in *The American Scene* to characterize the luxury hotel. Everything is "terrible" in this tale, and the violence of the images prepares us for the violent suicide at the end.

The infernal conditions, the dominance of the skyscraper, the noisy hotel suggestive of Pandemonium, the betrayal, the suicide, and the prevalence of New York's plague, influenza, made "the remarkable, unspeakable" city both as attractive and repulsive to James as hell was for Milton, expressed in terms remembered and inherited from the seventeenth-century writer. "A Round of Visits" is truly an interlude in hell.

The Romance of Finance: Some Icons Parsed

James's revulsion at what America was becoming, described vividly but coldly in *The American Scene* and clearly presented in "The Jolly Corner" and "A Round of Visits," fits the conventional pattern of the reclusive expatriate James. His ambivalent attitude toward American commercialism and the pursuit of money and especially power (already touched on in "The Jolly Corner") is not so widely appreciated. His bitterness in *The Ivory Tower* is offset by the rich, romantic description of Aurora Coyne in *The Sense of the Past* and the attractiveness of the alter ego in "The Jolly Corner." James's romance with finance can be properly illuminated if we look at the meaning of some fictional icons that appear in the late works.

The Panic of 1907 and John Pierpont Morgan in "A Round of Visits"

"A Round of Visits," the last tale published by Henry James and reprinted in his last collection of short tales, *The Finer Grain*, in 1910, is part of a complex with such various connotations and associations that it can be read for multiple reasons and points to the pluralistic universe that James's world became in the twentieth century. For instance, among *The Finer Grain* tales, each story can be read as following a variety of tracks. "The Bench of Desolation" can be read as a reflection of the breach of promise suit that was being filed against Morton Fullerton (see *The Master*), James's and Edith Wharton's friend. We can also read it either as a black fairy tale or as a story influenced by George Gissing's world (see chapter 4). So, too, "A Round of Visits" in that volume can be read as a reflection of a Miltonic version of Hell placed in the modern world or in the form of a "round" in response to Arthur Schnitzler's *Reigen*—a "round" in which the plague of syphilis from the Viennese play is suggested by the influenza epidemic in New York City.[2]

2. Adeline R. Tintner, *The Cosmopolitan World of Henry James* (Baton Rouge, 1991), 270–76.

But it also can be viewed as a reflection of the financial panic of 1907 in New York City.

The reader of the tale is thrust immediately at the onset into a daily calendar account of the arrival of Mark Monteith, the hero, in New York City from Europe. We are told: "He had got in on Tuesday; he had spent Wednesday for the most part down town, looking into the dismal subject of his anxiety" and "it was through information reaching him on Wednesday evening . . . that he had measured his loss. . . . He had waked up on Thursday morning . . . with the sense . . . of a blinding New York blizzard and of a deep sore inward ache" (XII, 427), that is, both from the influenza and from his financial injury. After a few pages telling us the reasons for Monteith's coming to the metropolis, the betrayal by his financial agent, we are told that he continued to be sick with influenza on Thursday and that "at last, on Sunday, he decided to leave his room" (XII, 430).

The careful itemization of the better part of a week of anxiety for a man who had been the victim of financial betrayal conjured up for the contemporary reader of 1910 the memory of the severest week in the history of the New York financial world up to that date. Although James may not have paid attention to the "downtown" world before, except tangentially, as in "Guest's Confession" of 1872, as in *The American,* where Newman, after making a fortune, wishes to buy up souvenirs of Europe, or in the character of Adam Verver, who, in *The Golden Bowl,* has forgotten his business world and now collects art, in James's last tale, he grapples with the type of "absconder" seen in the midst of financial speculations or at least in the wake of those speculations. James summons up events that did take place in New York in October of 1907 during what was to be known as the Great Panic.

The panic of 1907 took place all within one week (as did Mark Monteith's), following Theodore Roosevelt's famous talk at the Gridiron Club attacking the "malefactors of great wealth" (CH, 112) and following excessive speculation in copper mining and railroad stocks. It was the recklessness of the trust companies that triggered it, for what had been safe investments had become by 1907 extremely speculative. Through legal loopholes, trust executives operated like stock market plungers. By October, a large proportion of bank loans in New York used only securities as collateral. It was during the week beginning Monday, October 21, 1907, that the collapse in copper undermined the entire existence of trusts. Thousands of depositors of the Knickerbocker Trust stormed its doors, and the next day, Tuesday, October 22, the Knickerbocker Trust failed. A few weeks later, Charles Barney, president of the Knickerbocker Trust, shot himself after he was refused help by John Pierpont Morgan (CH, 122–23). On Tuesday night, Morgan met with the Secretary of the Treasury, who pledged financial support. On Wednesday, October 23, Morgan met with the presidents of the trusts and created a rescue pool. By Thursday, October 24, after stock trading was halted, twenty-five million dollars had been guaranteed by the government. On Friday night, October 25, Morgan told religious leaders to preach sermons on Sunday to calm the terrified New York investors.

This was the week in which the financial crisis was met by J. P. Morgan. It dominated all the newspapers, including both the New York *Times* and the London *Times,* and Henry James, who had the London *Times* delivered in the morning and an evening paper as well, must have been aware of it.

As we have seen, this week is curiously but carefully reflected in "A Round of Visits." There is described, day by day, a week in which the hero has learned that his own kinsman and financial agent, Phil Bloodgood, has absconded with the greater part of his money. It is interesting that during the week in which Morgan saved the financial future of America he was also suffering from a severe cold for which his doctor "plied his throat with sprays and gargles" (CH, 126) as he dozed from this illness during an emergency meeting (CH, 126). It seems quite probable that the suicide of the president of the Knickerbocker Trust is reflected in James's tale in the suicide of Newton Winch, one of the "absconders" (XII, 434), who, unlike Monteith's own broker, has "stayed to take" his punishment (XII, 457).

If we follow the text of the story, we find a series of phrases and words that, in a subdued way, stage the "downtown" scene. The hotel expresses for Monteith "the whole bustle of the market" (XII, 431). Although Mrs. Folliott has lost ten thousand dollars from her and Monteith's "agent," Phil Bloodgood, her "crowd" ignores Monteith's whole episode, either because there had "been no hue or cry for him" or because there had been too many other absconders in "the interval" (XII, 434). Mrs. Ash, who has troubles other than financial, wants to do without "horrible proceedings" (XII, 439) in her plans for a separation from her husband. The word *agent,* the official Wall Street term for the man who represents investments for individuals, occurs a few times. Bloodgood is Mrs. Folliott's "confidential American agent" (XII, 431). The word *trust* is presented in Monteith's having "abjectly trusted" Bloodgood (XII, 429). We find it again in "some admonition finer than any it might trust to chance for" (XII, 443). We also find "treacherous" (XII, 429); "faithless" (XII, 444); "an act of bad faith" (XII, 445); "appropriator of *her* securities" and "swindle" (XII, 452); "betrayal" and "the education of business" (XII, 457). These terms are inconspicuously scattered throughout this tale of the dismay of a betrayed investor whose "agent" was his kinsman and childhood friend—an agent who had absconded and whose "engaging, treacherous face" (XII, 429) belied his criminality, one who had fled "for parts unknown" (XII, 430). These terms do manage to recreate the atmosphere of a week of a panic when the trusts and the trust of the country in its financial foundations had suddenly all collapsed.

The suicide of Newton Winch, the main "absconder" of this tale, may be a reflection of Charles Barney's suicide at the time the Knickerbocker Trust had failed, after Morgan had ignored his personal appeal. Winch's suicide in the story is actually facilitated by Mark Monteith, who, in his innocence and need to ventilate his anger at his trusted agent's betrayal, revealed his inability to forgive the man who had deprived him of part of his income. Realizing no one would have mercy on him, Winch kills himself as a direct result of Monteith's insensitivity to his own betraying agent.

The situation is clearly James's only attempt, since "Guest's Confession" in 1872, at showing how the imagination of financial disaster operates. The ingredients that went into it were those that were beginning to distinguish the behavior of "the securities" market, a term also found in the tale (XII, 449), a pattern that climaxed in the later financial collapse of 1928, which resulted in a depression of more than ten years, and in the many situations of the 1980s when junk bonds were created and failed. In 1907, the disaster affected thousands of investors who had put their trust in the trusts, which had become more and more devalued by greedy speculators such as Phil Bloodgood, even though he was of "good blood," and Newton Winch. Winch, however, who had always affected Monteith as vulgar, crude, and lacking in human feelings, becomes a hero in the last hours of his life.

When we pay attention to Winch, James's only full-length portrait of a Wall Street embezzler, we come up with a solid, physically delineated personality, much more clearly defined than any other character in the tale. Not only do we have a picture of him as he appears when Monteith visits him, but we also have a picture of what kind of man he was before he received "the education of business" (XII, 457). We also see him in his milieu, so we can estimate his taste. We know he is tall, for he has "long legs" (XII, 454) and "long fingers" (XII, 450) that are also "fine" (XII, 444). His eyes are "passingly depressed and quickened" (XII, 454). Monteith sees a man totally different from the Winch he knew years ago in his law-school days when Winch had been "clever only for uncouth and questionable things" (XII, 444) and he had been known as "coarse" and "common" (XII, 445). Now he has been "mysteriously . . . educated" (XII, 444). But one of the chief changes is that earlier he had worn "one of the vulgarest of moustaches" (XII, 447) and now he has shaved. His face has become improved. His shaving was the "key to . . . the capture of refinement" (XII, 448). His surroundings show now an interest in objects of decoration and visual satisfaction. Some "glaringly false accents" (XII, 444) are still there. James uses the phrase "a wild strike," slightly altered as "striking a little wild" (XII, 444), to refer to the discovery of contemporary art. This display of costly objects proved to Monteith that Winch was rich, made visible in a "great hearth-rug that was a triumph of modern orientalism" (XII, 451) and "the low, luxurious morocco chair—it was of the finest orange colour" (XII, 457), a testament to his taste as a collector and a decorator, reflecting a refinement different from the Winch of the past. It has been an education in the arts, as well as "the education of business" (XII, 457). The man presented clearly has certain contradictory characteristics, but his concrete figure is established in a way Monteith's is not and in a way Mrs. Ash's is not, though Mrs. Folliott's is also physically represented because of her likeness to a François Boucher painting (XII, 432).

From such a description of Winch, it is not too farfetched to see that James is resurrecting the main figure in the panic of 1907: John Pierpont Morgan. It was he who had single-handedly saved the nation, but as a self-sacrificer, unlike Winch, though the figure of Morgan has clothed the figure of Winch. Both were six feet tall. Both were accustomed to wearing at one time "the vulgarest of moustaches," and both were educated by business and by the arts. James never in his fiction mentioned Morgan, though he vaguely invokes his presence in his comments in *The American Scene* when he discusses the policy of the Metropolitan Museum (*AS*, 191).

James suggests Morgan later on in the character of Breckenridge Bender in *The Outcry* as the collector with the limitless checkbook.[3] James is known to have visited Junius, Pierpont's father, in his house in London and perhaps to have thought of Morgan as someone behind the character of Adam Verver in *The Golden Bowl.* But in the contradictions within their characters (the businessman versus the art collector), in the nervousness of both men, in the fact that both Winch's and Morgan's first wives had died early in their marriages, and in their common interest in decor (Winch's bachelor apartment and Morgan's house), there are many points of similarity between the fictive character and the financial tycoon. It is as if James is saying that if Morgan had been in such a position, perhaps he too would have revealed his more sensitive characteristics. The reader might ask, if this is a portrait of Morgan, why wasn't a large nose referred to, since that was the popular clue to Morgan? But that was not James's way. The nose was the source, it is true, of many Morgan anecdotes, but the florid features and the coarse appearance were just as much a giveaway, though not as obvious or detectable. To make Newton Winch sport a large nose would have betrayed James's source too easily. The portrait, therefore, would have to be a hidden one and one simply inferred because of certain associations—the associations of finance and of the "handlebar moustache" and the plunging tactics of a speculator, both of which Morgan displayed early in his career—and the wide distribution of photographic images of a world-famous financier. Of course, the portrait is not consistent because Morgan did just the opposite of embezzlement during the panic of 1907. He rescued the failing trusts and the country at large. The character of Newton Winch combines both the external attributes of Morgan and the internal attributes of Charles Barney, the president of the Knickerbocker Trust and a suicide.

So one might look back upon this portrait of Newton Winch as a composite one—one that conflates the hero of the crisis of the panic of 1907, John Pierpont Morgan, with one of the victims of that panic. The portrait is made up of fragments of the disaster: the sudden loss of income for so many depositors and investors and the loss of trust between friends and kinsmen. The meaning of the financial "trust" lost its simple, direct connection with the word *trust* as we know it. That James was intrigued by this aspect of "downtown" business is further shown in the unfinished novel *The Ivory*

3. Henry James, *The Outcry* (New York, 1911), *passim.*

Tower, which remained unfinished because of the outbreak of World War I but which carried to another level the financial victimization of the hero, who also returns from Europe only to be exposed to greedy speculators. The criminal aspects of society began to engage James's imagination in the new century.

Morgan as a young man was also a reckless investor, so that Winch's earlier resemblance to the younger Morgan is not too farfetched, for Morgan had the same "false accents" that Winch displayed in his apartment. The great financier was partial to "polka dotted vests, bright cravats, and checkered pants" (CH, 20). Born in 1837, six years before James, Morgan, as a young man, entered into "rash, unauthorized speculation" in 1859. "He gambled his firm's capital on a boatload of Brazilian coffee that had arrived in port without a buyer. He bought the entire shipment and resold it at a quick profit" (CH, 20–21). At this time, he sported his "handlebar moustache" and was characterized by "full lips and an intense gaze. . . . He already seemed restless" (CH, 21). Witness Winch's "pale, nervous" face (XII, 444). Morgan also engineered an equivocal deal of carbines during the Civil War, which he saw "as an occasion for profit, not service" (CH, 22). During the war he also engaged in highly speculative dealings (CH, 22). His recent biographer continues, "If Pierpont seemed corrupted by rowdy wartime Wall Street, he could also be unexpectedly tender-hearted" (CH, 22), for he fell in love with Mimi Sturges, a gentle, tubercular girl, like Minny Temple, but after a few months of marriage, she died. Winch also, we are told in James's tale, had been married to a wife who "had died only two years after marrying" (XII, 435).

This fusion of two main participants in the 1907 panic—Charles Barney providing the suicide when Morgan refused to save the Knickerbocker Trust, and Morgan providing the flamboyant and coarse financier with a tender heart and refined taste—marks an advance in James's formulation of the double personality, the kind he had written about two years before in "The Jolly Corner." In that story, Spencer Brydon, the expatriate, confronts his alter ego, the man who stayed in the United States and became a financier, who is himself transformed into an "evil, odious, blatant, vulgar" person (XII, 226). In "A Round of Visits," Newton Winch combines the two personalities, Barney the suicide, about whom we know very little, and the often-characterized, striking, idiosyncratic figure of J. P. Morgan, six feet tall, nervous, and always smoking cigars (Winch had offered Monteith "cigars, cordials, ash-trays" [XII, 444–45]); the two men are blended together.

The change in Winch seems also to repeat the change in Morgan himself, who became transformed from a coarse, aggressively dressed young man (and we see his taste for polka-dots lasted as late as the famous Steichen photograph) to the mediator and single-handed saviour of the country from the financial tight spot it was in in 1907. Like Morgan, Winch had "suddenly and mysteriously been educated" (XII, 444). It had been, Monteith realized at last, "the education of business, of which the fruits were all around them" (XII, 457)—those fruits that were like the fruits of Morgan's wild buying sprees, which were gathered in his home. Newton affects Mark as "the most distinguished of men" (XII, 446), for what "his pale, nervous, smiling, clean-shaven host had undergone since their last meeting [was] some extraordinary process of refinement" (XII, 444).

We can see even more easily how James's financier in "A Round of Visits," one who cheats and behaves criminally toward his investors, would be formed also by other aspects of Morgan's persona: the vulgar moustache, the aggressive expression we see in all photographs of Morgan's face, his height and his appearance of restlessness, his hands, which "beat a tattoo on his thighs" (XII, 450). Newton declares himself a "nervous beast" (XII, 449) and is seen "violently shaking keys or money, in his trousers pocket" (XII, 453).

What James may be saying in his portrait of Newton Winch is that the victim and the victor can be the same man, depending on how fortune favors or destroys him. We have seen from the early years of Morgan how the speculator in him almost ruined him and how in 1907 his productive ability to orchestrate certain reserves for the control over financial uncertainty was all part of his speculative manipulation, only this time it worked for the benefit of the country. Charles Barney sacrificed his life partly because Morgan did not stretch out a hand to help him, just as Newton Winch kills himself partly because Monteith indicates to him that he would not have mercy on his own betrayer. Monteith, therefore, takes on the characteristic of the historic Morgan in not extending his help to a man in need, who, because of this failure of human kindness, kills himself. The figure of Morgan as *the* power behind the financial world in America at this time hovers over both men in James's last tale and provides a physical and psychological foundation for James's well-developed portrait of a Wall Street speculator caught in criminal activities and paying the supreme price for his exploitation of those who trusted him.

In addition to this block of matter, there exists a close literary forerunner, an Edith Wharton story, the plot of which James follows and adapts to his purpose. The Wharton story is "A Cup of Cold Water" in *The Greater Inclination,* published in 1899, which James read, since her sister-in-law, Mary Cadwalader Jones, a friend of James, had sent him the volume. James had answered this gift of two books of E. W. and thanked Mrs. Jones for *The Greater Inclination,* though he never mentioned this story. In Wharton's tale, Woburn, ruined financially and morally, goes to a ball knowing that his fiancée is unaware of his business crimes. Wharton's tale, like James's "A Round of Visits," is set in New York on a frosty windy day. The hero makes a round of visits from the cold outside into warmly lighted social interiors, just as Monteith does. The Wharton tale is told from the point of view of the criminal, not the victim, and it is the embezzler who comes into the warmth from the cold. The encounter with a policeman and the suicide attempt that we meet in James's tale both have occurred first in Wharton's story, but her hero prevents the suicide. Monteith does not in James's tale. In fact, the last line of James's tale is: "I really think I must practically have caused it" (XII, 459). Wharton's hero redeems himself by saving a woman's life and being able, by this act, to give himself up.

James has made certain alterations in what is the same basic plot in order to meet the demands of his special preoccupations. Mark Monteith, self-absorbed expatriate, returns to New York to investigate his having been defrauded by a relation. Trying to get some sympathy from two lady friends (one of whom has shared the same kind of financial disaster, only not so badly) but finding himself giving it instead, he finally unloads his woes on an unexpectedly sympathetic embezzler who commits suicide once he realizes how bitter an exploited client can be and how disastrous his imminent arrest will be for him. James also implies that if the two women had allowed Monteith to express his unhappiness, he would not have been put into the position of unwittingly causing a suicide.

In both Wharton and James, we find the subject is the financial embezzler, but for James's story the scandal of the panic of 1907 was right before him, and we can see how certain popular crimes caught his attention. An interest in crime suddenly appears in his life two years before his death and right before World War I, an interest that will be treated later in this book.

"A Great Modern Master": Edward Steichen's Photograph of John Pierpont Morgan and "The Jolly Corner"

It has in the past been assumed that the appearance of the coarse and aggressive alter ego in "The Jolly Corner" in 1908 in its resemblance to a "portrait by a great modern master" might refer to some work by John Singer Sargent.[4] The relevant quotation reads: "So Brydon, before him, took him in; with every fact of him now, in the higher light, hard and acute . . . his queer actuality of evening-dress, of dangling double eye-glass, of gleaming silk lappet and *white linen*, of pearl button and *gold watch-guard* and polished shoe. No portrait by a great modern master could have presented him with more *intensity, thrust him out of his frame with more art*, as if there had been 'treatment' of the consummate sort, in his every shade and salience" (XII, 225; italics added). When he sees him first with his hands before his face, Brydon observes that he "had lost two fingers, which were reduced to stumps, as if accidentally shot away" (XII, 225). Then, when the hands "began to move, to open," the face was left "uncovered and presented." The impression is stunning:

> Horror, with the sight, had leaped into Brydon's throat . . . for the bared identity was too hideous as *his*. . . . The face, *that* face, Spencer Brydon's?—he searched it still, but looking away from it in dismay and denial, falling straight from his height of sublimity. It was unknown, inconceivable, awful. . . . The face was the face of a stranger . . . for the stranger, whoever he might be, evil, odious, blatant, vulgar, had *advanced as for aggression*, and he knew himself give ground. Then harder pressed still, sick with the force of his shock, and falling back as under the hot breath and the *roused passion of a life larger than his own*, a rage of personality before which his own collapsed. (XII, 225–26; italics added, except for "*that* face")

None of Sargent's portraits of men that have been suggested, such as those of Asher Wertheimer or of John D. Rockefeller, exhibit any of the

---

4. Viola Hopkins Winner, *Henry James and the Visual Arts* (Charlottesville, Va., 1970), 74.

characteristics of this kind of image that James has described for the reader, but there is one picture that does. It is not a painting but a photograph by an equally "modern master"—a master of photography—the twenty-eight-year-old Edward Steichen, who had become well known during these years in London, creating a likeness that can measure up factually and psychologically to the impression of James's alter ego. Steichen had taken this photograph of John Pierpont Morgan in 1903 in a two-minute exposure, but Morgan, sensitive to his own crude appearance, which had little to do with a man of his sensibility and taste, destroyed the first print (Figure 11). Steichen describes the setting and its consequences:

> I suggested a different position of the hands and a movement of the head. He took the head position, but said, in an irritated tone, that it was uncomfortable, so I suggested he move his head to a position that felt natural. He moved his head several times and ended exactly where it had been "uncomfortable" before, except that this time he took the pose of his own volition. But his expression had sharpened and his body posture became tense, possibly a reflex of his irritation at the suggestion I had made. I saw that a dynamic self-assertion had taken place, whatever its cause, and I quickly made the second exposure, saying, "Thank you, Mr. Morgan," as I took the plate holder out of the camera.
>
> He said, "Is that all?"
>
> "Yes, sir," I answered.
>
> He snorted a reply, "I like you, young man. I think we'll get along first-rate together." Then he clapped his large hat on his massive head, took up his big cigar, and stormed out of the room. Total time, three minutes. . . .
>
> When I took the proofs to Morgan, he thought the one I had retouched for Encke was fine, and he ordered a dozen prints. Then he looked at the other print that I had made for myself. He said, "Terrible," and tore it into shreds. This act of tearing up something that did not belong to him riled my blood. I was not angry because he did not like the picture but because he tore it up. That stung very deep.
>
> I made the twelve prints that he had ordered and sent them to him, but I took the good negative with me when I went back to Paris and made an enlarged negative. Then I worked for a long time before I got what I considered the best possible print. . . . The next time I came back to New York, I brought this print along and presented it to [Alfred] Stieglitz. Later he included it in an exhibition of my photographs. Belle da Costa Greene, Morgan's librarian, was a constant visitor to 291 [Stieglitz's gallery], and when she saw that print of

Morgan, she became very excited. She said it was the best portrait of him that existed in any medium, and she asked Stieglitz to let her take it to show Mr. Morgan. The next morning she reported that, when she showed the picture to Morgan and told him how wonderful she thought it was, he said he never had seen this picture. Apparently he had forgotten that he had torn up my proof. . . . Morgan told Belle da Costa Greene to buy the picture for him. She said she was sure Stieglitz wouldn't sell it, but Morgan said to pay him well for it. He even suggested offering him five thousand dollars, if necessary. Stieglitz, of course, turned down the offer.

When Morgan found out that he couldn't buy that print, he wanted me to make some prints for him. . . . For about two years, cablegrams and letters kept arriving, but I ignored them. This was my rather childish way of getting even with Morgan for tearing up that first proof. About three years later, I did make a group of prints for him. . . .

Over the years people have referred to the insight into Morgan's real character that I showed by photographing him with a dagger in his hand. But this was their own fanciful interpretation of Morgan's hand firmly grasping the arm of the chair. . . .

The experience of photographing J. P. Morgan taught me an important lesson. . . . In photographing the dynamic personality of Morgan, I found that, when he sat in the pose he habitually took for the painter, all I saw was the map of his face, blank and lifeless. But when he was irritated, even by a trifle, something touched the quick of his personality and he reacted swiftly and decisively. The lesson was that a portrait must get beyond the almost universal self-consciousness that people have before the camera.[5]

Morgan had allowed the photograph to be published, and published it was in *Camera Work* in April of 1906 as a *Special Steichen Supplement, Plate 2*, by Alfred Stieglitz at 1111 Madison Avenue. Just at this time in 1906, Henry James was seeing young Alvin Langdon Coburn, also a young photographer and great friend of Steichen, to do his photographic illustrations for the New York Edition in June of 1906 and again on July 3 of that year at Lamb House. Coburn and Steichen were considered the two outstanding young photographers in London at that time. It is probable that when Coburn visited James he brought with him the Steichen *Supplement*

5. Eugene Steichen, *A Life in Photography* (New York, 1963), sec. 3; *New York, Stieglitz and the Photo-Secession*, unpaginated.

of *Camera Work*. Surely in July, when Coburn visited James again, he must have shown his own portraits in Number 15 of *Camera Work*, published in July, which contained five photographs by Coburn. Later on, *Camera Work* produced many issues with Coburn photographs. We also know that James (*MA*, 313) could not sleep during the night of August 3, 1906, for he wrote in his head all night long the story he was to call "The Jolly Corner."

What is of interest for us is that we find that Henry James signed his name on July 31, 1906, in the guestbook at J. P. Morgan's Prince's Gate House in London, and it was on August 3, during the night, that he found himself kept awake by the idea for a story of "himself *as he might have been* had he stayed at home" (*MA*, 312–13). He had made this visit to Morgan's house in the company of his friend, Dr. Henry White.[6] We do not know whether he had met Morgan personally and had been exposed to his some-what intimidating presence. Yet it does seem highly significant that three days later he had his troubled night. By being in Morgan's house, he might have been exposed, if not personally to the man, for we are not sure he saw him there, but possibly to the photograph that may have been exhibited. It is more likely that Coburn showed Henry James the photo in the portfolio devoted to Steichen's portraits in 1906. It is significant that there clearly is a connection between Morgan's personality, including his role as the chief financial titan in New York at the time, and the alter ego in "The Jolly Corner."

From Coburn's autobiography we learn that Steichen, in his early twen-ties, was a "dynamic personality with promise of his later achievements" and that in 1900, at the age of twenty-five, he had held an exhibition at the Royal Photographic Society, which consisted of 375 photographs in which there were "21 by Steichen and 9 by [Coburn]."[7] In October of 1906, Coburn went to Paris to do James's frontispieces. "Early in November Henry James came up to London," and "in the middle of December" he was in Venice.[8] Certainly during this year James must have been made aware of recent avant garde photography as never before, and as we know from the preface to

6. Communication from Jean Strouse, author of *Morgan* (New York, 1999), to Adeline R. Tintner, May, 1992. See also *Morgan*, 653.

7. *Alvin Langdon Coburn, Photographer: An Autobiography*, ed. Helmut Gernsheim and Alison Gernsheim (New York, 1966), 14, 16.

8. *Ibid.*, 54.

Volume 24 of the New York Edition, he credits Coburn by name as having been the perfect illustrator of his edition.

"The Jolly Corner" was published in December of 1908 in *The English Review* and then made it just in time to be part of one of the volumes of the New York Edition. If we look at the illustration of Steichen's portrait of Morgan (Figure 11), it is not hard to see that it is a closer likeness than any of the proposed Sargent portraits in hand. Edward Steichen is quoted as saying, "Meeting his black eyes was like confronting the headlights of an express train bearing down on you," suggesting the aggressive personality of both Morgan and James's alter ego.[9] What we do see, a certain point that does correspond in a way to James's description of the alter ego, is that no modern master could "have presented him with more intensity, thrust him out of his frame with more art" (XII, 225), as if there had been "treatment," as James continues, "of the consummate sort, in his every shade and salience." This does not necessarily refer to the treatment by a painter. It might also describe the treatment by a brilliant photographer who must manipulate chemicals in his processing of the image. "Shade and salience" would express the difference between the bright-faced, winged collar, the "gold watch-guard," as well as the vivid light shining on the arm of the chair on which Morgan sits and the darkness of his suit. It is clear that Morgan's hands resemble the "two fingers, which were reduced to stumps" (XII, 225) of James's figure. In none of the photographs of Sargent's paintings that have been widely published do we see such a good example of a gold watch-guard. "The stranger, whoever he might be, evil, odious, blatant, vulgar" (XII, 226), might seem to be visibly portrayed in the unfortunate face that Morgan was given: the large nose of bad shape and surface and the glaring eyes. Morgan, in the photograph, looks as if he is about to propel himself with his seemingly mutilated hand out of the chair in a "roused passion of a life larger than" Brydon's own, with "a rage of personality before which his own collapsed" (XII, 226). One would not like to meet the J. P. Morgan shown in Steichen's photograph in an empty house late at night.

I am suggesting that in the story as he framed it in that August of 1906 during the time that he began to know and work with Alvin Coburn, James,

9. Cass Canfield, *The Incredible Pierpont Morgan: Financier and Art Collector* (New York, 1974), 94.

who saw things in concrete terms, would be conjuring up this product of "a modern master," a master of photography, that form with which James was highly involved during 1906, a year during which this great portrait by Steichen was finally revealed to the public and made accessible to James. A few weeks after July 3, 1906, Coburn again visited Lamb House, possibly carrying with him the *Camera Work Supplement* featuring the Steichen photograph of Morgan. Since James had just gone to the house of the intimidating titan of finance, the photograph would have intensified Morgan's legend and clearly showed "the roused passion of a life larger than his own, a rage of personality before which his own collapsed" (XII, 226), the image of a man over six feet tall and of extraordinary financial and personal power, John Pierpont Morgan.

Morgan was a fascinating figure. In 1907, as we saw, he had saved the United States government from bankruptcy. He was a financial genius. In a sense, because of his supreme control over the financial resources of the country, he seemed to exude an evil aura, but at the same time, he was a very greedy art collector. Perhaps this greed and this lack of control over his impulse to buy everything he saw was a recompense to him for the tight control he had to have over his financial machinations. In 1904 James criticized Morgan's policy in the acquisition and the de-acquisition of pictures in the Metropolitan Museum without quoting his name, but he had become critical of that institution because of Morgan's presidency, which occurred during the year 1904, when James visited America. He may not have lost fingers like James's alter ego, but his face was vulgar and ugly, and his expression truculent. The photograph by Steichen surely shows him poised for aggression, and he looks as if he holds a dagger or knife in his left hand. But the left hand also looks as if it might have lost its fingers, a characteristic apparently of all the portraits by Sargent of these men. It is what happens when the hand of the sitter is posed on a chair.

But Morgan was also a hero in his genius for financial control. We have seen reflections of him in Newton Winch in James's last published story, "A Round of Visits." In the aftermath of his New York trip from 1904 through 1905, Henry James had found a new subject, "downtown" and the romance of finance, which he had ignored during most of his writing period. For although it was cruel and it was brutal, it smacked of adventure and it was in this vein that he had the heroine of "The Sense of the Past" represent the buccaneers of Wall Street.

James's Fictional Photographic Album

When James was young, he asked his friends for photographs of themselves and for photographs of art objects they saw on their European tours. When James was old, he continued to beg for photographs of his new friends, and the walls of Lamb House were filled not by works of art but by photographs of friends and family. However, photographs do not appear in his fiction until very late, and it is only in 1896 in "The Way It Came" (later titled "The Friends of the Friends") that a photograph becomes the keystone of the plot and an accessory to its denouement.

In this story, the female narrator has tried for years to have a man friend meet a woman friend of hers, since both have seen a parent at the point of death in a psychic experience. These especially gifted people shared a "perversity in regard to being photographed," reflecting in a rather sophisticated form the primitive fear of having their spirit "caught," or "captured." However, the woman narrator will only become engaged to the man if he has his photograph taken, and this photograph rests on her mantelpiece when the psychically sensitive woman friend comes to call. The latter looks long at the photograph of the man whom she has been unable to meet, and then "she turned [it] . . . over to see the back" (IX, 379). This maneuver gives her his address, and thus the photograph, with its information for her as to where he lives, provides the essential information on which the problem of the story depends. When the woman finally visits him in his rooms, the question is, was she already dead or is she still alive? The narrator believes her woman friend was already dead and that her fiancé was visited by a ghost. The narrator's "unextinguished jealousy" (IX, 397), which had become an obsession with her, and her belief that her two especially gifted friends had a ghostly experience make her break off her plans to marry the man. Six years later the mysterious death of the man only reinforces the narrator's belief that he had responded "to an irresistible call" (IX, 401) on the part of the dead woman. This is the first time a photograph is used as the keystone to the plot and as an icon relating to the psychically sensitive couple and their similar tastes.

In *The Golden Bowl* Maggie tells Amerigo that when the curiosity shop dealer came to her to say he had overcharged her for the bowl, he waited "downstairs—in the little red room." While he was waiting, he looked at the few photographs that were exhibited there and recognized two of them. "Though it was so long ago, he remembered the visit made him by the lady and the gentleman, and that gave him his connexion. It gave me mine," Maggie recounts (NYE, XXIV, 197).

Along with the photographs mentioned in *The Golden Bowl*, there is the preface to it where James speaks of the photographs he has chosen for the New York Edition. He wanted a "couple of dozen decorative 'illustrations' " (*AN*, 331). He writes that the "essence of any representational work is of course to bristle with immediate images" (*AN*, 331). He is against the tendency "to graft or 'grow' . . . a picture by another hand on [his] own picture" (*AN*, 332). He liked "expressions of no particular thing in the text, but only of the type or idea of this or that thing" (*AN*, 333), "small pictures of our 'set' stage with the actors left out" (*AN*, 333). His frontispieces would render "certain inanimate characteristics of London streets" (*AN*, 334).

Just about the same time that he was involved with choosing photographs for his New York Edition, he wrote "Crapy Cornelia" in 1909, five years after *The Golden Bowl*. It again shows James using photographs as a key to the plot's evolution and the real meaning of the story. Cornelia Rasch, an old friend of the hero, White-Mason, has a collection of "small sallow carte-de-visite photographs" taken at the time of their youth, now "spectrally faded" (XII, 360), which moved the man to choose her hearth rather than the brilliant home of Mrs. Worthingham for his future. The photograph of Mary Cardew especially ties him to old memories and makes him choose Cornelia's flat filled with old memories stimulated by her old photographs.

In "A Round of Visits," the hero, Mark Monteith, travels with a small leather "show-case" in which there are "half a dozen old photographs stuck into a leather frame" that he sets "up on a table when he stayed anywhere long enough" (XII, 429). In it, the "at last exposed 'decoy' of fate" (XII, 429) is prominently exhibited: the photograph of Phil Bloodgood, the villainous cousin who has cheated Mark out of a fortune and has absconded with the savings of his victims. The photo enters as the visible icon of the betrayal by a cousin and intimate relation. Monteith's complaints about him to Newton Winch, another embezzler, drives the latter to his suicide.

The Renaissance Princess in *The Sense of the Past*

Henry James's attraction to and his simultaneous revulsion from the American scene of money and business in New York poured forth in profusion in his late fiction. His late heroines, like Lily Gunton, Aurora Coyne, Milly Theale, and Maggie Verver, all in fiction published after 1900, are not merely rich; they are fabulously wealthy, and they are the feminine exemplars of the power that money can buy. They outlive the robber barons, merchants, and bankers of the same period, and they represent the continuity of wealth.

Aurora Coyne in *The Sense of the Past*, in James's incomplete novel, is presented with a romantic attraction stemming from her close connection with Wall Street finance, something that we have never seen before in James's fiction. Aurora, or Mrs. "Stent" Coyne, a young widow, is so rich that the suitor for her hand, Ralph Pendrel, cannot woo her with the fortune he does not have, since she has all the money she might want. It is only something unusual that he can offer her. One might translate the name Aurora Coyne as "the dawn of the dollar princess." She is a perfectly clear pre-vision by James that not only was the wealth of America in the twentieth century going to be held by women, the daughters and widows of the rich men, but her wealth means power for such women because their wealth gives them that power. There is no other heroine in James's work like her in this respect, for Isabel Archer, who inherits some money through the intervention of her cousin, does not have the wealth that Aurora Coyne seems to command, a fortune that gives her the power to buy anything at all in the world, except adventure and ancient lineage. Milly Theale, equally rich, has no power because she is dying. Maggie Verver, who cares nothing for her wealth, is interested only in her father, child, and husband. Perhaps Aurora's ancestor in some way is Miss Gunton of Poughkeepsie in James's story by that name, for courted by a prince of the Colonna family, she treats herself, James implies, as if she were of the same social rank as he is and refuses to make the moves everybody else must make in honor of the prestige of his family. But she is not likened to a Renaissance princess. It is the prince in this tale of 1900 who seems to have been drawn mostly on the impression we know James had received of the "great Titian . . . the formidable young man in black, with the small compact head, the delicate nose and the irascible blue eye," who inspires romance: "You may weave what romance you please about it, but a romance your dream must be. Handsome, clever, defiant, passionate, dangerous, it was not his fault if he hadn't adventures and to spare" (IT, 552).

What connects Lily Gunton with Aurora Coyne is that the latter seems to have been developed on a suggestion placed in this tale by James. Lady Champer explains to the stricken prince that Lily did not love him. What she loved was "all the rest": his "great historic position, the glamour of [his] name and [his] past," for "She has a sense of such things and *they* were what she loved" (XI, 92). In other words, Lily has "the sense of the past," and for that she is seen as a preliminary model for Aurora Coyne.

Aurora Coyne differs from the other three heroines in that she seems to be a symbol of great wealth rather than an individual; she proudly inherits the prestige and privileges of the fortunes that her grandfather, father, and husband have augmented, for she is in effect presented by James as an empress of the Wall Street empire. Therefore, she is consciously associated with "downtown" as the other rich heroines were not.

The New York that had been deserted by the rich for Europe in the 1870s, now, in the first decade of the twentieth century, has its great wealthy class living in mimic Renaissance palace townhouses on Park Avenue, its new avenue of the super rich, the avenue on which Aurora lives. James disparages this class in The American Scene, but in his uncompleted fiction, he shows that its imperium has struck his hero Ralph Pendrel, who has a historical imagination, as an analogue to the Italian Renaissance, a period when the great mercantile princes flourished. Aurora is a flower of American wealth: "The roots of her flowering were watered by Wall Street, where old Mr. Coyne and her maternal grandsire, both still in the field and almost equally proud of her, conspired to direct the golden stream; though the plant itself seemed to spring from a soil in which upheavals—when upheavals occurred—offered to panic at least a deeper ground than a fall in stocks" (SP, 7–8). This reference to the functioning of Wall Street finance comes at a time when James had just finished writing "A Round of Visits," in which he gives the dire effects of some of the activities of the financial absconders during the panic of 1907. In that story, however, clearly *about* the panic of 1907, the word *panic* itself is never used. Not only does he use it here, but he shows that the sources of Aurora's wealth were much more stable than those of Mark Monteith and Mrs. Folliott in "A Round of Visits." As for Aurora, her appearance and her solid wealth put her above "panic."

Aurora Coyne, Ralph thought, had a "resemblance to some great portrait of the Renaissance," and "That was the analogy he had . . . fondly and consistently found for her: she was an Italian princess of the *cinque-cento,* and Titian or the grand Veronese might, as the phrase was, have signed her image. She had a wondrous old-time bloom and an air of noble security" (*SP,* 7–8). He goes on: "Large calm beauty, low square dresses, crude and multiplied jewels, the habit of watching strife from a height and yet looking at danger with a practised bravery, were some of the impressions that consorted with her presence" (*SP,* 8). When she refuses his proposal of marriage, Pendrel feels "a sad sense of having staked his cast, after all, but on the sensibility of a painted picture" (*SP,* 8).

It is not an imaginary portrait he conjures up but a picture that so closely resembles the portrait by Titian in the Uffizi Gallery of Eleonora Gonzaga della Rovere (Figure 12) that the reader familiar with it cannot but recognize it. The clues to identifying Aurora with this picture are seen in certain details James uses to describe her—details that fit definite details in the Titian portrait. He refers to her "grand thick-braided head" (*SP,* 10) as well as to "crude and multiplied jewels." It is this description that indicates that this Titian may be the portrait James has in mind as the one Aurora resembles, for it is significant that the gold bows made out of solid precious metal are multiplied all over Eleonora's dress, costly ornaments to which James's description of Aurora's "crude and multiplied jewels" can refer. One can see they are raised *above* the surface of the cloth, not woven into it. In addition, she wears heavy chains and a belt with heavily gilded and jeweled tassels, and in her right hand is a martin muff with a gold animal's head and jeweled eyes. It is the *ne plus ultra* of a Renaissance portrait of a rich and powerful woman, as a member of the Gonzaga family was bound to be, and her age and the consciousness of her wealth correspond to Aurora Coyne's age (thirty) and *her* consciousness of great wealth. What may be conflated with this portrait is another portrait by Titian in the Pitti Palace called *La*

Bella, painted when Eleonora was younger, but the portrait in the Uffizi seems to be closer to someone already a widow. In fact, the description of this picture reminds one of James's description of Agnolo Bronzino's Lucrezia Panciatichi in *The Wings of the Dove,* where he mentions "her recorded jewels," a phrase that specifically though obscurely refers to the chain with the recorded words "Amour Dure Sans Fin" that Bronzino shows us around Lucrezia's neck. In this later case, the specific reference is to the "multiplied jewels," which appear to be rather crude as jewels but are clearly solid gold bows distributed all over the dress Eleonora wears. There is no other well-known Renaissance portrait by Titian of a lady bearing such costly gems as these "crude and multiplied jewels."

It is significant in our attribution of the well-known portrait of Eleonora Gonzaga della Rovere by Titian that it contains the earliest and perhaps most famous representation by Titian of a table clock, seen in the left-hand side of the picture (Figure 13). This was an expensive and rare object purchasable only by the distinguished, powerful, and very rich in Italy at this time. There are seven or eight portraits painted later by Titian that show a variation of this clock. There is one of a man with a book, if James could have seen it, in Copenhagen. With the book shown close to the clock, the combination of objects would have made a pertinent analogue for Ralph Pendrel. But the clock in the portrait of Eleonora Gonzaga, which we know he saw since he was familiar with all the portraits in the Uffizi by Titian, is most significant because of the implication of the "sense of time," which is the idea behind *The Sense of the Past.* Erwin Panofsky, in his *Problems in Titian, Mostly Iconographic,* sees in the clock a rare and expensive, even chic item for the time, symbolizing the earlier sense of *memento mori* combined with a sense of temperance.[10] Perhaps the little figure of a man who seems to be in triumph on the top of the clock could stand for Ralph Pendrel in James's mind as he watched this picture, the man who tried to conquer the past. Pendrel very clearly could not conquer it and had come out from under it with great difficulty, an achievement in itself, for he overcame the threat of being swallowed up by the past once it had been resurrected.

In his late period, more than ever, James uses, whenever he can, some work of art or architecture to create an analogy for his main theme. In this

10. Erwin Panofsky, *Problems in Titian, Mostly Iconographic* (New York, 1969), 88–90.

case his seeming reference to a Titian portrait is distinguished by the fact that its opulence is expressed by the multiplied solid-gold bows, the concrete evidence of the gold standard that lies behind the power of the Wall Street princess—a power that determines Ralph Pendrel to engage in his extraordinary adventure, which depends on a power even greater than money, on his "sense of the past." It is also as the figure from the past, as a powerful princess painted by Titian with all the signs of her great wealth distributed over her clothes, that Ralph Pendrel sees Aurora Coyne, who is translated into her modern equivalent. If this is not the romance of finance, created in his last years, what is it indeed?

New Artistic Epiphanies: The Widening of James's Taste

James's impressions of the American scene do not comprise only a litany of horrors. Their challenges also called forth certain positive happy responses, occasioned by two unanticipated encounters involving his sensitivity to art. The first made him reverse his judgment of Impressionist paintings and the second made him react more strongly to Greek art than he had in the past. Neither Greek art nor Impressionist paintings had previously, in his long career of incorporating art objects into his writing, entered significantly into his fictions.

"The Sudden Trill of a Nightingale": James's Reaction to the Farmington Impressionist Paintings

It was in the twentieth century in 1904 (reinforced again in 1910) that James experienced the third of the three great artistic epiphanies in his life. He experienced them when he was under the influence of a restricted environment of plastic art. The first took place when he was eleven, when he entered the Galerie d'Apollon with his brother William, an experience he has left a record of in *A Small Boy and Others:* "The wondrous Galerie d'Apollon . . . seem[ed] to form with its supreme coved ceiling a prodigious tube or tunnel through which I inhaled little by little . . . a general sense of *glory*" (*AU*, 196). This is in praise of the great environment dominated by Eugène Delacroix's ceiling of Apollo, or art vanquishing the monster of ignorance.

The second epiphany through art came to him through another painter's invented environment in the library in the Siena Cathedral. Pinturicchio, an early Renaissance painter, devoted a cycle of ten paintings, confined in a small room, to the life of Pope Pius II, Aeneas Sylvius Piccolomini, an experience that James recorded in his *Italian Hours* (in both the 1875 and 1909 versions), an experience that, in 1874, seemed "to stand there for your own personal enjoyment, your romantic convenience, your small want and aesthetic use," so "One could possibly do . . . what one would with it" (IT, 528). In both these cases, James did what he would with his epiphanies, for the Galerie d'Apollon reappears transformed, as does the library of the Siena Cathedral, in *Roderick Hudson* (*LE,* 105–24).

The third epiphany occurred late in James's life when the same kind of overwhelming effect of an artifacted environment hit him all unexpectedly, as he has recorded it in *The American Scene.* He was introduced to a great collection of French Impressionist paintings at Hill-Stead, a private house in a small New England town. It was the unexpectedness of this experience that struck James with an intensity about which he wrote a couple of years after he returned to England. One reason for the intensity was that he had never experienced before the power and beauty of Impressionist painting through the canvases of its greatest exponent, Claude Monet, and the most striking paintings in the drawing rooms at Hill-Stead are three Monets of the late 1880s, including *The Bay and Maritime Alps at Antibes* and *The Haystacks* of 1888 and 1890.

All we know about James's prior opinions about Impressionist painting depends on a review he wrote for the New York *Tribune,* on May 13, 1876, of the second Impressionist exhibition, in which he criticized this school of painting, then in its early manifestation. James began his review by saying "But the effect of it was to make me think better than ever of all the good old rules which decree that beauty is beauty and ugliness ugliness. . . . The young contributors to the exhibition of which I speak are partisans of unadorned reality and absolute foes to arrangement, embellishment, selection, to the artist's allowing himself . . . to be preoccupied with the idea of the beautiful." He compares them to the English Pre-Raphaelites but to the detriment of the Impressionists. "They send detail to the dogs and concentrate themselves on general expression. Some of their generalizations of expression are in a high degree curious."[11]

11. *Henry James, The Painter's Eye* (London, 1956), 114–15.

In the fall of 1904, James was taken by one of his Emmet cousins, perhaps Bay Ellen Temple Emmet, to visit Hill-Stead. In 1910 he returned for a second visit. This house had been completed a couple of years earlier in 1901, when Alfred Pope, an industrialist from Cleveland, his wife, and his daughter Theodate commissioned McKim, Mead, and White to build a country house in Farmington, Connecticut, where his daughter had gone to Miss Porter's School and where she had been very happy (Figure 14). J. H. Whittemore, who had been influenced in buying Impressionist pictures by Mary Cassatt, introduced the American painter to the Popes. She single-handedly was responsible for influencing the great American Impressionist collections, including the magnificent Havemeyer Collection, now in the Metropolitan Museum, all purchased from 1888 and 1889 on into the 1890s. Durand-Ruel and Boussod, the most important French dealers in Impressionist painting, realized that newly rich Americans were out to buy complete collections, something that most cultured Europeans with money rarely did since their painting collections were usually begun by their forebears and did not therefore constitute a complete environment of paintings bought almost all at once as the American collections were. What made Pope's collection at Hill-Stead different from the others was that it was not arranged in a gallery but was hung on the walls of lived-in rooms. After the Popes' deaths, Theodate, their daughter, took the house over and kept it very much the way her parents had left it, so that today spectators can relive the impression made on James.

James had in a tale called "Flickerbridge," published in 1902, two years before his trip to the United States, described the equivalent effect of a total environment on a young Impressionist painter fresh from Paris, who recognized the experience, which he had previously had "in Italy, in Spain, confronted at last . . . with great things desired of or with greater ones unexpectedly presented" (XI, 334).

James did not care for the Impressionist pictures when, as a young man, he attended their exhibition. He did, however, admire the work of John Singer Sargent, his friend, who practiced a kind of modified Impressionism, and he modeled his young Impressionist painter, Charles Waterlow, on Sargent in the 1888 novel *The Reverberator,* written just about when Pope was buying his first Impressionist pictures. Waterlow did not paint like Claude Monet, with the object deconstructed in sunlight; instead, he was a portraitist, as Sargent was. He had studied with Carolus Duran, Sargent's teacher, and had made a trip to Spain with him as Sargent had.

In 1901 the Popes finished their house, which had partly been designed by Theodate, and the pictures bought in 1888 and 1889 and later in 1892 were hung on the walls immediately. The Claude Monet *Bay and Maritime Alps at Antibes* was bought in 1889 and was probably the first Impressionist picture to enter Pope's collection. Of the three Monets in this collection, one is from his very early period, before he was even called an Impressionist.

The passage from *The American Scene* that James devotes to his impressions of this collection shows very clearly what happened. This beautiful array of pictures that begins with the 1888 *Bay and Maritime Alps at Antibes* (Figure 15) and ends within sight of it with *The Haystacks* (Figure 16) of 1890 at the far end of the dining room, impressed James with the impact of a total environment (Figure 17), the kind of phenomenon Monet was later to give to the rooms at the Orangerie and at other exhibitions in which the series of paintings *The Waterlilies,* all devoted to a simple motif, was exhibited.

James first expresses his impression of what is known as "the classic mile" of Farmington (Figure 18), a row of eighteenth- and early nineteenth-century New England domestic buildings. He saw these houses as making "no vulgar noise" about their excellent condition and described them in a "long double line" as being like "gentlewomen seated against the wall at an evening party" (*AS*, 42). The houses in Farmington confess to "the sweet shyness of veracity," though he could find a certain "inscrutability of the village street . . . in any relation but its relation to its elms," and asked, "What secrets, meanwhile, did the rest of the scene keep?" (*AS*, 43). He felt in this scene "the quantity of absence," whereas "the present, the positive, was mainly represented by the level railway-crossing" (*AS*, 44). There was a "visible vacancy" about the effect of these houses. The street seemed to be fairly empty and the people seemed to be "all of one kind," wearing a kind of "negative garment" (*AS*, 45). As a spectator, or, rather, as what he called the "restless analyst," he wondered "what may be behind, what beneath, what within, what may represent, in such conditions, the appeal of the senses of the tribute to them; what, in such a show of life, may take the place . . . of amusement, of social and sensual margin, overflow and by-play?" (*AS*, 45). That is his introduction to his experience: "Never was such

by-play as in a great new house on a hilltop that overlooked the most composed of communities; a house apparently conceived . . . on the lines of a
magnified Mount Vernon, and in which an array of modern "impressionis-
tic" pictures, mainly French, wondrous examples of [Edouard] Manet, of
[Edgar] Degas, of Claude Monet, of [James] Whistler, of other rare recent
hands," faced him (AS, 46). He felt that a "large slippery sweet" had been
"inserted, without a warming, between the compressed lips of half-con-
scious inanition." For him, in fact, "nothing else had been . . . prepared to
anything like the same extent; and though the consequent taste . . . was of
the queerest, *no proof of the sovereign power of art could have been, for the
moment, sharper. . . . It made everything else shrivel and fade: it was like
the sudden trill of a nightingale, lord of the hushed evening"* (AS, 46; italics
added).

Those who know James's lack of interest in Impressionism up to this point
must be impressed by the intensity of his reaction. Part of it, as we see from
his introduction to the passage, is due to the fact that he did not expect this
shock of color and the modern Parisian civilized painted world to be behind
the walls of this impersonal-looking, colonial-type country house, which had
been, after all, prepared and designed to fit in with "the classic mile" of
houses that James had looked at before he entered the Popes' residence.
His experience of Impressionism had been with the paintings of Sargent,
but Sargent did not break up his brush strokes or cut off the visual scene
the way Monet, Degas, Alfred Sisley, and Camille Pissarro did, even though
Degas's brush strokes were conventional and Manet did not wish to and
never did show with the Impressionists. An illustration of how the paintings
were placed in the reception rooms of the house and of the pictures themselves can make us see exactly what James saw (Figure 19). The Monets are
particularly interesting because, no matter what James has written about not
having felt the Impressionist style, one of his tales, "The Chaperon," from
1891, in its language anticipates the cathedral series of Claude Monet, not
begun until the next year, 1892. How the façade of the Milan gothic cathedral looks as the characters approach from the piazza is described in these
words: The characters "strolled . . . across the big, amusing piazza, where
the front of the cathedral makes a sort of builded light" (VIII, 105). The
façades of Monet's cathedrals are built only out of colored light, in fact, out
of a "builded light." Monet shows at Hill-Stead in the canvases of *The Bay*

and Maritime Alps at Antibes and *The Haystacks* that light can be "builded" by paint (Figures 15 and 16). The light through color builds the foreground as well as the background of *The Bay and Maritime Alps at Antibes.* The haystacks of the second painting are also constructed through color and light. There is no outline, but the color, created by light, does the work. But as far as his taste in Impressionism went, before his trip to Hill-Stead in 1904, James had preferred a modified impressionist like Charles Waterlow in *The Reverberator* or Frank Granger, his Impressionist painter in "Flicker-bridge." The latter sees Addie Wenham, a middle-aged spinster, as a figure suggestive of an ancient world. His "impression" of her was "alien to his proper world, so little to be conceived in the sharp north light of the newest impressionism." Instead, "he had been treated, of a sudden, in this adven-ture, to one of the sweetest, fairest, coolest impressions of his life—one, moreover, visibly . . . complete and homogeneous" (XI, 334). But Frank is, above everything else, a portrait painter, and he paints fat, rich, American ladies. Therefore, in spite of the fact that the world from which he comes is contrasted to the medievalized world of the Flickerbridge spinster, his impressionism is, like Sargent's, diluted, a style easily assimilable by James and his friends. For it was Emile Charles Lambinet, one of the "little mas-ters" of the landscape school prior to Impressionism, really a proto-Impres-sionist, who was James's ideal contemporary French landscape painter in 1903 when he wrote *The Ambassadors.* However, a year later his reaction to the Popes' collection of Impressionist paintings, now much more highly developed from Impressionism in 1876, especially in the case of the Monets exhibited, corresponds in its character and intensity to Frank Granger's re-action to the kind of visual scene that inspired Edward Burne-Jones, rather than Monet.

The effect of the Impressionist paintings at Hill-Stead took place too late to have any effect on James's novels of his last period, nor do we find it operat-ing in any of his last tales. James's relation to Theodate Pope continued, and in 1910 she took some photographs of James (Figure 20). But the effect of the paintings does occur in his works, for it leaps up at us in that section of *The American Scene* in which he describes the New England countryside, "New England: An Autumn Impression." It was published first in 1905 in the April–June issue of the *North American Review,* and as a description of nature, it is unparalleled in any of James's other writings, including later parts of *The American Scene*. James's attitude toward writing about nature has been influenced, it seems, by his recent experience with the Impressionist paintings that reveal those painters' view of nature. He saw this in the brilliant paintings by Monet, Manet, and Whistler in the Pope collection. Nowhere else in James's work do we see such passages as the following ones from the first chapter in his *American Scene*. He writes of the "freshness of eye, outward and inward" in his preface to the book, where he described how he was bent on "his gathered impressions, since it was for them, for them only, that [he] returned." In Chocorua he finds that he had hitherto been "deprived to excess . . . of naturalism in *quantity*" (*AS*, 15). He found it here in "such quantity" that it might "by itself be a luxury corrupting the judgment" (*AS*, 15). We must remember that this writing took place *after* he had seen the Hill-Stead pictures. He notes that the "light . . . cast an irresistible spell" and that "the leaves of the forest" produced "the enhancement of this strange conscious hush of the landscape, which kept one in presence of a world created, a stage set, a sort of ample capacity" (*AS*, 15). Yet even though he is entranced by nature, he here cannot avoid comparing his impressions with those he would have in a drawing room. "The two or three gaps of the old forgotten enclosure made symmetrical doors, the sweet old stones had the surface of grey velvet, and the scattered wild apples were like a figure in the carpet" (*AS*, 16). Although he sees in the solitary maple on a woodside an object "that flames in single scarlet," he is reminded of "the daughter of a noble house dressed for a fancy-ball, with the whole family gathered round to admire her before she goes" (*AS*, 17). Nature here reminds him of his social indoor life; still, the fiery red maple is something that gets his attention most likely because of the impression that the Monet fiery bush in the landscape *View of the Bay and Maritime Alps* made on him, which he is now rewriting with his own Jamesian vocabulary.

But even with the return to indoor metaphors in a description of nature, there is here a James who devotes pages to a description of the autumn landscape. In section three, which leads up to the Farmington experience, we find at least twenty-two mentions of the word *impression*. Cape Cod features for James as "a pictured Japanese screen or banner; a delightful little triumph of 'impressionism' which . . . never departed, under any provocation, from its type" (*AS*, 34).

However, in spite of these descriptive words echoing the pictorial expression of the Impressionist pictures he has seen, it is typical that James never forgets "the human, the social question," making him "before each scene, wish really to get *into* the picture, to cross, as it were, the threshold of the frame" (*AS*, 35). Is not this here a question of the influence finally of the retinal view on his imagination, which he is now able to absorb into his own sensibility?

On his way to Farmington, while looking out of the windows of the train coming down from Boston, he sees "the land grow mild and vague and interchangeably familiar with the sea, all under the spell of the reported 'gulf-stream,' those mystic words that breathe a softness wherever they sound" (*AS*, 36). Does not this sentence reveal the essence of the Impressionist view of nature, especially in Monet's version of it, and does it not reflect the water scenes from the Farmington collection of paintings? Proust, in his *Remembrance of Things Past*, described the Monet element in his invented painter, Elstir, in the classically accepted version of Impressionism. "Elstir had prepared the mind of the spectator by employing, for the little town, only marine terms and urban terms for the sea." There are "masts which had the effect of making the vessels to which they belonged appear town-bred, built on land, an impression reinforced by other boats moored along the jetty" (*P*, 894). The churches, in "a powdery haze of sunlight and crumbling waves, seemed to be emerging from the waters . . . and enclosed in the band of a variegated rainbow, to form an ethereal, mystical tableau. On the beach in the foreground the painter had contrived that the eye should discover no fixed boundary, no absolute line of demarcation between land and sea" (*P*, 894–95). Is not the experience of the remarkable collection of Impressionist pictures at Farmington responsible for James seeing this scene in Massachusetts and Connecticut in September?

> The mere *fusion* of earth and air and water, of light and shade and colour, the almost shameless tolerance of nature for the poor human experiment, are so happily effective that you lose all reckoning of the items of the sum, that you ensured finding your draught, contentedly, a single strong savour. . . . Objects remarkable enough, objects rich and rare perhaps, objects at any rate curious

and interesting, emerge, for genial reference from the gorgeous blur, and would commit me, should I give them their way, to excesses of specification. So I throw myself back upon the fusion, as I have called it—with the rich light hanging on but half a dozen spots. (*AS*, 40)

What is remarkable is that this early chapter in *The American Scene*, written almost immediately after James experienced the Farmington pictures, reflects in the writing itself a phenomenon unique in his work, an impression of nature that corresponds to the view that the Impressionists, particularly Monet, took of the interrelationship of land, sea, and air.[12]

"A Fine Greek Thing . . . Seen . . . in America"

Henry James was now open to art he had never paid much attention to before. This included classical Greek art. Just as James did not fully appreciate the French Impressionists until he saw them in America, so he learned to taste fully the beauty of ancient Greek sculpture only when he saw it transported to his native soil. He himself gives this as a reason for the powerful effect on him of a small head of Aphrodite, called "The Bartlett Aphrodite," which he came upon in the Museum of Fine Arts in Boston on his trip there in 1904 (Figure 21). It was, among a "collection of fragments of the antique," one fine piece. "Here the restless analyst found work to his hand—only too much; and indeed in presence of the gem of the series, of the perhaps just too conscious grace of a certain little wasted and dim-eyed head of Aphrodite, he felt that his function should simply give way, in common decency, to that of the sonneteer" (*AS*, 252). Here he must be thinking of Keats.

For it is an impression by itself, and I think quite worth the Atlantic voyage, to catch in the American light the very fact of the genius of Greece. There are things we don't know, feelings not to be foretold, till we have had that experience—which I commend to the *raffiné* of almost any other clime. I should say to him that he has not *seen* a fine Greek think till he has seen it in America. . . .

12. Susan M. Griffin, in *The Texture of the Visual in Late James* (Boston, 1991), considers the Hudson River School, and especially the paintings of Thomas Cole, to be the great influence on James's descriptions of nature in *The American Scene* (128, 142 n. 30, and see her Chapter 3).

The little Aphrodite, with her connections, her antecedents and references exhibiting the maximum of breakage, is no doubt as *lonely* a jewel as ever strayed out of its setting; yet what does one quickly recognize but that the intrinsic lustre will have, so far as that may be possible, doubled? She . . . has lost . . . her company, and is keeping . . . the strangest, but so far from having lost an iota of her power, she has gained unspeakably more. . . . She has in short, by her single presence, as yet, annexed an empire. . . . Where was she ever more, where was she ever so much, a goddess—and who knows but that, being thus divine, she foresees the time when, as she has "moved over," the place of her actual whereabouts will have become one of her shrines?" (*AS*, 252–53).

The effect on James was so strong that he reacted to it the way he had reacted to the impact of the Impressionist paintings in Farmington. Until this experience, James had really not brought Greek art into his oeuvre. For James, it was the antique art of Rome that enlisted his search for analogues and icons from the ancient world as in "The Solution" in 1889, "Adina" in 1874, when he used a precious gem, a topaz from the reign of Tiberius, and "The Last of the Valerii," also in 1874, in which the marbles of the Vatican gallery, including mostly Roman antiquities populated and gave an edge to his tale. But as far as the art of Greece went, it took a back seat (except for mention of the Elgin Marbles in *The Princess Casamassima*) until his visit in 1904 to the Museum of Fine Arts in Boston.

This situation changes after he sees the "Bartlett Aphrodite." Her effect on James has in a way helped make "these shores," to which the little Aphrodite has "moved over," become her "shrine," for he has brought her influence into his tale "The Velvet Glove." That tale of 1909 is constructed around an Olympian theme, with the characters assuming the roles of the Olympian gods in a metaphorical sense. The scribbling Princess who wishes to buy her preface from the young American playwright is a "Diana bending over the sleeping Endymion" (XII, 260), and her lover, the young Lord, is likened to "a perfect-headed marble Apollo" (XII, 245). Atlas and Hebe are made classical appendages of other characters and, though Aphrodite herself is not invoked, the Princess herself "was Olympian—as in her rich and regular young beauty, that of some divine Greek mask overpainted say by Titian" (XII, 244).

In her own overblown fiction, the Princess does mention the greatest

Greek sculptor of the period, for "the loveliness of the face . . . was that of the glorious period in which Pheidias reigned supreme" (XII, 249). But the Olympian metaphor surrounding the entire tale is a tribute to Greek art of the classical period, stimulated, one speculates, by the great aesthetic impression that James received from the lovely damaged "Bartlett Aphrodite" in Boston on his American sojourn. "The Velvet Glove" is a kind of offering by James to that fragment of Aphrodite that had so touched him.[13]

13. Beryl Barr-Sharrar called attention to Henry James's comments in *The American Scene* about "a Greek marble head in the Boston Museum of Fine Arts" in a review she wrote of "the Greek miracle," a loan exhibition of Greek antiquities at the Metropolitan Museum, New York, November 22, 1992–February 7, 1993. See Beryl Barr-Sharrar, "The Greek Miracle: Classical Sculpture at the Met," *The New Criterion*, II, no. 9 (1993), 18–23.

1. The Century Club, 7 West Forty-third Street, New York City. Designed by McKim, Mead, and White, 1888. *Courtesy the Museum of the City of New York*

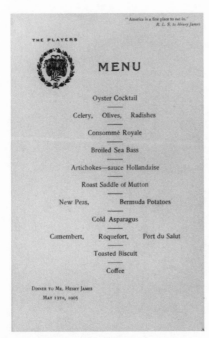

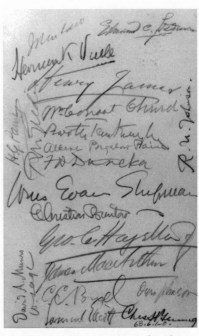

"America is a fine place to eat in."
R. L. S. to Henry James

THE PLAYERS

MENU

Oyster Cocktail
———
Celery,   Olives,   Radishes
———
Consommé Royale
———
Broiled Sea Bass
———
Artichokes—sauce Hollandaise
———
Roast Saddle of Mutton
———
New Peas,   Bermuda Potatoes
———
Cold Asparagus
———
Camembert,   Roquefort,   Port du Salut
———
Toasted Biscuit
———
Coffee

DINNER TO MR. HENRY JAMES
MAY 13TH, 1905

2. Autographed Menu of "Dinner to Mr. Henry James," May 13, 1905. The Players Club, Gramercy Park, New York City. *Author's collection*

3. The Façade of the Metropolitan Museum of Art, 1902. *Courtesy the Metropolitan Museum of Art, New York City*

4. Julia in the Metropolitan Museum. Illustration by W. T. Smedley, in *Julia Bride* (1909)

5. The Villard Houses, Madison Avenue and Fiftieth Street, 1882–1886. Designed by McKim, Mead, and White.

6. The Exterior of the Waldorf-Astoria, Thirty-fourth Street and Fifth Avenue, 1903. *Collection of the New-York Historical Society*

7. The Waldorf-Astoria, Royal Suite, Louis Quinze Bedroom, 1903. *Collection of the New-York Historical Society*

8. The Waldorf-Astoria, Main Foyer, 1903. *Collection of the New-York Historical Society*

9. The Waldorf-Astoria, Interior of the South Palm Garden, 1903. *Collection of the New-York Historical Society*

10. A. C. David, "The studio of Mr. Henry W. Ranger, Sturgis and Simonson, architects." *The Architectual Record,* Vol. XIV, No. 4 (1903), 238.

11. J. Pierpont Morgan, photograph by Edward Steichen. *Courtesy Archives of the Pierpont Morgan Library, New York*

12. *Eleonora Gonzaga,* by Titian, in the Uffizi Gallery, Florence. *Alinari / Art Resource, New York*

13. Detail of the Table Clock from Titian's *Eleanora Gonzaga. Alinari / Art Resource, New York*

14. View of Hill-Stead, Exterior View, Western Façade, 1906. Designed by McKim, Mead, and White. *Courtesy Hill-Stead Museum, Farmington, Connecticut.*

15. *The Bay and Maritime Alps at Antibes,* by Claude Monet, 1888. *Courtesy Hill-Stead Museum, Farmington, Connecticut*

16. *The Haystacks,* by Claude Monet, 1890. *Courtesy Hill-Stead Museum, Farmington, Connecticut*

17. Dining Room at Hill-Stead, 1910. *Courtesy Hill-Stead Museum, Farmington, Connecticut*

18. *The Classic Mile* of Farmington, Connecticut, photograph by Karl Klauser. *The Farmington Library, Farmington, Connecticut*

19. View of the Living Room at Hill-Stead and Claude Monet's *The Bay and Maritime Alps at Antibes. Courtesy Hill-Stead Museum, Farmington, Connecticut*

20. Henry James, photograph by Theodate Pope, *ca.* 1910. *Courtesy Hill-Stead Museum, Farmington, Connecticut*

21. "The Bartlett Aphrodite," in the Museum of Fine Arts, Boston. *Francis Bartlett Donation of 1900. Courtesy Museum of Fine Arts, Boston*

22. "How badly you wrote!," "How badly you write!" Cartoon of Henry James the Younger and Henry James the Older, by Max Beerbohm, 1936. *By permission of the Houghton Library, Harvard University*

23. *Niobe,* in the Uffizi Gallery, Florence. *Alinari / Art Resource, New York*

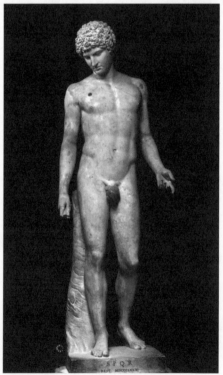

24. *Antinous,* in the Capitoline Museum, Rome. *Alinari / Art Resource, New York*

25. *Faun*, by Praxiteles, in the Capitoline Museum, Rome. *Alinari / Art Resource, New York*

26. *The Rout of St. Romano,* by Paolo Uccello, 1455, in the National Gallery, London. *Alinari / Art Resource, New York*

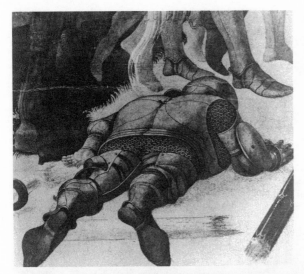

27. Detail of Armor from Uccello's *The Rout of St. Romano.* *Alinari / Art Resource, New York*

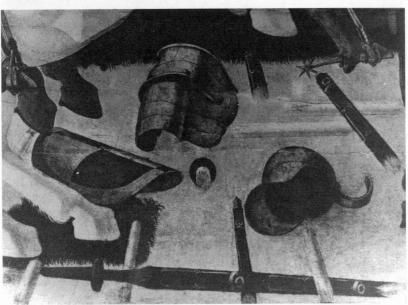

28. Detail of Pieces of Change from Uccello's *The Rout of St. Romano. Alinari / Art Resource, New York*

29. *King Charles I on Horseback,* by Anthony Van Dyck, *ca.* 1635–40, in the National Gallery, London. *Alinari / Art Resource, New York*

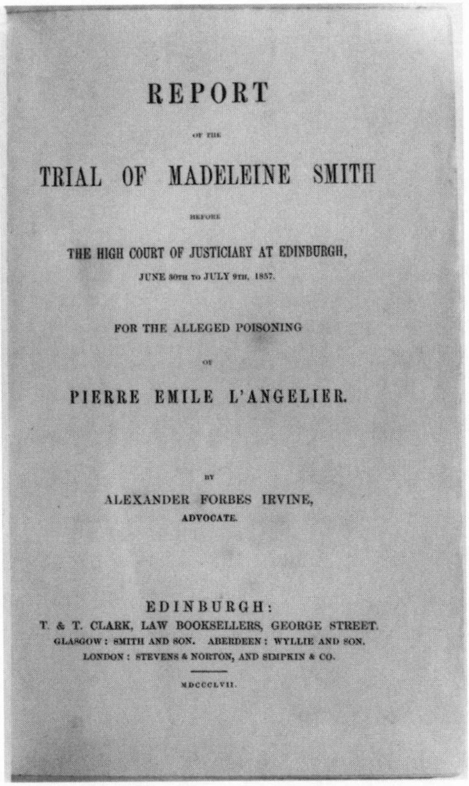

REPORT

OF THE

TRIAL OF MADELEINE SMITH

BEFORE

THE HIGH COURT OF JUSTICIARY AT EDINBURGH,

JUNE 30TH TO JULY 9TH, 1857.

FOR THE ALLEGED POISONING

OF

PIERRE EMILE L'ANGELIER.

BY

ALEXANDER FORBES IRVINE,
ADVOCATE.

EDINBURGH:
T. & T. CLARK, LAW BOOKSELLERS, GEORGE STREET.
GLASGOW: SMITH AND SON.   ABERDEEN: WYLLIE AND SON.
LONDON: STEVENS & NORTON, AND SIMPKIN & CO.

MDCCCLVII.

30. A Report of the Trial of Madeleine Smith, Title Page (Edinburgh, 1857). *Author's collection*

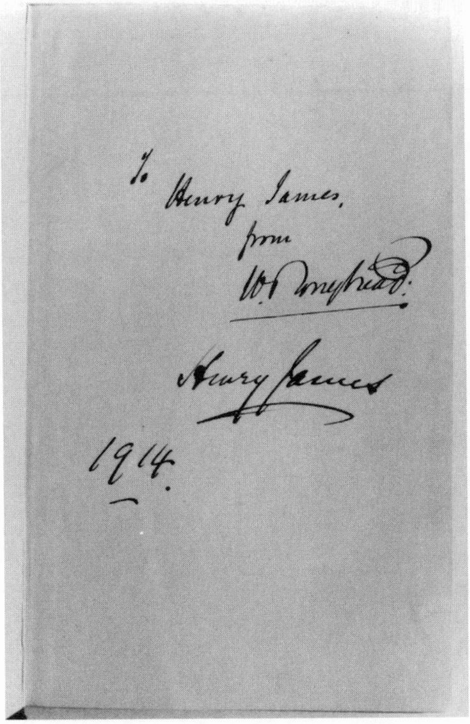

31. The Madeleine Smith Report, Flyleaf, Inscription by William Roughead to Henry James (Edinburgh, 1857). *Author's collection*

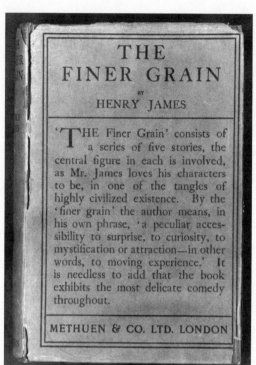

THE
FINER GRAIN

BY
HENRY JAMES

'THE Finer Grain' consists of
a series of five stories, the
central figure in each is involved,
as Mr. James loves his characters
to be, in one of the tangles of
highly civilized existence. By the
'finer grain' the author means, in
his own phrase, 'a peculiar acces-
sibility to surprise, to curiosity, to
mystification or attraction—in other
words, to moving experience.' It
is needless to add that the book
exhibits the most delicate comedy
throughout.

METHUEN & CO. LTD. LONDON

32. Dust Jacket for *The Finer Grain* (London, 1910). *Author's collection*

NOTES ON
NOVELISTS

❦

HENRY JAMES

This volume is a collection of studies of eminent
writers of fiction which have appeared at various
times and in various periodicals from upwards of
twenty years ago to date ; to which are affixed
two or three studies of dramatists and of minor
writers. The range is thus from R. L. Stevenson
to Matilde Serao, taking Flaubert, Zola, George
Sand, Balzac and D'Annunzio by the way, and
presenting two of these authors in the light of
considerations of them, on the occasion of new
commemorative publications, renewed after in-
tervals and at different dates. Robert Browning,
Dumas fils and Ibsen, being of the Dramatists,
the book is concerned, it will be seen, but with
names of the first order.

33. Dust Jacket for *Notes on Novelists* (London, 1914). *Author's collection*

34. Henry James's Interview for the *New York Times* Sunday Magazine Section, March 21, 1915. *Author's collection*

(1)

ts of the war which ought to be taken
which it has given the general public
in anything approaching a personal
An outstanding personality of this
irty years at least he has enjoyed a
utation;he has written and published
-of novels, tales and belles lettres;
l himself a master of reticence as
e has reached the age of seventy
publication or seen his name
s in other than the literary
tly after the outbreak of war
f the American Volunteer Motor-
r taking three months to think about
t an interview to a representative
departure from the convictions
xpressed, in the
in the following words:

said,speaking very slowly
ion as well as his words be
mpathy to the cause of
ngly than to say that it has
av... overcome an insurmountable aversion to be being
interviewed,which all my life has been absolute and
uncompromising;based upon the fact that anything which I can't
say myself,by myself and for myself isn't worth my saying at
all;I being in possession of a vehicle of expression which
I seem to myself to give away when, if expression is in question
for me, I don't employ it."

35. Henry James's Interview for the *New York Times* Sunday Magazine Section, March 21, 1915, with annotation by his nephew, Henry James, III. *Author's collection*

2

Cameos of James's Friends in His Late Fiction: The Extension of His Personal World into His Work

In James's twentieth-century universe, his texts have become endowed with a greater density of references of all kinds. Among these are the cameo portraits he drew of his friends in his last novels. If not to the reader, at least to the sitter himself, the identity might be obvious, but then again he might never know he had been included. It was part of the real world James was now including in his fictive world.

Mr. Crichton and Sir Sidney Colvin

The Wings of the Dove, though published before *The Ambassadors,* exhibits this tendency to plant actors in the drama of James's life squarely within his fictive drama. This novel of 1902 includes Minny Temple, who here becomes Milly Theale, doomed to early death as Minny Temple had been. Morton Fullerton, who was a close friend of James during these years, becomes Merton Densher, who has been pledged by Kate Croy to marry Milly for her money, and Annie Fields, the widow of James's Boston publisher, becomes Mrs. Susan Stringham (*PW,* 226–27).

Henrietta Reubell, an eccentric but generous friend of James, is the figure behind Miss Barrace (the name rhymes with Paris) and represents the spirit of that city. In *The Ambassadors,* through her character she protects her fellow countrymen visiting that city, observing all through her tortoise shell eyeglass and finding everything "wonderful." Leon Edel sees the young artist John Little Bilham as resembling Jonathan Sturges, to whom Howells had said, "Live all you can," which is the theme of the novel (*MA,*

114). Edel also sees Waymarsh, the Washington lawyer and Strether's friend, as a combination of William James, Henry Adams, and Mark Twain (*MA*, 72).

But it is in *The Golden Bowl* that James inserts a number of the portraits, one of which has been folded in without any real connection to the plot. Mr. Crichton, "the custodian of one of the richest departments of the great national collection of precious things" (NYE, XXIV, 146) in the British Museum, who introduces Maggie to the documents relating to the family of her husband, the Prince, seems to be a portrait of James's old friend Sir Sidney Colvin. He is discreetly but recognizably characterized in James's ornamental, bantering late style. Although in volume one of the novel Maggie has been once to the British Museum with Fanny Assingham to check on the historical glories of the Prince's family, there is no mention, according to the one reference to the visit Fanny makes to her husband, that Mr. Crichton had been their sponsor. "Go to the British Museum," she tells Bob. "I went one day with Maggie. We looked him up, so to say. They were most civil" (NYE, XXIII, 80). However, in volume two James seems to have realized that it might be entertaining to transform the impersonal "they" from volume one to a specific character, Mr. Crichton, who would be a disguise for his friend Sidney Colvin. So in the second volume James makes Mr. Crichton retroactively involved. "It was at his invitation, Fanny well recalled, that Maggie, one day, long before . . . paid a visit" to see the records of the Prince's family (NYE, XXIV, 147). This personal invitation is news to the reader. Although unmentioned in volume one as Maggie's sponsor to the museum, Mr. Crichton is now introduced to the story and given a role, since it is "some renewed conversation with Mr. Crichton" (NYE, XXIV, 148) that gives Maggie "the idea, irresistible, intense, of going to pay at the Museum a visit to Mr. Crichton" a second time, just when she is reaching a crisis in her awareness of her husband's adultery (NYE, XXIV, 146).

What is the evidence that Mr. Crichton (whose name, like Colvin's, also begins with a "C") is a portrait of Sir Sidney Colvin? First, he is described as "the most accomplished and obliging of public functionaries, whom everyone knew and who knew everyone," and as the "custodian of one of the richest departments of the great collection of precious things" at the museum (NYE, XXIV, 146). Colvin was keeper of the Department of Prints and Drawings at the British Museum from 1884 to 1912 and the host of "a literary and artistic centre."[1] It is true that Maggie is not going to the Department of Prints and Drawings, Colvin's territory, to look up Amerigo's family records, but that discrepancy is easily overcome by James. Mr. Crichton is made to introduce Maggie to the authorities concerned with her project; "though not sworn of the province toward which his friend had found herself, according to her appeal to him, yearning again, nothing was easier for him than to put her in relation with the presiding urbanities" (NYE, XXIV, 148). The following excerpt clinches the resemblance between Mr. Crichton and Colvin: "He had desired, Mr. Crichton, with characteristic kindness, after the wonderful show, after offered luncheon at his contiguous lodge, a part of the place, to see her safely home; especially on his noting, in attending her to the great steps, that she had dismissed her carriage" (NYE, XXIV, 154). We know that Colvin's Keepership came "with a residence within the museum precincts," which, in Colvin's case, "gradually became a literary and artistic centre" and which corresponds to Mr. Crichton's "contiguous lodge, a part of the place."[2] Robert Louis Stevenson, Colvin's very close friend, called it, incorrectly, "the many-pillared and the well-beloved," for as Colvin pointed out, Stevenson described it "as though the keepers' houses stood within the great front colonnade of the museum, which they do not, but project in advance of it on either flank."[3] James's description of the lodge as "contiguous" is correct.

Mr. Crichton is characterized by James as a "custodian" who "could feel for the sincere private collector and urge him on his way even when condemned to be present at his capture of trophies sacrificed by the country to parliamentary thrift" (NYE, XXIV, 146). According to E. V. Lucas, Colvin managed to keep the Malcolm Collection for the museum ("the most notable achievement of Colvin's Keepership"), for "it was due to his personal enterprise and exertions that the Government was persuaded to give a special grant and thus secure the collection for the nation." Apparently "he never spared efforts to persuade possible givers to enrich the nation in this way, often with success.[4] Colvin, as a museum official, considered it "a chief

1. E. V. Lucas, *The Colvins and their Friends* (New York, 1928), 184.
2. *Ibid.*
3. Sidney Colvin, *Memories and Notes of Persons and Places* (New York, 1921), 143.
4. Lucas, 182, 183.

part of his duty to win the regard and confidence of private collectors, to help and stimulate them in their pursuits."[5] Mr. Crichton's attitude resembled Colvin's as well:

> [Crichton] carried his amiability to the point of saying that since London, under pettifogging views, *had* to miss from time to time its rarest opportunities, he was almost consoled to see such lost causes invariably wander . . . into . . . the wondrous, the already famous fold beyond the Mississippi. There was a charm in his "almosts" that was not to be resisted, especially after Mr. Verver and Maggie had grown sure—or almost again—of enjoying the monopoly of them; and on this basis of envy changed to sympathy by the more familiar view of the father and the daughter, Mr. Crichton had at both houses, though especially in Eaton Square, learned to fill out the responsive and suggestive character. (NYE, XXIV, 146–47)

James also seems to be suggesting with tongue in cheek that in preferring Eaton Square (Maggie's home) to Portland Place (Verver's home), Mr. Crichton prefers the company of the ladies to that of the gentlemen collectors. This is continued a few lines further on: "Visits of gracious ladies, under his protection, lighted up rosily, for this perhaps most flower-loving and honey-sipping member of the great Bloomsbury hive, its packed passages and cells" (NYE, XXIV, 148). What could be a more poetic, almost Keatsian tribute, to Colvin, James's good friend and the biographer of John Keats, the social, courtly, most "obliging of public functionaries" (NYE, XXIV, 146), than this figure of a bee extracting honey (or money) for the museum from rich flowers?

The character of Mr. Crichton may affect the reader as being a gratuitous intrusion into the plot, which at this point, after 548 pages, is about to reach its first climax in the confirmation of Maggie's suspicions of the Prince's and Charlotte's adulterous relationship. It is as if James could not resist writing in a part for his friend and, to justify the intrusion, has given the character a double function. One is to usher Maggie into the repository of the history of her husband's family, and the other is to release her into the Bloomsbury quarter, where she will come upon the golden bowl, the proof of the flaw in her marriage.

5. Colvin, 205.

Sidney Colvin probably never recognized his portrait, for he wrote in his *Memories and Notes:* "In creative literature, I do not remember any special instance of a character in whom the collecting passion is incarnate except that famous one of Cousin Pons in Balzac's *Les Parents Pauvres*."[6] This suggests that he never made the acquaintance of Adam Verver or, probably, of Mr. Crichton. It is equally sad that Fanny Sitwell, who became Mrs. Colvin, probably missed a naughty but recognizable version of her name in Fanny Assingham, who also seems to resemble her in character and personality. Hugh Walpole's tribute to Lady Colvin describes a woman very much like Mrs. Assingham. "[She] joined so eagerly in the experiences of other people that you were amazed that she had time or energy left for her own. . . . Her curiosity was never greedy; she loved to hear all the details but passed on from them always to give fully her pity, her admiration, her praise and her irony."[7] In addition to the silver salver Henry James gave the Colvins when they married in July, 1903, he may have also thought of *The Golden Bowl* as a wedding present, for during that summer of the Colvins' wedding James was writing the novel in which he put them both.[8]

Prince Amerigo and the Marchese Simone de Peruzzi de Medici

Prince Amerigo, the young Italian nobleman in *The Golden Bowl* secured by the Verver millions for Maggie's hand, seems to be largely drawn from the Marchese Simone de Peruzzi de Medici, who had married Edith Story, the daughter of the rich American sculptor William Wetmore Story. In 1903, the year before *The Golden Bowl* appeared, James had published Story's biography and he had had much to do with Edith and her noble husband. It is not surprising that the marchese lends details from his history to the background of James's Prince Amerigo, since, as we have seen, other personages drawn from James's own circle appear disguised in this novel.

Some facts about Amerigo's lineage are given by Mrs. Assingham: "One of the Prince's baptismal names . . . was Amerigo; which . . . was the name

6. *Ibid.*, 205–206.

7. Lucas, 351.

8. Adeline R. Tintner, "Sidney Colvin and *The Golden Bowl:* Mr. Crichton Identified," *Colby Library Quarterly,* No. 7 (September, 1974), 428–32.

. . . of the pushing man who followed . . . in the wake of Columbus and succeeded . . . in becoming godfather, or name-father, to the new Continent" (NYE, XXIII, 78). This, of course, is Amerigo Vespucci. Although James's Amerigo bears the same baptismal name as Vespucci, the reputed discoverer of America, his more important distinction is that he is a descendant of another, though here unnamed, noble Italian family, the Medici. This corresponds to Simone de Peruzzi de Medici's connection with that family.

The clue is given by Maggie when she reminds her husband that he would be nowhere without the "archives, annals, infamies" of "the generations behind [him], the follies and the crimes, the plunder and the waste—the wicked Pope, the monster most of all, whom so many of the volumes in [his] family library are all about" (NYE, XXIII, 9–10). The pope she refers to probably is the same pope later alluded to by Adam when he compares himself favorably as a "Patron of the arts," to Leo X, the Medici pope. The mention of this Medici pope strengthens the connection of Amerigo's link with the family whose political crimes and art patronage involved spending a fortune. He answers Maggie's question, "Where, therefore . . . without your archives, annals, infamies, would you have been?," with "I might have been in a somewhat better pecuniary situation" (NYE, XXIII, 10).

The explanation of how the Vespuccis co-joined the Medici family is made through Mrs. Assingham's further review of the Prince's history for her husband. When Colonel Assingham asks, "But where does the connexion come in?," she answers, "By the women—that is by some obliging woman, of old, who was a descendant of the pushing man, the make-believe discoverer. . . . A branch of the other family had become great—great enough, at least, to marry into his" (NYE, XXIII, 79).

This recounting of the transferral of a house as great as the Medici to the Prince's family, the Vespucci, makes the source of the Prince as Simone de Peruzzi de Medici plausible. Mrs. Assingham's explanation repeats almost verbatim Edith Story's version of how the Medici name came to be appended to her husband's name, which occurred during James's own lifetime, in an interview she gave to the New York *Sun* in 1913:

When the last of the reigning line of the Medici, Anna Maria Luisa, 1667–1743, lay dying in the Pitti Palace she made her will naming the Peruzzi nearest of kin as heir to her property, with the promise that he should assume the name and the titles of the Medici. For some time the Peruzzi refused to do this, claiming that the Peruzzi title and record was as great if not greater than the Medici. Finally the King expressed a wish to have it done. He felt that both families had done so much, their names were so closely interwoven in the history of Italy, that neither should be allowed to be unrepresented. It was at King Humbert's especial request that my husband added the Medici.[9]

The only difference between the fictive and the actual report is that in the novel the Medici are linked to the Vespucci family, whereas in the true family history of Edith Story's husband, the Medici are linked to the Peruzzi.

James's interest in the Medici family seems to have centered chiefly on their great pope, Leo X. He knew the classic life of the pope by William Roscoe since it is cited in *Roderick Hudson* (*RH*, 298). In this way we know that James was familiar with that author's account of the perfidy of Leo, whose "safe-conduct" passes were not only no guarantee of safety but were instead a precondition of an assassination, information that G. F. Young repeats in his *The Medici* and that is indicative of Pope Leo X's reputation for wickedness.[10] So much for the "infamies" and "crimes" of Amerigo's family.

James was also interested in this Medici pope's role as a "Patron of the arts," though Adam, also a patron of art, is made to deplore his treatment of Michelangelo: "No pope, no prince of them all had read a richer meaning, he believed, into the character of the Patron of Art," and Adam had "never so climbed to the tip-top as in judging . . . where Julius II and Leo X were 'placed' by their treatment of Michael Angelo" (NYE, XXIII, 150).

The Medici association is reinforced in the description of Amerigo's "Castello proper, described by him always as the *'perched'* place," that had, as Maggie knew, "formerly stood up, on the pedestal of its mountain-slope" (NYE, XXIII, 164; italics added). We know from the Story biography that the American sculptor owned "an old deserted house, built centuries ago by the Medici as a stronghold and hunting-box," which James himself had visited in "this admirable altitude." James also visited the "admirably placed

9. "Romance of Beautiful American Marchesa Peruzzi de Medici, Daughter of Sculptor Story; Revisiting This Country After Half-Century's Absence She Talks of Many Famous Persons Among Her Friends," New York *Sun*, Sunday, April 27, 1913, p. 4.

10. G. F. Young, *The Medici* (New York, 1910), 410.

summer home" of Edith Peruzzi de Medici and her husband, which he described as "the high-perched Lago di Vallombrosa, in Tuscany, more than two thousand feet up from Pontassieve."[11]

The Peruzzi family itself is invoked by reference to another association with the Medici pope Leo X. The pope had commissioned in 1520 the architect and builder Baldassare Peruzzi to make a Greek cross plan for St. Peter's, but it was never realized. The great works actually built by Peruzzi were palaces.

This Peruzzi, the builder of palaces and ancestor of Simone de Peruzzi de Medici, is connected with Amerigo in James's novel when the Prince realizes that his gaining a fortune by marriage to an American millionaire's daughter is just another chapter in his family's history. He says that he is assured of "more money than the palace-builder himself could have dreamed of" (NYE, XXIII, 10). This seems to be an allusion to the one Peruzzi to be remembered in history, Baldassare Peruzzi, "the palace-builder" and the most distinguished ancestor of Edith Peruzzi's husband.

James's knowledge of the Italian higher nobility seems to have come from his intimacy with Simone de Peruzzi when the author was preparing the biography of the Marchese's father-in-law. James wrote to Edith Peruzzi after her husband's death, "I . . . have not ceased to be glad I knew the last of your husband's beautiful dignity and courtesy."[12] For this reason Prince Amerigo is a more concretely realized Italian nobleman than James's earlier attempt in Prince Casamassima, the Neapolitan nobleman who appears in both *Roderick Hudson* and *The Princess Casamassima*.

The intensely close relationship that Adam Verver enjoyed with his daughter is central to James's novel. Maggie discusses with her father "our beautiful harmony" (NYE, XXIV, 74). She also "felt her communion with him more intimate than any other" (NYE, XXIV, 72). That same degree of intense intimacy also existed between William Wetmore Story and his daughter, who said that "even as a child" she and her father were "very close friends": "I don't believe such perfect sympathy exists very often between a

11. Henry James, *William Wetmore Story and His Friends* (2 vols.; London, 1903), II, p. 333.

12. *Henry James to Edith Peruzzi de Medici, n.d.;* access made possible by Leon Edel, August, 1977.

girl and her father as we felt for each other."[13] This triadic relationship found among prince, daughter, and father in both the Verver family and in the Story family strengthens my belief that the source for Prince Amerigo's lineage is to be found in Edith Story de Peruzzi de Medici's husband's lineage and that *The Golden Bowl* owes much of its inspiration to the Story material that James had found himself involved with when he was commissioned by the sculptor's children to write their father's official biography. That *The Golden Bowl* followed on the heels of the biography makes the close connection readily explicable.[14]

13. New York *Sun*, p. 4.

14. See Adeline R. Tintner, "A Source for Prince Amerigo in *The Golden Bowl*," *Notes on Modern American Literature*, II, No. 3 (1978), n. 23.

3

The Usurping Consciousness

> The artist is present in every page of every book from which he sought so
> assiduously to eliminate himself.
>
> —Henry James

The Older James Looks at the Younger James

The twentieth century in its first decades was concerned above all
with the notion of consciousness. What William James had termed "the
stream of consciousness" was to be the concept behind James Joyce's *Ulysses* and was to take over completely *Finnegans Wake*. Henry James was
himself to respond to the demands of this concern at this time in various
ways. One form this awareness of human consciousness took was in the
revised edition of most of his novels and tales of the New York Edition. This
conscious artistic overhauling was made permanent and documentary in the
twenty-four prefaces that introduced the volumes. The whole enterprise
becomes thus a monument to the awareness of fictional creation. The prefaces document the problems of invention, along with their initiating germs,
and both give a candid revelation of what the author dredges up out of his
consciousness, or even his unconsciousness, to justify the particular conditions of his fiction making (Figure 22).

James's revision from 1905 to 1909 turned him into an authority on
James; it taught him how to take charge of his work and how to canonize it.
The operation of his consciousness on the fictions he had constructed many

years before reveals certain emendations as fitting in now with his new consciousness, that of 1905 through 1909. An investigation of what he chose to change in a number of these productions will tell us how Henry James became a man of the new century.

Henry James's Revisions in *Roderick Hudson* and *The American*

The revisions of *Roderick Hudson* from 1905 to 1907 show the fruit of James's visual experiences and impressions—impressions of architecture and art received from his trip home in 1904 and 1905 and from the tour of the States made as if he were a visiting foreigner. So many of his changes and additions are metaphoric references to images received from art and from the new society he observed that they make a different book from the 1875 *Roderick Hudson*.

His attention to the matters about art has increased. Guercino's *Aurora* now has one of those "stored patiences that lurk in Roman survivals" (NYE, I, 84), a phrase that probably means that thirty years after the earlier *Roderick Hudson*, popular taste has revived this artist. James has removed the word *corrupt* to describe Gloriani's work in order, possibly, to accommodate him as he appears here to the later admirable Gloriani of *The Ambassadors*. He now calls the sculptor's work "elegant and strange, enigmatic and base" (NYE, I, 107), for he is now in 1907 seen as a symbolist artist of the fin-de-siècle, a note amplified in the added paragraph about Salomé in which Roderick's head is "on his charger." The insertion of a few passages about Salomé filled with puns and verbal arabesques shows James's interest in Gustave Moreau's paintings and watercolors dealing with the Salomé legend and James's almost open dependency on Oscar Wilde's *Salomé*, which he owned in a first edition (NYE, I, 189–90). Andrea del Sarto, as well as Sassoferrato, has been eliminated (*RH*, 405), probably because they are not tastes of the twentieth century. There are also richer references to American art, no doubt also stimulated by James's trip, and the electric bell now makes its appearance anachronistically in a novel supposedly taking place in the 1870s (NYE, I, 372). The introduction of six metaphoric figures related to Honoré Daumier's engravings of the Saltimbanques, performers at fairs, shows the "torch of analogy" James fashioned from representational art and used as a device underlying the pathetic and the tragic history of his hero and heroine (*LE*, 125–32).

In the revision of his next novel, *The American*, there are changes in the New York Edition that also represent the pluralistic drives of the twentieth-century James. Royal A. Gettmann has pointed out that in James's 1907 revision of *The American* the old Marquis's confessional paper included an additional motive for Madame de Bellegarde's murder of her husband and the marrying off of her daughter to M. de Cintré. "It's in order to marry my beloved daughter to M. de Cintré *and then go on herself all the same*" (Gettmann's italics).[1]

Gettmann himself was uncertain that this added sentence fragment proved the fact of Mme. de Bellegarde's adultery. After the publication of this article, Leon Edel made available the play text of 1890 and a fragment of a new fourth act, composed in 1892, of the dramatization of *The American*. In them, James makes perfectly clear that M. de Cintré had been Mme. de Bellegarde's lover (*CP*, 232, 249). As a result, the question arises (as Oscar Cargill in his study of James's fiction states it): "Did James restore an original feature of the crime or add an implication after dramatization had revealed the weakness of Mme. de Bellegarde's motivation?"[2]

A close reading of chapter 8 of the early versions of *The American* (1877 and 1879) seems to answer the question. Newman has encouraged Valentin de Bellegarde to talk to him about his sister, Claire. "Well," says Valentin, "we are very good friends; we are such a brother and sister as have not been seen since Orestes and Electra."[3] The alert reader will immediately recognize that the significant fact about Orestes and Electra in this context is that their mother was Clytemnestra, not only the murderer of their father and her husband, King Agamemnon, but also the lover of Aegisthus, whom she set on her murdered husband's throne. The implication is clear that Mme. de Bellegarde, Claire's and Valentin's mother, is an adulteress as well as a murderess. This appears to have been James's intention from the start.

At the end of the same chapter that begins by giving us the above infor-

---

1. Royal A. Gettmann, "Henry James's Revision of *The American*," *American Literature*, XVI (1945), 291–92.

2. Oscar Cargill, *The Novels of Henry James* (New York, 1961), 53.

3. Henry James, *The American* (New York, 1963), 96.

mation, after Valentin has pointed out to Newman how strange his family is, James added in the 1907 revision the following sentence: "We're fit for a museum or a Balzac novel" (NYE, II, 162). This reference to Honoré Balzac inserted thirty years later should be viewed as an additional literary reinforcement of the theme of adultery, linked in the earlier editions with the reference to the House of Atreus. In one of the best known short stories in *La Comédie humaine,* "Les Secrets de la Princesse de Cadignan," Diane de Maufrigneuse is also the victim of an adulterous mother who married off her daughter to her lover so she can "go on herself all the same." In *Le Curé de village,* Véronique Graslin, a character deeply loved by James, repents after having spent a life of concealed adultery, having collaborated in a murder with her lover. By the reference to Balzac, the aura of his more melodramatic examples of both adultery and murder serves to extend the meaning of Valentin's not wholly ironic statement about his family. "Old trees have crooked branches, old houses have queer cracks, old races have odd secrets" (NYE, II, 105).

The first part of the quotation, "We're fit for a museum," seems to place emphasis on the introductory scene of the novel where Christopher Newman opens his story. "On a brilliant day in May, of the year 1868, a gentleman was resting at his ease on the great circular divan which at that period occupied the center of the Salon Carré in the Museum of the Louvre" (NYE, II, 1). Since Newman, the gentleman just seen, has admired the copies "more than the originals," we know a man with such taste is going to make a mistake in choosing a wife from what he considers the "masterpieces" of French aristocracy. He will be wrong, as he is wrong to attach himself to Noémie Nioche, the copyist, and to introduce her into the Bellegarde circle, for she brings death to young Valentin de Bellegarde. James has caught up in Valentin's sentence the two areas where the Bellegarde family secrets can be allegorically situated. Noticeably, the pictures Newman commissions the pretty French copyist to copy for him are all marriage pictures, pointing iconographically to his purpose in coming over to France to obtain a beautiful and aristocratic wife. As the marriage pictures are copies, so the real thing, the marriage itself, will not take place. "We're fit for a museum" brings us back to the illusions about Newman's ideal marriage, which he receives from his visit to the Salon Carré, and reminds us of how those illusions get rudely shattered. From Newman's dreams of museum masterpieces, we arrive at the monstrous history of the Bellegarde family, and in 1907 James feels free now to stress the debased character of that family.

The Retouched *Portrait of a Lady,* 1906–1908

Of the two versions of *The Portrait of a Lady,* the first published in 1881 and the second in 1908, the latter, the revision for the New York Edition, offers us in many ways another novel. The plot has not changed, but certain insertions have been made that alter the sensibility of Isabel Archer and bring her consciousness and imagination up to the expanded imagination of her author. What has happened to James since 1881 is not only that his penchant for making metaphoric analogues has become a permanent characteristic of his style but that those analogues take the form, for the most part, of precious objects. He had just written *The Golden Bowl* in 1904, two or three years before he revised *The Portrait,* and that novel is a paradigm of the aesthetic metaphor. Valuable objects coexist in a metamuseum, or collector's paradise, of "just-as-ifs" and "just likes," from Maggie's pagoda to the aesthetic form in which every person in the novel appears to its art-collector hero, Adam Verver. His daughter in his eyes is a figure from the Capitoline; his son-in-law, a Palladian church; his grandson, a piece of *pâte tendre,* and so on.

This particular new-century habit of analogy alters the 1908 *Portrait of a Lady.* Of more than forty additions, at least thirty are taken from art or from an aestheticized realm, and certain suggestions made in the 1881 *Portrait* are extended. Further, some of the newer icons did not exist in the world of 1881 and represent changing tastes, such as those for Eastern and Etruscan art. Also, the Watteau in the Touchett Collection has been demoted to a Lancret, probably because by the first decade of the twentieth century it was unlikely that a genuine Watteau would be found in the private collection of Mr. Touchett, an American banker who was rich but not by any means a multi-millionaire. A figure in a Lancret *école galante* landscape served James's purposes equally well, for Ralph Touchett's character was to emerge by being set beside a pleasure-seeking cavalier in this painted, somewhat morbid world.

Art objects already mentioned in the 1881 novel are kept, and new ones are added. James has introduced in his twentieth-century *Portrait* a Juno and a Niobe to describe how Madame Merle affects Isabel's imagination. James's ingenuity in prefiguring her tragedy is expressed in Isabel's opinion that the way Madame Merle does her hair "arranged somehow 'classically,' " is "as if she were a Bust . . . a Juno or a Niobe" (RP, 152). A classical bust can now be thought of as part of a private collection rather than of a public museum, though in the reference to Niobe we are probably expected to think of the famous full-length statue in the Uffizi of Niobe clinging to her last surviving daughter just as she is about to be killed (Figure 23). The joining in Isabel's mind of the goddess Juno and the boasting mother Niobe appears to be a planned union to indicate that whereas Madame Merle is a Juno insofar as she is a mother (for Juno is the matchmaker, the goddess of fertility and of marriages), she is also, in oxymoronic form, a Niobe, a mother who is deprived of her children. The little Niobe reminds one also of the statuesque Madame Merle's undersized daughter, Pansy. The Niobe reference is insisted on, for Isabel again thinks of Niobe when she later quotes Lord Byron's line on Rome from *Childe Harold:* "Ought I dislike it because, poor old dear—the Niobe of Nations, you know—it has been spoiled?" (RP, 238).

The concentration on the relationship of the *Dying Gladiator* in the Capitoline Museum to the wounded Warburton is at once emphasized and diluted. It is emphasized because James inserts, "it was absurd that he [Warburton] . . . should cultivate a scar out of proportion to any wound" (RP, 191). It is diluted because it no longer is the only identified masterpiece that Isabel admires in that particular room of the museum. Instead of "Isabel glanced at the circle of sculpture" (*PO,* 279), James has now added, "And she glanced at the Antinous and the Faun" (RP, 253) (Figures 24 and 25). Those pieces of sculpture seem to be related to the presence of Osmond, the victor in the competition for Isabel's hand, for the *Antinous* and the Praxitelean masterpiece display characteristics just the opposite to those of the Gallic warrior from the North. They are sensuous, indolent youths representing the ripest, perhaps the too-ripe, development of canons of beauty—canons to which Osmond has devoted his life. As the *Dying Gladiator* signified Warburton, "the Antinous and the Faun" iconify Osmond.

James had refined his own tastes in the twenty-five years since he wrote the first *Portrait.* He had spent many weekends at such houses as Osterley

Hall, one of the finest Adam houses in England; Waddesdon Manor, which Baron Ferdinand de Rothschild had filled with eighteenth-century art from royal French collections; and Mentmore Towers, Lord Rosebery's home inherited from Sir Mayer de Rothschild.[4] These experiences in private homes of princely status may have contributed to the further refinement of the precious china analogues. For example, the information Osmond withheld from Isabel "marked him for her as by one of those signs of the highly curious that he was showing her on the underside of old plates (RP, 220). Isabel is the apt pupil of Osmond the connoisseur, for she is learning to understand him through the collector's tricks he is teaching her. Special collections are introduced in an insertion in which Osmond's ideas are compared to precious walking sticks. "He uttered his ideas as if, odd as they often appeared, he were used to them and had lived with them; old polished knobs and heads and handles, of precious substance, that could be fitted if necessary to new walking-sticks—not switches plucked in destitution from the common tree and then too elegantly waved about" (RP, 233). James had seen a collection of beautiful ceramic tops for walking sticks at Waddesdon and even had by that time his own collection of carefully chosen walking sticks.

Of all the main characters in the first version, only Caspar was not given his own vivid icon, and this defect is remedied in the revision. Isabel sees Caspar as an armored warrior in terms of the individual pieces making up the suit of armor. She "saw the different fitted parts of him as she had seen, in museums and portraits, the different fitted parts of armoured warriors—in plates of steel handsomely inlaid with gold" (RP, 106) (Figure 26). The image is reenforced later when Caspar's eyes "seemed to shine through the vizard of a helmet" (RP, 135), and "he was naturally plated and steeled, armed essentially for aggression" (RP, 136). James inserts the word *hard* more than twice and refers to Caspar's "hard stiffness." The reader sees the armor as "pieces of change," the technical term for the separate articulated elements of the suit. As well as allowing the steel-clad warrior to move easily, they could be quickly replaced in battle when individual sections of the armor were damaged. Around the turn of the century these pieces of change were greatly sought after by collectors, echoed in the way Isabel's image

4. Adeline R. Tintner, *The Museum World of Henry James* (Ann Arbor, 1986), 210–11.

focuses on the articulation of the plates of armor rather than on the whole suit (Figures 27 and 28).

This interest in armor coincided with an exhibition at the Metropolitan Museum during 1904, the year James visited the United States, of the remarkable armor collection of Maurice de Talleyrand-Perigord. Bashford Dean in his handbook on the collection has called it "the most valuable collection of arms and armor in America," rivaling Sir Richard Wallace's collection in London. Since Isabel mentions seeing such armor not only in museums but in "portraits," one of those might be the National Gallery portrait, by Anthony Van Dyck, of Charles I on horseback, fully clothed in armor, the pieces of which are distinctly and clearly articulated (Figure 29). It was a portrait that James had suggested when Biddy Dormer in *The Tragic Muse* thinks of Peter Sherringham as resembling Charles I.

Another source for Isabel's metaphor might have been the collection of pieces of armor at Waddesdon. Even when Baron Ferdinand owned it, there were trophies of arms and various articles on the walls of the billiard room corridor, though the great pieces were bought by Alice de Rothschild beginning around 1902. An exquisite helmet, or burgonet, and a pair of cowters, or elbow pieces, of the finest workmanship in blued steel and gilt, all having belonged once to Emperor Charles V, and a pair of eighteenth-century shoulder and arm defences known as spaudlers and vambraces from the Duke de Giove's armor are the choicest pieces of a collection in which the armorer's art is represented by only a few superb things, but those things illustrate admirably Isabel's metaphor.

Osmond, too, has now been carefully gilded and adorned with new, rather complex analogies to make more precise his peculiarities: "He suggested, fine gold coin as he was, no stamp nor emblem of the common mintage that provides for general circulation; he was the elegant complicated medal struck off for a special occasion" (RP, 194).

At Waddesdon there is a precious silver-gilt medal of Ferdinand I by Hans Reinhart, dated 1539, Leipzig, also acquired by Alice de Rothschild, another version of which is in the Victoria and Albert Museum, struck when Ferdinand had been elected king of Hungary and Bohemia. The profile is so suggestive of Osmond's resemblance to a sixteenth-century portrait and so imbued with a princely hauteur that if James saw it, it might be a concrete analogue for Isabel's husband. Ferdinand's face in profile suggests Osmond's refined features and elegantly contoured beard "cut in the manner of the portraits of the sixteenth century." He, too, is "dressed" like one who has "no vulgar things." This is the kind of commemorative medal that lies behind James's figure.

The complexity of the icons that James now invents to increase the visual precision with which he wishes to describe a characteristic is apparent in the extension of a simile designed to summon up for the reader the piercing fixity of Henrietta Stackpole's eyes. In the 1881 version, they are described as "large, polished buttons" (PO, 78). In the revision James adds, "buttons that might have fixed the elastic loops of some tense receptacle" (RP, 80). The reader is to see Henrietta's eyes as opposing any interference with the same kind of resistance that buttons offer when secured by taut elastic loops on a tightly packed case or traveling kit. This extension into the metaphor of a packed container intensifies the tenacity of her glance. Ralph, from whose imagination this image comes, is abashed by the glance of those "button" eyes—a glance that made him feel "more dishonoured, than he liked" (RP, 80).

Other important art icons from the first version of The Portrait, including the "Dresden-china shepherdess" (an analogue for Pansy) and the cups and saucers (one for Touchett and another for Madame Merle), are now somewhat refined in the twentieth-century version of the novel. They are made more specific and rare so as to focus on the specialty of connoisseurship. In the revised Portrait there is an intensification of James's stress on that science, which was beginning to develop and which James was to concentrate on in his last complete novel, The Outcry. First, James brings in additional allusions to "curious pieces," a "collector's piece," or a "valuable piece." An image that usurped his imagination even after he had revised the novel appears in his preface to the revision as "the rare little piece" that "a weary dealer in precious odds and ends" handles. The "rare little piece" is Isabel Archer, of whom the "dealer" is "conscious" in the "dusky, crowded, heterogeneous back-shop of the mind." Although he claims that this might be "a somewhat superfine analogy" for the kind of character suggested for Isabel, he finds it most illuminating to think of her as being a "precious object locked up indefinitely" until ready for use (AN, 48).

He introduces a paragraph that amplifies Osmond's delight in seeing that Isabel not only appreciates him as her suitor but will announce that fact to the outside world. He expresses this thought in terms of the successful attribution of a hitherto unacknowledged museum masterpiece that is joined to a personification of that work. "If an anonymous drawing on a museum wall had been conscious and watchful it might have known this peculiar pleasure of being at last and all of a sudden identified—as from the hand of a great master—by the so high and so unnoticed fact of style" (RP, 255). Here is an example of the wit of the later, twentieth-century James in his attribution of consciousness to a minor work of art, as well as his empathy with the "feelings" of a work of art, an individual form of personification. In *The Outcry,* published two years later, James has young Hugh Crimble, his first professional expert, identify a Vermeer that had been hanging on the walls of Dedborough Castle and until his attribution had been considered to be by Albert Cuyp, a painter much lower in the hierarchy of modern taste.

James introduces two painters in the revised *Portrait,* one, an artist of his own day, the other, an eighteenth-century artist at that time appreciated only by experts. The first painter is George Frederic Watts, whose famous *Sir Galahad,* alluded to indirectly by James but not named, was at the time very popular. Forgotten for the next seventy years, it has surfaced once more in the present revival of Victorian art. Watts painted it in 1862 and made three additional versions, the last in 1903. It is probably the version painted in 1897 that James draws our attention to, since it has always been viewable in the college chapel at Eton. Isabel thinks of Mr. Bantling, the English suitor of Henrietta Stackpole, when he greets her at the station on the eve of Ralph's death, as "a beautiful blameless knight." A cultivated reader of the revised version would understand that it is only Sir Galahad who can be a "blameless knight" and that Watts's famous picture at Eton, so highly praised and reproduced, would be the image Isabel saw, for in this later version of *The Portrait* Mr. Bantling's connection with Eton has been stressed by James's insertion of a bit of additional information about him. Not only did he as a good Etonian know Latin well but Henrietta's suitor in 1908 had also read the novels of George John Whyte-Melville, the novelist known to concentrate on Eton and the sporting scene.

The second painter, who was then being revived but was not to become a popular taste until the 1930s, is Pietro Longhi, the eighteenth-century Venetian painter of small scenes that are aristocratic in subject matter and serve as stage sets for people waiting for the action to begin. Longhi was the favorite painter of the playwright Carlo Goldoni, who appreciated the theatrical quality of his little panels. James originally devoted a paragraph to describe the shabby servant waiting on the Osmonds in their house in Italy: "He might, tarnished as to livery and quaint as to type, have issued from some stray sketch of old-time manners." Now James adds that he had "been 'put in' by the brush of a Longhi or a Goya" (RP, 226), indicating a twentieth-century taste that has not even, at the end of the century, reached its full growth. Perhaps Francisco Goya is added (and it is here alone that Goya's name appears in James's fiction) because James felt he would be more familiar to his readers than Longhi was. In the 1890s James's familiarity with paintings by Pietro Longhi probably came from his visits to the Palazzo Barbaro, the home of his friends, the Curtises, in Venice. One Longhi painting in their collection, *A Visit to Grandmama,* has just such a servant and two little girls of the age of Pansy, who "had watched these proceedings with the deepest interest" (RP, 226).[5]

The most interesting of all is the insertion of the aesthetic analogues, which are in essence tastes only of the twentieth century, in a novel whose date of action is the 1870s. These include references to a Buddha; to an Etruscan cinerary urn; to musical instruments and race horses treated as aesthetic objects rather than as music makers or animals of the chase or racecourses; to antique clothing as aestheticized collectibles; and, finally, to certain constructs of modern twentieth-century life, such as electric street cars. It is the intrusion of these signs of the new century that makes the revised novel different, written by a man whose vision is far advanced beyond 1881.

We notice an insertion early in the book of a statue of Buddha when Ralph Touchett says how differently he would take the responsibilities of Lord Warburton's position. "For me, in his place, I could be as solemn as a statue of Buddha" (RP, 69). This reference represents a burgeoning interest in Eastern art taking place in the United States, accelerated by the arrival of the new Japanese adviser to the Boston Museum, Okakura Kakuzo. Mrs. Jack Gardner took him in hand in 1904, and since she saw James frequently during his trip that year to the United States, her enthusiasm for Eastern

5. See Terisio Pignotti, *Pietro Longhi* (London, 1969), 283. See also *LE*.

art would have been conveyed to her friend. The Bigelow Collection in the Museum of Fine Arts in Boston included a number of pieces of oriental sculpture; the great orientalist, Ernest Fenollosa, had worked on the collection. Exhibited publicly in the 1890s, it stimulated a taste always dormant in New England because of the China trade—taste that was to snowball as the new century progressed. The introduction of this phrase, "a statue of Buddha," indicates a twentieth-century taste beginning its first stage in the Boston area.

In 1896 an Etruscan cinerary statue of the third century B.C., a fine example of its type, had been presented to the Metropolitan Museum. James may have seen it during his recent visit to the museum, to which he devoted many pages in *The American Scene*. For the specific observations we must turn to a page in the revised *Portrait*. The figure of an Etruscan urn appears in an inserted clause when Isabel, near the close of the book, goes to Gardencourt to see the dying Ralph. She feels "so detached from hope and regret, that she recalled to herself one of those Etruscan figures crouched upon the receptacle of their ashes" (RP, 458). Her mind has become the 1908 mind of James, who had recently been in America and who had been sensitive to some of the new artistic acquisitions. He was precocious in his appreciation of Etruscan art, for it was not to become generally valued until the 1930s when D. H. Lawrence's book, *Etruscan Places*, published in 1932, helped popularize it.

In addition, James introduces a taste for medieval art. In the sentence "she would have been as smooth to his general need of her as handled ivory to the palm" (RP, 254), the author clearly suggests the kind of small ivory pieces that J. P. Morgan was collecting, chess pieces and detached ivory religious plaques, which could be seen at either of his two British houses. A bishop of ivory, given by Morgan to the Metropolitan Museum, or a leaf of an ivory diptych might be so described, for it almost invites the spectator to hold it in the palm of his hand.

Isabel refers to Madame Merle's "interest in life" as she travels as being "professional . . . carried about in its case like the fiddle of the virtuoso, or blanketed and bridled like the 'favourite' of the jockey" (RP, 269). In this one sentence James indicates a new attitude toward musical instruments and toward horses. The later twentieth-century popularity of the eighteenth-century horse painter George Stubbs is anticipated by James's interest in the horse as a cared-for, precious object. As for musical instruments, once objects designed principally to produce sounds, they are now themselves objects of aesthetic contemplation. Twentieth-century collections of musical instruments, like the Crosby Brown Collection in the Metropolitan Museum, consisting eventually of three thousand items, first exhibited in the late 1880s, proudly on show in 1904, and perhaps enjoyed by James on his visits, would stimulate in him a collector's appreciation of the surface appearance of musical instruments, the case of the violin, the shape of the harp. The reference to exquisite musical instruments focuses now on their appeal to the eye rather than to the ear. The harp, which was enjoying a revival of interest, partly for its archaic harpsichordlike tone and partly for its beautiful contour, is the instrument James brings into his metaphors. Isabel, at the beginning of chapter 17 in both versions, is described as "trembling." But in the revision she is described as being subject to "vibration": "She found herself now humming like a smitten harp. She only asked, however, to put on the cover, to case herself again in brown holland" (RP, 142–43). This romantic attitude is supported by the change from Ludwig van Beethoven to Franz Schubert in Madame Merle's piano repertory.

Another iconic analogue appears when Mrs. Touchett tells her son Ralph that Isabel is "capable of marrying Mr. Osmond for the beauty of his opinions or for his autograph of Michelangelo" (RP, 230). The latter icon is appropriate to the 1908 version because just around this time J. P. Morgan, as well as the British Museum, was buying Michelangelo autographs and manuscripts from the Azzoli Collection, though the actual date of the sale has not been verified. Mrs. Touchett is supposed to be talking during the mid-1870s, so her comment is strangely anachronistic. Since it is too early for such autographs to be on the market for private collectors and surely for one as poor as Gilbert Osmond, Mrs. Touchett is leaping out of her century into the next.

There is another whole category of aesthetic objects expressed metaphorically that are pleasure-giving partly because of their luxury. One seems to derive from the ornamental outdoor sculpture of the great country houses. What had been "the kindest eyes in the world" belonging to the Misses Molyneux in 1881 become in 1908 "as she [Isabel] thought, eyes like the balanced basins, the circles of 'ornamental water,' set, in parterres, among the geraniums" (RP, 72). This image shows the effect of twenty-five years of country-house weekends and their training in the ornate. When a dog now appears in a metaphor, it is an elegant dog, "a poodle" that "splashes after a thrown stick." The Countess Gemini, once a "bright shell," is now a "bright rare shell" (RP, 368). James elevates his characters to a superior class through his descriptive analogues. Pansy, once a little duchess, now becomes "a little princess" (RP, 228) and a "little pearl of a peeress" (RP, 342). Osmond is now presented, when in a bad mood, as "looking at such hours like a demoralized prince in exile" (RP, 206). Instead of a "most efficient duenna," Madame Merle is now described as "lady-in-waiting to a princess circulating *incognita*" (RP, 268). It no longer suffices to say that her values are simply "different from Isabel's"; they are now specified as having "been acquired at the court of some kingdom in decadence" (RP, 269). James's mind collected impressions of the most beautiful things that money could buy. He did not own them, but as a house guest of the privileged classes, he saw them with a sharp eye, and they entered the later version of his novel, giving the aestheticized atmosphere a costlier tone. Prices also have gone up. Rosier now realizes fifty thousand dollars on his collection, whereas in the earlier *Portrait* he sold it for forty thousand dollars.

Another twentieth-century taste that James now includes in his book is the collecting of clothing. When the Countess Gemini describes the clothes of her mother, the American Corinne, in the sentence "Her mother used to wear a Roman scarf thrown over a pair of bare shoulders," James adds, "timorously bared of their tight black velvet" and the phrase "(oh the old clothes!)" (RP, 369). The last words make the difference in the later description of the costume of the 1820s. It is an attitude expressed by the author, as well as by the Countess, so that the reader may appreciate with him the taste for clothes of a past generation—a taste that is now universal. From the middle years of the last century, American painters in Italy wore Renaissance costumes to paint in, and the Pre-Raphaelites liked to dress in medieval clothes; but to admire the clothes of the Napoleonic and Louis Philippe periods was original.

At the same time that James admires antique clothing, he draws his icons from city life, not the museum. The chariot ruts in Rome had reminded Henrietta in 1881 of "the iron grooves which mark the course of the American horse-car" (*PO*, 265), but in 1908 they remind her of "the overjangled iron grooves which express the intensity of American life" (RP, 240). It is no longer a "horse-car." The word *overjangled* tells us that the horse-car has been replaced by the electric car and that American life has achieved an "intensity." Since life has changed, the metaphor has changed.

The Isabel Archer who is now a young woman with a taste for Etruscan art and for the beauty of old instruments is not the Isabel Archer of 1881. The twenty-two-year-old Isabel has become the sixty-five-year-old James, for she sees herself as James had seen her in his preface. She tells us, after she has become an heiress, that she "felt older—ever so much, and as if she were 'worth more' for it, like some curious piece in an antiquary's collection" (RP, 270). Isabel's revised interpretation of her days in Rome is couched in a figure far beyond the capacity of a young woman of the most creative imagination. Her sojourn "she might musingly have likened to the figure of some small princess of one of the ages of dress overmuffled in a mantle of state and dragging a train that it took pages or historians to hold up" (RP, 257). The notion of "dress" as having had an "age" and as being attached to a small royal personage, to which is added the sense of history in the pun in "pages" (small boys holding up the little princess's train and / or the pages of history written by historians), makes the analogy very complex. Since it occurs in the scene during which Osmond proposes marriage, James has extended Isabel's capacity for poetic flights to make it more credible that Osmond has caught her imagination.

After the sentence "Happy things do not repeat themselves" from the 1881 novel (*PO*, 285), James put in Isabel's mind a remarkable landscape, reminiscent of Victorian neoclassicism, such as we find in the paintings of Lord Leighton: "Her adventure wore already the changed, the seaward face of some romantic island from which, after feasting on purple grapes, she was putting off while the breeze rose" (RP, 257).

Isabel has even taken on the sensibility of James the dramatist, who by 1908 had lived through the play-writing period and was still to write four plays and a dramatic monologue before he died. Where Isabel in 1881 thought of Madame Merle's and Osmond's conversation "almost as a dramatic entertainment," in the revision she expands this into an elaborate image of "distinguished performers figuring for a charity" (thus also conforming with the social upgrading of James's characters in the later novel). She "sat there as if she had been at the play and had paid even a large sum for her place. . . . Madame Merle appealed to her as if she had been on the stage, but she could ignore any learnt cue without spoiling the scene" (RP, 208–209). Stage business is added to the social implications of an expensive special performance. For Isabel, fresh from a provincial girlhood, to envision such a scene is another amusing proof of the identification with the seasoned playwright and spectator Henry James.

Isabel's imagination in the revised novel shows a tendency to imitate her husband's habit of seeing people, events, and things in terms of their resemblance to art works. Are we to believe that this is evidence of her basically aesthetic view of the world or that in her marriage to Osmond she has caught his obsession? Or are we to see it as another demonstration that Isabel is Henry James himself? The Isabel of 1908 comes across as equipped with a more highly developed intelligence and imagination, just as James himself has now perfected an ingenious machinery for reproducing iconic analogies of a high level of variety and dexterity, as demonstrated in *The Golden Bowl*. It will become the chief narrative strategy of the modernist novelist Marcel Proust.

Isabel is shown (if we consider it a conscious choice on the part of James to make her imagination produce this proliferation of aesthetic analogues) as a woman trapped by her own ideas. Her cultivation of a highly developed sense of beauty and her collection of impressions of art works produce a "house of suffocation" rather than a house of life. This is a narrative strategy of the later James. The moral may be that such a predisposition should encourage Isabel to turn into a writer. Her sensibility has become that of the artist who created her. The net effect of this sophistication of Isabel's consciousness on this reader is to place the book in its revised form alongside the great novels of the world.

The Isabel who affronts her destiny in the later version is indeed a much greater affair. In it, James stressed Isabel's disillusionment with her marriage in a remarkable series of aesthetically downgraded icons. The facts of the true relationship between Madame Merle and Osmond revealed by the Countess Gemini appear in both versions of the book in the shape of objects that no connoisseur of the beautiful would touch, for they consist of "a bale of fantastic wares some strolling gypsy might have unpacked on the carpet at her feet," an image highly suggestive of a genre painting (RP, 445). Isabel then knows that she has been a "dull unreverenced tool" in the 1881 *Por-*

trait, but in the revision her feeling of utter degradation is more fully developed through iconic elaboration. She now becomes "an applied handled hung-up tool, as senseless and convenient as mere shaped wood and iron" (RP, 451), in no way a work of art but simply a thing for the use of others. The "Things" have become just *things*, now that the magic of Isabel's illusions has been shattered. The truth Isabel has heard about her husband and his former mistress is expressed by the detritus of the world, followed by ashes in an urn and by the "dregs of the banquet." Even these, however, are some of the "enrichments of consciousness."

What seems sometimes "a somewhat superfine analogy" is an attempt not to avoid reality but to place reality in some other, more concrete form alongside a thought, which is an abstraction of reality. By comparing the abstraction with a concrete form of a highly visible or palpable character, James elucidates through comparison. Metaphors are part of a method not to hide or to evade the truth but to increase knowledge, as well as the density of the prose. What is perhaps most important is that metaphors are used as the chief carriers of the aesthetic point of view. That it gets out of control with Osmond is demonstrated in James's characterization of him. That it destroys Isabel's freedom is the burden of the original tale.

James wrote that it "is dreadful to have too much, for any artistic demonstration, to dot one's i's and insist on one's intentions" (AN, 56). In presenting the argument that Isabel's imagination has become that of the later James, I have taken the liberty of doing the dotting and insisting for him. For the things piled in "the dusky, crowded, heterogeneous back-shop" of James's "mind"—the things that stem from a poeticizing drive to multiply metaphors—for both the explication of the text and the adornment of the prose are the things of Isabel's mind, too. The Isabel of the second *Portrait* might well say, reversing Gustave Flaubert's dictum about Emma Bovary, "Henry James, c'est moi!" The revised *Portrait of a Lady* paves the way for the modernist novel.

Revisions of Certain Recurrent Characters: Gloriani and Rodin

James's recurrent characters undergo certain revisions in the twentieth century. They do not remain the same; they grow. Christina Light, who appears first in *Roderick Hudson*, keeps her characteristics and becomes the star character in *The Princess Casamassima*. She continues her baleful influence, for her magic hastens the death of a young, talented person because of her whimsical and selfish behavior. Another of James's characters, the courier Engenio, while a fairly young man, is in the service of a maiden doomed to death in his first story, "Daisy Miller," completed in 1879. Later in *The Wings of the Dove*, he has moved into another class, for he has become a professional, a great organizer who manages the Palazzo Leporelli and Milly's whole life.

The third character to reoccur in James's fiction and perhaps the most important one is Gloriani, and Viola Hopkins has thoroughly examined these reoccurrences.[6] The first Gloriani appears in *Roderick Hudson*, and he is known to be an American sculptor with an Italian background who lives in Rome. "He was a man of forty, he had been living for years in Paris and in Rome, and he now drove an active trade in sculpture of the ingenious or sophisticated school." He had spent his money "recklessly, much of it scandalously, and at twenty-six had found himself obliged to make capital of his talent" (NYE, I, 106). What Rowland liked in the man "was the extraordinary vivacity and frankness, not to call it the impudence, of his opinions." Gloriani had "a definite, practical scheme of art, and he knew at least what he meant. In this sense he was solid and complete" (*RH*, 88). As for his statues:

Corrupt things they certainly were; in the line of sculpture they were quite the latest fruit of time. It was the artist's opinion that there is no essential difference between beauty and ugliness; that they overlap and intermingle in a quite inextricable manner. . . . They were extremely elegant, but they had no charm for Rowland. . . . The artist might have passed for a Frenchman. He was a great talker, and a very picturesque one; he was almost bald; he had a small bright eye, a broken nose and a moustache with waxed ends. When sometimes he received you at the lodging he introduced you to a lady with a plain face whom he called Madame Gloriani—which she was not. (*RH*, 88–89)

In the New York Edition, James makes certain changes. By this time he had already written *The Ambassadors*, in which Gloriani has become an

6. Viola Hopkins, "Gloriani and the Tides in Taste," *Nineteenth Century Fiction*, XVIII (June, 1963), 65–71.

entirely different kind of sculptor. Therefore, James inserts in the revision of *Roderick Hudson* that "Gloriani's effects, elegant and strange, exquisite and base, made no appeal to Rowland as a purchaser" (NYE, I, 107). In this way he brings Gloriani's early work up to the standards of Art Nouveau, which apparently James outgrows by the time he reaches the twentieth century. For when we get to *The Ambassaors*, there is an entirely different figure behind Gloriani, a real figure, and it is very possible that this figure is Auguste Rodin, who was then, in 1900 when the book was being written, considered the greatest artist in the world. When we get to the description of Gloriani, we see the sculptor has become an entirely different man, so that his character and personality now agree with the personality and genius of Rodin. Strether is being taken to see "the great Gloriani, who was at home on Sunday afternoons and at whose house, for the most part, fewer bores were to be met than elsewhere" (NYE, XXI, 193). Strether is introduced to him and notices his appearance:

> [He has] a fine worn handsome face, a face that was like an open letter in a foreign tongue. With his genius in his eyes, his manners on his lips, his long career behind him and his honours and rewards all round, the great artist, in the course of a single sustained look and a few words of delight at receiving him, affected our friend as a dazzling prodigy of type. Strether had seen in museums—in the Luxembourg as well as, more reverently, later on, in the New York of the billionaires—the work of his hand; knowing too that after an earlier time in his native Rome he had migrated, in mid-career, to Paris, where, with a personal lustre almost violent, he shone in a constellation: all of which was more than enough to crown him, for his guest, with the light, with the romance, of glory. (NYE, XXI, 196)

Strether was to remember later how the sculptor's eyes held him: "He wasn't soon to forget them, was to think of them . . . as the source of the deepest intellectual sounding to which he had ever been exposed. . . . Was what it had told him or what it had asked him the greater of the mysteries? . . . The deep human expertness in Gloriani's charming smile—oh the terrible life behind it!—was flashed upon him as a test of his stuff" (NYE, XXI, 197). According to Little Bilham, this great artist also has "some awfully nice women . . . and in particular the right *femmes du monde*. You can fancy his history on that side—I believe it's fabulous: they *never* give him up. . . .

Never too many—and a mighty good thing too; just a perfect choice" (NYE, XXI, 199). This portrait resembles Rodin in many respects. In the first place, Rodin was the outstanding artist around 1900. He was well known for his amorous exploits and his relation with all kinds of superior, aristocratic, and talented women. From the photographs by Edward Steichen and Gertrude Käsebier, one can see how the eyes were extremely intense. Gloriani's origin now has been changed from being an American to being a native of Italy, and although he is the same artist, the portrait of him has been revised as James's tendency in the twentieth century is to revise everything he wrote.

The same Gloriani, the person who was probably Rodin, reappears in "The Velvet Glove" and is called "the great Gloriani," and we are now as readers supposed to remember the Gloriani of *The Ambassadors:* "The great Gloriani somehow made that law; his house, with his supreme artistic position, was good enough for anyone" (XII, 238). Mrs. Gloriani here has fat, begemmed hands and looks to be a portrait of the great hostess, Countess Fitz-James, whom he met when he visited with Edith Wharton in 1907 and 1908 just before writing this story, which is an Edith Wharton story.[7] The Countess Fitz-James has been described as such in Wharton's *A Backward Glance.* However, Countess Fitz-James was not fat, but she was one of the greatest hostesses of the period (*BG*, 282). Her salon has also merged with Rodin's as the host. According to Edith Wharton, her society was the most intellectual and most distinguished in Paris at the time, and although Wharton doesn't mention Rodin, we can assume that if he is a great and celebrated sculptor, he has to be Rodin, just as the great dramatist in the tale has to be Edmond Rostand, if he is to be anyone. Along with them the princess in the tale appears to have to be Edith Wharton.

It is also interesting that in 1902, which was just before *The Ambassadors* was published, James wrote an essay on Balzac in which the monumental figure he describes metaphorically to convey the importance and the impact of the French writer on him suggests the monumental and celebrated figure of Balzac by Rodin, which only in 1939 was put in place in Paris but which in the 1890s, when it was exposed at the salon, became a *pièce de scandale.* Because he knew what this figure looked like through its great publicity,

7. Adeline R. Tintner, "The Metamorphoses of Edith Wharton," *Twentieth Century Literature,* XXII (December, 1975).

James probably modeled his great metaphor around it.[8] The photographs of Rodin by Steichen in 1902 show the brilliant eyes that James selects as the salient feature of Gloriani's face. The suggestion of Rodin also may stem from James's interest in Steichen's portrait of J. Pierpont Morgan as well.

The reader of "The Velvet Glove" in 1909 would have to conjure up only one sculptor who would fit the description of occupying the "supreme artistic position," and that sculptor would have been Auguste Rodin. As far as we know, James never mentioned Rodin in any of his writings or in any of the letters that have been so far published, but Rodin was a worldwide celebrity, part of the social group to which Edith Wharton had introduced James when he had visited her in 1907 and 1908 in her rue de Varenne apartment in Paris. Henry Adams has written a letter showing that he had met, through Edith Wharton, the famous French sculptor and that he was somewhat upset by Rodin's interest in women and his unsavory reputation in sexual matters.[9]

That Gloriani could be considered by James to be a portrait of Rodin in "The Velvet Glove" is supported by certain contemporary assessments of Rodin's genius. According to Norman Bryson, Rodin "reinvented the figure of the Sculptor," and he "elevated his trade to the status of myths," the key elements among which are "the Sculptor as superhuman creator (Prometheus, Titan, demiurge)" and "the Sculptor as genius."[10] We see this in the way James elevates the commercial Gloriani of *Roderick Hudson* to the genius of *The Ambassadors* and later to the titan of "The Velvet Glove" whose guests are culled from Mount Olympus. The entire tale is a mock-epic in which Olympians foregather. How did James intuit this role that Rodin was playing in the first decade of the twentieth century—a role that was not part of Rodin criticism and appreciation until the last decade of that century? If it is true that James had in mind Rodin for the last avatar of Gloriani (though it is sheer speculation on my part to think so, it is also a reasonable speculation), then although James had a mind "too fine for ideas," his mind was sufficiently fine to evaluate concrete reality.

8. Adeline R. Tintner, *The Book World of Henry James* (Ann Arbor, 1987), 313–18.

9. *Henry Adams, Selected Letters,* ed. Ernest Samuels (Cambridge, Mass., 1992), 396, 494.

10. Norman Bryson, *Times Literary Supplement,* April 8, 1994, p. 12.

James as a Modernist

Autobiography as "Experimental" Fiction: "The Usurping Consciousness" as Hero of James's Memoirs

Henry James's memoirs, *A Small Boy and Others* in 1913, *Notes of a Son and Brother* in 1914, and *The Middle Years* in 1917, represent a new form of fiction, creative autobiography. James was aware that he was involved in an experimental method and defended himself against the charges that he had tampered with the literal familial records from which the memoirs were constructed. He himself wrote that his autobiography was a new kind of "idea" that would devote itself to the consciousness of the artist independent of and free of all other characters in the novel. If *A Small Boy and Others* is to be interpreted correctly, it must be seen in a perspective that includes Proust's *Swann's Way*, published in 1913, and Joyce's *A Portrait of the Artist as a Young Man*, published in 1916.

It was a form dominated by what James called "the usurping consciousness" in his preface to the New York Edition of *The Tragic Muse*, written a few years before *A Small Boy and Others*. In creating a form of fiction based on a *"usurping consciousness*," James anticipated and paralleled the structure that "the new novel" was assuming at that time. "No character in a play," James wrote, has "a *usurping* consciousness; the consciousness of others is exhibited exactly in the same way as that of the 'hero' " (*AN*, 90). It is necessary to point out that the consciousness that usurps is different from the single point of view. For instance, *What Maisie Knew* is told from the point of view of a small child, but the events of the story are to be perceived by our consciousness of things the child cannot know, and therefore the novel becomes a participation between the reader and a child whose consciousness is limited yet exposed to adult sophistication; this could only *distort* reality. It is this distortion that makes the story. In *The Golden Bowl* there is a further reduction to two consciousnesses, those of the Prince and the Princess.

The perfect example of a "novel" in which only one consciousness "usurps," in which all progress is devoted to the growth and development of the single consciousness of the writer, is James's autobiographical trilogy.

Triggered by his sister-in-law's wish that he write down all he was telling her about her recently dead husband, William, and his own childhood, he found that memories swarmed at the touch. As reported by his amanuensis, Theodora Bosanquet, James would browse over some old documents for not more than hour, and then the "sentences would gush forth." Perhaps it was the first time in his writing career that he didn't "redo" to some extent other works of art, both literary and artistic, but simply exposed himself to his own consciousness, presented directly and not analogically. He goes straight to the effect of life on his consciousness.

His first volume, a "family book," *A Small Boy and Others*, had a kind of preliminary tryout. In 1906, Elizabeth Jordan, editor of *Harper's Bazaar*, had invited James to write for the composite novel *The Whole Family*. The idea, originally suggested by William Dean Howells, was to publish a novel of twelve chapters, each written by a different author. The novel finally appeared in *Harper's Bazaar* from 1907 to 1908. Eight of the dozen writers were women. The men, in addition to Howells and Henry James, were Henry Van Dyke and John Kendrick Bangs. The novel is a remarkable tour de force, extremely entertaining even today, amazingly fluent from character to character, except where James's irreducibly idiosyncratic prose seems suddenly to stop the flow and to make his chapter a soliloquy almost Shakespearean in its associative and ruminative character.

Each chapter tells the story of the reaction of a member of the large Talbert family to Peggy Talbert's engagement. Her fiancé is involved with her young aunt. James's chapter (chapter 7) concerns the "ambassadorial" project of Charles Edward, Peggy's brother, to find her fiancé and to get from him a declaration of his intentions. This brings Charles to New York and provides James with a chance to use the New York scene of the first years of the twentieth century, something he had just begun to do in two stories, "The Jolly Corner" and "Julia Bride," and that he would use again a year later in his last two stories of New York, "Crapy Cornelia" and "A Round of Visits." The chapter is done almost completely from the point of view of Charles (or James), and the author was irked by the restrictions necessarily created by chapters 6 and 8.

James's letters to Elizabeth Jordan show that he was entranced by the idea from the beginning, that not only did he enjoy doing his own chapter, "The Married Son," but he yearned to do the chapters on the mother, on

Eliza, the flirtatious aunt, and on everyone in the volume. He writes that he "tends to burst [his] bonds of [his] frame. . . . But to prevent this uneasy consciousness [he] should have had to do them *all* [himself]!" (*BL,* 44). Having been prompted to view in a fictional form a family very much like his own, with a number of children, parents, an unmarried aunt, and grandmother all living under the same roof, he seems to have discovered from this chore in 1907 the possibility for his own family book four years before "the germ" for his own memoirs was sown by William's widow.

In one of his letters to Miss Jordan, he gives her at her request his favorite fairy tale (to be published with those of other representative men), which also has a direct bearing on *A Small Boy and Others.* His choice is "Le Petit Poucet" as his "small romance of yearning predilection." He remembers "the enchanting heroism of the small boy, smaller than oneself," which "gave one's fond fancy the most attaching of possible companions" (*BL,* 50). The extraordinary power of the small boy who saves his brothers and sister and becomes the hero of the family depends on his thinking up a technique of spreading little pebbles, which enables the children to find their way out of the forest. In James's *Whole Family* chapter he makes use of the plot of "Le Petit Poucet" in a figure of speech: "Yet wishing not to lose my small silver clue, I just put it here for one of the white pebbles, or whatever they were, that Hop o' My Thumb, carried off to the forest, dropped, as he went, to know his way back" (*WF,* 173). In his own *Small Boy* (and note how his title repeats his descriptive words to Miss Jordan), he uses "clues," as he calls them, and they, too, become silver and golden when they trigger the great experience of his childhood; they, too, are dropped like the pebbles of "the small boy" of the fairy tale, so that he can find his way back to his childhood consciousness and to the impressions that formed it.

There are pieces of evidence that clearly point to James's thinking of his autobiographies as works of imaginative art, works of fiction rather than simply-told memoirs following the line of truthful events of the family. The evidence emerges during his writing of and after he has finished the second volume and finds he has to defend to his nephew the liberties he has taken with the literal text of his brother William's letters.

He wrote to Mrs. Alice James after he had finished *Notes of a Son and Brother* in October, 1913, "It's better than its predecessor (through superiority of substance for it's quite in the same 'general style')."[11] His nephew, Henry James, III, however, objected to the tampering with the textual accuracy of the letters of his father, William. James's letter of defense clearly shows that he felt he was writing a novel, not a documentary memoir. He wrote, "At no moment, with regard to my Book use of any letter was I, by the very nature of the case, able to say in advance, whether, or how much, it would or could come in: This depended wholly on what concomitant comment I should be able to accompany it with, and *that* question so intensely on the current and contexts of my composition, as they bore me along and determined my possibilities." The form of the work, in other words, determined which letters he would use. He deplores in these unpublished parts of the letter the "absence of your entering into the only attitude and state of feeling that was possible to me by my mode of work, and which was so distinct, by its whole 'ethic' and aesthetic (and indeed its aesthetic, however discredited to you in fact, *was* simply its ethic)." If, however, James had been "handling [his] material as an instalment merely of the great correspondence itself . . . the case would have been for [him] absolutely of the plainest—[his] own ethic, with no aesthetic whatever concerned in the matter, would have been the ideal of documentary exactitude, verbatim, literatim et punctuatim—free of all living back imaginatively . . . into one's earliest and most beguiling . . . contemporaneities with the writer." He adds then he would have done a job of "*rigid* editing which would have been the sole law of the matter, with no relations for the letters but their relation to their utter text." Instead, he argues, his job and intentions are quite other:

> But that wasn't in the least what I felt my job, from its very germ; my superstitions were wholly other, and playing, such as they were, at every point—the part of my matter, my *book-matter,* that the letters . . . as I fallaciously hoped . . . were to constitute, was in a related state to innumerable *other* things, the things I was to do my book *for,* which were all of the essence of the artistic ideal that hovered before me, and all tainted . . . with that conception of an *atmosphere* which I invoked, as, artistically speaking, my guiding star. By so much as atmosphere would have nothing to say . . . to any concern with the presentation of the correspondence as a whole, by so much did it have every-

---

11. Henry James to Mrs. William James, Lamb House, October 18, 1913; access made possible by Leon Edel, January, 1977.

thing to say to my sense of the little backwater of the past in which my scant bundle might play its part.[12]

That germ, he goes on, and we read from now on in Percy Lubbock's edition of James's letters, had "dated from those words of your Mother's, which gave me the impulse and determined the spirit of my vision" and, he continues with emphasis, "a spirit and a vision as far removed as possible from my mere isolated documentation of your Father's record." Henry James and Mrs. William James had talked of the "Family Book," so "by the time [he] came away [he] felt [he] had somehow found [his] inspiration, though the idea could only be most experimental, and all at the mercy of [his] putting it, perhaps defeatedly, to the proof." Then he makes reflections on works of fiction that had their own laws, their own "figure in the carpet": "It was such a very special and delicate and discriminated thing to do, and only governable by proprieties and considerations all of its own, as I should evidently, in the struggle with it, more and more find. . . . Everything the letters meant affected me so . . . as of *our* old world, mine and his alone together . . . that I daresay I did instinctively regard it at last as all *my* truth, to do what I would with" (LU, II, 346–47).

But Lubbock stops here and has left out the very passages that testify to James's consideration of this book as a work of art, not to be confused with a documentary record of his life with his brother. Lubbock left them out probably because he saw the book as a factual autobiography, in spite of the emphasis James makes and in spite of the directional clues James gives us to his aesthetic purpose. In the next long deleted passage, James writes:

I have no doubt that if you do make the comparison, in detail, yourself, I shall strike you as having been much more excessive—as to changes—than I intended. . . . you may find they are, in their slightness, pretty frequent. . . . I am perfectly willing therefore that my effect on the pages embodied shall be pronounced a mistake—that I quite inevitably, by my irrepressible "aesthetic," lost the right reckoning, the measure of my *quantity* of amendment, and that this makes my course practically an aberration. Yet I think I am none the less right as to the passages hanging better together so with my own text, and "melt-

12. Henry James to Henry James, III, November 15–18, 1913; access to unpublished portions made possible by Leon Edel, January, 1977. A copy of the letter with the ellipses restored can be found in *HJL*, IV, 800–804.

ing" so with my own atmosphere, than if my superstition had been . . . of the opposite and the absolutely hands-off kind. . . . *That* really will have been my mistake, I feel—there it will have begun; in thinking that with so literary, so compositional, an obsession as my whole bookmaking impulse is governed by, any mere merciless transcript might have been possible to me.[13]

Later in the letter he adds, "I know the difference between dealing with such things *in an imaginative connection and in a non-imaginative,* between an application of them *determined by some special and unique relation to their subject-matter,* and one determined by the preoccupation of simple literalism" (LU, II, 347; italics added). It was *his* "truth" that he stuck to as his objective in his book. It was to be an *imaginative* record and therefore subject to the laws of what James called his "usurping consciousness."

If we accept James's own defense of the two autobiographic novels as "experimental" artistic works, with "germs" like his other fiction, we read them as novels in which "the consciousness" of the writer himself "usurps" and becomes the hero. The novel demonstrates the education of this consciousness through experience in the shape of "impressions" that are avidly and greedily devoured by the healthy and active imagination. Since James in many places wrote that each work of art has its own conditions and follows its own laws, a close reading of *A Small Boy* reveals a very definite form, which follows that of the novel as it was at the same time appearing in Joyce and Proust.

James begins appealing "to memory" mainly "for particulars" of his family environment with "aspects" which "began to multiply and images to swarm." He continues: "To knock at the door of the past was in a word to see it open to me quite wide—to see the world within begin to 'compose' " (AU, 3–4). His first "impressions," and the book is made up of these, are those made on his eyes, nose and mouth: vivid images, smells, and taste. His book opens with "the vivid image and the very scene; the light of the only terms in which life has treated [him] to experience" (AU, 4). James pitches his memories by reliving his very earliest sensations and the fruits of that awareness of his environment. The word *glimmer* occurs countless times, for to "glimmer" means to twinkle and glow and suggests all kinds of illuminations into the dim past, with its faltering glow lighting up certain places more than others. Each chapter leads on from the preceding one, usually

13. *Ibid.*

by the repetition of the last sentence or thought. Early in the book he tells of his first and most precocious consciousness, when he was in his nurse's arms; he became aware of the portico of the hotel at New Brighton as a "Greek temple" with "the splendour of a white colonnade and a great yellow pediment" (AU, 18). As he writes, he "dawdles and gapes" and relives the infancy of his consciousness. He tracks down "little clues," ending a chapter by thinking he lost one, beginning the next by finding it. He astounded his family by having a toddler's memory of the Place Vendôme and of Napoleonic glory, a note that is not only an important clue for his growing attitude to all the wonders of the Empire he would see shortly in the Louvre but also one that will be picked up again on the first page of *Notes of a Son and Brother* when the family arrives in Europe. The consciousness he writes about in this book is the "Family" consciousness, determined by his father's laissez-faire attitude to formal education.

The "impressions" of his childhood are carefully graded in relation to what he could absorb at different ages. An early chapter concentrates on the New York house with his father's distinguished friends whom he becomes aware of through their presence, their portraits, and their legends in family gossip. At this point his memories become analogized so that they become interpretable by the small boy as well as by the older man telling the story, through reference not only to the literature that he was reading at this period but even more to the illustrations accompanying the books. It was Charles Dickens by way of Phiz who resurrects the vision of his dentist. *Godey's Lady's Book* furnishes images of his activities. The "smell" of English books now takes its place beside the taste of peaches. The growth and depth of his impressions now advance to a combination of city life, spectacles, literature, visual excitements, all contained in the rich and varied theater that New York of the 1850s offered New Yorkers and that James's parents encouraged the whole family to enjoy. What acts as the clue here is the memory of James himself staring at the huge Fifth Avenue "poster"; the vision it invokes insists on "swarming" with his early theatrical memories. For Joyce in *Portrait of the Artist* the poster or playbill was part of his ugly environment. The imaginations of James and Proust would be fired by a playbill: James would actually go to the theater; Proust would only dream in front of the Morriss column on which theatrical notices were placed. But Joyce was repelled by the posters, a young man ashamed of his environment.

Then the form of James's family memories, activated by these theatrical memories, takes on the shape of drama. The recollection of his early experience with Shakespeare in the theater now changes the next part of the book into a dramatized recounting. His Albany relations dispose themselves into a dramatic format. Albert, Helen, and Henry are part of a "drama" with Dickensian analogues, enriching James's memory of the young consciousness as it develops. The Barnum poster, the catalyst of the great experiences, reemerges as an image, taking the form of a magnified playbill (AU, 65), and we are standing in front of "the Fifth Avenue poster" with James again, as his chapter on Dickens, circuses, vaudeville, and trapeze artists (AU, 65) expands his and our lives out from his childhood's thrilling moments.

That James is organizing his "plot" in order to project the growth of his consciousness is nowhere better evidenced in this book than in his shift from his experiences in the theater, both legitimate and vaudevillian, back to his relations and cousins. He picks up "the thread [he] left dangling" (AU, 99) after his spectatorhood of plays so that the reader, too, can be aware of how James had arrived at his first great illumination about literary creation. It takes place when a young cousin is reprimanded for "making a scene" by defying her father. "Life at these intensities clearly became 'scenes,' " concluded the gaping James, "but the great thing, the immense illumination, was that we could make them or not as we chose" (AU, 107). "The passage itself," he continues, "had been itself a scene, quite enough of one, and I had become aware of a rich accession of possibilities" (AU, 107).

After this "illumination" (similar to Joyce's "epiphanies"), James turns to the other aspect of his growth, the ability to see and use images of a pictorial nature. After the vision of the performance, the vision of the work of art was built up for him by his exposure to the pictures of Europe. The paradox and inversion of his late fiction are nonexistent here because he goes straight to the source of the creative energy, and his aim is to describe it in its truth as much as possible. The art is to flow from the pure and rare vision of what took place, as seen through his consciousness. Halfway through the book, he defines the conditions and the soil that affected the boys' education. Morality was "made hay of in the very interest of character. . . . Pedantries . . . were anathema. . . . Method certainly never quite raged among us" (AU, 124). At the age of twenty-three, as a reaction, James was attempting to invent a method for constructing his first short stories. He always felt "almost uncomfortably stuffed," and he could not have "put more things into his consciousness" (*AU*, 125). Joyce's reaction to his father, who lost every-thing the family possessed (except the family portraits, to which he clung for dear life), was to put his entire biography, father's stories and all, into his work. In a manner close to Proust's, James again parallels the clues, the pebbles in the pockets, by putting into his pockets the "mounds of chopped cocoanut" that give "a reciprocity of contact" that he loses himself "in the thought of" (*AU*, 131). (The living back into the child's happiness in both candy and the making of scenes keeps the consciousness from too jerky an ascension.) When Joyce takes his family to the theater, he, too, fills his coat pockets with something delectable, squares of Vienna chocolate.

James now turns to the picture, the work of pictorial art that, though it surrounded him in its American form and through such exhibitions as "the 'primitives' in Bryan's Gallery of Christian Art" in New York (*AU*, 152), came chiefly from his early trips with his family to Europe. His first scene of "a castle and a ruin" in Switzerland paved the way, it occurs to the reader, for the important stage props of such earlier romantic fictions as "Daisy Miller" and "Four Meetings." Through the Pre-Raphaelites, John Everett Millais and Holman Hunt, the accumulated museum pictures of Europe, as well as the storytelling art of Paul Delaroche and Thomas Couture, begin to prepare the youthful James for his great experience of Eugène Delacroix in the Galerie d'Apollon, "a tube" through which he "inhaled . . . a general sense of *glory*," not only "beauty and art and supreme design, but history and fame and power" (*AU*, 196). The Louvre experience is placed at this point in the narrative, led up to by all the other preliminary art "gapings" of a more secondary emotional significance, to show the tremendous effect it had on the older James and to focus its role in the imagination of the mature artist, for it produced "the most appalling yet most admirable nightmare of [his] life" (*AU*, 196).

To see the Louvre passage as a part of a work of literary art, to understand its role in the aestheticized history of James's consciousness, is a different thing than to see it quoted out of context, which it is so often for other reasons. The art of the Louvre offered both boys "gold and silver" clues, and "it would have been stupid and ignoble" not to follow them (*AU*, 199). He and his brother "picked out the silver and the gold, attenuated threads though they must have been" (*AU*, 199–200). The scene of glory tapers off to Boulogne, where Napoleon, always the proponent of glory in James's life (even in his deathbed delirium), brings his historical presence to bear on the lapse of consciousness—a lapse brought on by a serious illness. As in *Finnegans Wake*, the last line of James's book harks back to the first page. "I fell into a lapse of consciousness that I shall conveniently here treat as a considerable gap." It also reminds one of the first sentence of *Swann's Way*, where the narrator falls asleep and has a lapse of consciousness.

Notes of a Son and Brother has its own aesthetic laws and morphological growth. It shows the young boy becoming a writer, and the infantile consciousness of *A Small Boy* is transformed into that of a practicing artist. The boy, now a writer, is also a son and brother, part of a family with two strong figures influencing his development. It contains half the number of chapters of the first volume yet is a third longer; its action is totally different. It creates its own tempo and rhythms, since James's consciousness is going to be interrupted by the introduction of letters written by his father and his brother. In a sense, these interruptions parallel the interruptions of Proust's or Marcel's "I" story by the story of Swann's love affair, not only in the arrhythmias produced, but by the analogic role that the story within the story plays. Since James has taken liberties with the documentary nature of the letters, their interruptions correspond, in a certain sense, to Joyce's villanelle that grows into a real poem and marks the passage from the amateur to the professional in *Portrait of the Artist*.

The impressions of *A Small Boy* now had to be backed by "science," and it is the manner in which the scientific underpinnings were offered to the young writer by his father and supported also by his brother's experiences in education that is shown by analogy in the way their personalities emerge from the letters. The letters are to be shown as James's truth, *his* truth, and they are pruned and trimmed to prepare the reader to see that Henry James, Sr.'s cheerfulness, his optimism, his conversion of everything to use, and his elimination of waste are characteristics his younger son imitated but that the father's chief interest in *being* rather than *doing* and his impatience with the literal are characteristics his younger son reacted against. The letters of father and brother are both foils and restatements of some aspects of the narrator's consciousness and, if carefully scrutinized, are seen to operate in that fashion, just as Swann's sufferings in love are a prefiguration of Marcel's sufferings in love. Joyce's competing for prizes was also an imitation of his father's delight in entering competitions; his singing, an imitation of his father's choral feats; and his adolescent refusal to study, a reaction to his father's wish to be atoned for by an academically successful son.

The main thrust of *Notes of a Son and Brother* exhibits James's growing authorhood. "To feel a unity . . . in one's impressions . . . *was* positively to face the aesthetic, the creative, even, quite wondrously, the critical life and almost on the spot to commence author" (*AU*, 253). He discovers the unity of art and that the arts were one. He and his brother both felt free of their father's ideas, since he freed them from pressure. "I saw that my father saw" (*AU*, 373), and although he claims that it was not the story's sake that moved him to gather his father's letters, the letters themselves show how his father's good-natured gregariousness and friendship with many of the great men of his time predisposed James toward his social life (*AU*, 385). They also indicate that his father, like Joyce's father, could and did provide him with material for stories (for instance, he contributed the germ of "Crawford's Consistency"). His was an imagination to which everything "signified obligingly," so that he could enjoy even the law lectures at Gore Hall back at Cambridge.

It is in chapter 11, close to the end of the volume, that James explains and includes within the book his creed and statement of purpose in composing the book, very much the way Marcel explains at the end of *Remembrance of Things Past* the justification for his long work, the discovery by the very writing of it that he is a writer. The discovery of Joyce's artistic vocation comes at the end of his first novel, *A Portrait of the Artist as a Young Man*, after which he is free, first, to make various consciousnesses his theme in *Ulysses* (which would correspond to *Notes of a Son and Brother*) and, second, to make the subconscious his hero in *Finnegans Wake*, the last of his three autobiographical novels. The climax of his artistic vocation is developed by James when he recognizes at the end of his life what the goal of his artistic apprenticeship was to be.

> The personal history . . . of an imagination . . . had always struck me as a task that a teller of tales might rejoice in, his advance through it conceivably causing at every step some rich precipitation—unless it be rather that the play of strong imaginative passion . . . constitutes in itself an endless crisis. . . . Wouldn't the light in which it might so cause the whole scene of life to unroll inevitably become as fine a thing as possible to represent? The idea of some pretext for such an attempt . . . haunted me; the man of imagination . . . showed . . . for the hero of a hundred possible fields. . . . Who and what might he prove, when

caught, in respect to *other* signs and conditions? . . . I had in a word to draw him forth from within rather than meet him in the world before me, the more convenient sphere of the objective, and to make him objective, in short, had to turn nothing less than myself inside out. What was *I* thus, within and essentially, what had I ever been and could I ever be but a man of imagination at the active pitch?—so that if it was a question of treating *some* happy case, any that would give me what, artistically speaking, I wanted, here on the very spot was one at hand in default of a better. It wasn't what I should have preferred, yet it was after all the example I knew best and should feel most at home with—granting always that objectivity, the prize to be won, shouldn't just be frightened away by the odd terms of the affair. (*AU*, 454–55)

After this clear statement that he considered the ideal novel one in which the writer himself would anatomize himself, he now makes use of the very language of fiction to characterize the story he is telling. He has brought the reader over into the realm of fiction when he writes that in Boston "the plot began most to thicken for [him]" (*AU*, 475). He begins to write steadily, and the death of Nathaniel Hawthorne (who had made "an assault on his private consciousness") marks James's emergence as a professional with the "sudden sweet discovery that [he] might . . . stammer a style," and recalling the eating experiences that gave the "Small Boy" so much pleasure, he adds, "I pull out a plum from under the tooth of time."

His first stories gave him the greatest pleasure. He was proud of them for they were "quite 'good enough' to mix with the rest of one's society" (*AU*, 493); they were compounded, as he admits now after a long life of writing, "of borrowing and lending, taking and giving, not to say stealing and keeping" (*AU*, 495). Scholarship today is busily demonstrating what he admitted himself. The "borrowing" and "stealing" of Joyce and Proust—the way in which Joyce planted clearly recognizable structures from Balzac (the Maison Vauquer influence on *Portrait of the Artist*) and the insertions made constantly by Proust into his manuscript (*his* dependency on Balzac)—are techniques that none of the three disguised in order to launch their big machines. James's "secrets of the imaginative life" (*AU*, 494) referred to "actual concretions of existence as well as to the supposititious." He got his "joy of life . . . in the constant quick flit of associations, to and fro, and through a hundred open doors, between the two great chambers . . . of direct and indirect experience" (*AU*, 494). He now saw William's trip to

Germany as a "reflector of impressions" for himself. He ends the book with letters from Minny Temple, who (with Elizabeth Boott) becomes part of the "concretions of existence," memorialized in two of his greatest novels and who evidenced through her letters a consciousness trying to exist in spite of the gravest difficulties. With her death William and Henry "felt it together as the end of [their] youth" (AU, 544).

Whether or not James read Proust and whether he expressed his opinion about Proust's Swann's Way depend on the word of two people. Edith Wharton in A Backward Glance claims she "sent the book immediately to James, and his letter to me shows how deeply it impressed him" (BG, 323). She explains that James at this late date in his life was not easily interested in the fiction of others, "but in the presence of a masterpiece all of James's prejudices and reluctances vanished," and he "devoured it in a passion of curiosity and admiration." He "instantly recognized a new mastery, a new vision," and "the encounter gave him his last, and one of his strongest, artistic emotions" (BG, 324). Although the letter she refers to containing his comments has never turned up to prove her statement (MA, 496), one would like to believe her, especially since Proust himself, according to George Painter, claims to have received a letter from James "informing him that this was an extraordinary book for so young an author . . . and that it was a great pity he lived in advance of his time." Painter does not document this letter for the reader, though he quotes Proust's letter of April, 1918, to Lucien Daudet, in which he refers to Leon Daudet's not knowing "what Henry James, whom he admires, said about me."[14] Surely these unknown words of praise might have been James's, for comparison of the two works shows an extraordinary similarity. Since James, I argue, was structurally attempting a new kind of novel, he would have recognized the same intentions in Proust. According to Painter, he is also supposed to have written to Proust that Proust would "suffer the fate of Stendhal and not be recognised in his lifetime"; Proust was to be sharing his own fate, he must have felt, since his late work fell flat popularly and critically.[15]

Whether Leon Edel and Louis Auchincloss are right in being skeptical about James's ever having gotten around to reading Swann's Way doesn't

14. George D. Painter, Proust: The Later Years (Boston, 1965), 252 n. 2.
15. Ibid., II, p. 252.

really matter when one considers the striking parallels that exist between the two authors' autobiographical novels. What is interesting is that A. B. Walkley, in his review on December 4, 1914, in the *Times Literary Supplement*, of *Swann's Way* (published on November 14, 1913), compared the novel to James's recently published *A Small Boy and Others* (which appeared March 29, 1913).[16] Edel reports that James, early in 1914, was introduced by Walkley to Henri Bernstein, who talked to him about Proust's novel (*MA*, 496). James's essay "The Younger Generation," in the *Times Literary Supplement* in March and April of 1914, gives no indication that he had recently read a new master. In it James had given tepid praise to the young novelists writing in English (H. G. Wells, Arnold Bennett, Edith Wharton, and others), but he had regretted that there was no "leap into the arena of some great demonstrative, some sudden athletic and epoch-making authority" (*NN*, 323). Perhaps if James had read the novel by Proust, he would have recognized that authority he missed in the otherwise well-"saturated" authors.

The parallels between *Swann's Way* and the three autobiographical volumes by James are considerable. The three divisions of the Proust novel seem to correspond quite closely to James's three volumes. James's reconstitution of his childhood's consciousness matches the memories and sensations of the first parts of Proust's novel, "Overture" and "Combray." The more objective "Swann in Love" corresponds to *Notes of a Son and Brother*, where James pays attention to the personality, mind, and character of his father as well as of his brother, and *The Middle Years* would correspond to "Place-Names: The Name" because, like Marcel, who begins to experience his own passion for a woman in his feelings for Gilberte, James begins to experience by himself in his first trip to Europe his awareness of five great writers whom he encounters personally. His illusions and disillusionments about George Eliot and especially Tennyson would parallel Proust's memories of his relations to the Swann family when he gets into personal contact with them.

Beyond this resemblance, which might seem somewhat arbitrary, the opening lines of both novels show that the matter is the same: the awakening by memory of early consciousness. The words *consciousness, memory,* and

16. *Ibid.,* II, pp. 251–52.

impression occur with identical frequency in both. The first lines of Proust's *Swann's Way* are like the last of James's *A Small Boy;* in both of them the narrating personnages lapse from consciousness to unconsciousness. Marcel falls asleep, and James becomes unconscious from a severe illness. James's aroused memory on his first page makes "aspects" multiply and images "swarm." They "compose round the primary figure. . . . Such then is the circle of my commemoration . . . fused and united and interlocked" (*AU*, 3, 4). Proust writes, "When a man is asleep, he has in a circle round him the chain of the hours, the sequence of the years, the order of the heavenly host." When he awakes and loses his sense of consciousness, then "memory . . . would come like a rope let down from heaven to draw [him] up out of the abyss" (P, 4–5). Part of Proust's third sentence is that he himself "seemed actually to have become the subject of [his] book" he has been reading, an "impression" that "would persist" (P, 3). Then he follows with, "the subject of my book would separate itself from me, leaving me free to choose whether I would form part of it or not" (P, 3).

Whether it was because both Proust and James, irrespective of the generation gap between them, came from cultivated upper middle-class families where the life of the mind and the imagination were liberated by the money and sophistication of their parents, who exposed them to the same kinds of experiences (literature, art, and the theater), their approaches to these experiences, presented as first-person impressions, observations, and conclusions, are remarkably close. Both novels present the intensity of childhood sensations of taste. Proust wrote that the past is hidden somewhere "in some material object." James called this object a "clue," and his first volume is strewn with these objects operating as clues. The "sweet taste of Albany" (*AU*, 6), which in "long summer afternoons—occasions tasting of ample leisure . . . tasting of accessible garden peaches . . . tasting of many-sized uncles, aunts, cousins" (*AU*, 4–5), corresponds to the madeleine in the lime tea, which could be just a "crumb" for Proust, just as the "clue" that started off James's memory could be, he wrote, only a "tiny particle." In the very smallness of the crumb, Proust wrote, the strength resided, as it did for James. Both writers saw the resurgence of memory as operating mechanically in the same way.

There are certain amazing pertinent parallels. For instance, in "Overture," Proust annoys his father by not going to sleep without his mother kissing him, and the episode in which his father reverses himself and allows the mother to stay in his room "opened a new era" for the "I." The parallel situation in James's *A Small Boy*, almost as early as in Proust's novel, occurs when his cousin Marie at Linwood annoys her father (as Marcel has done) by not wanting to go to bed. When her mother tells her, "don't make a scene," it becomes an "epoch-making" event in the life of the "I," for it "told me so much about life." The "great thing, the immense illumination," was that "we could make them [scenes] or not as we chose" (*AU*, 107). In this way the possibility of artistic creation dawned on the "small boy." Both writers see people as works of art and works of literature. Indeed, perhaps no other modern author has assembled these analogic structures to make a system of personal definitions the way Proust and James have. For both artists it was the picture and the drama, the written word and the painted image, that created analogic models to present their characters and to epito-mize psychological behavior.

Constantin Guys appears in Proust, as Gavarni does in James, in order to define a social scene. Giotto takes the place in Proust of Delaroche and Cou-ture, whose paintings were even earlier aesthetic experiences for the peripa-tetic James children. No other modern author has so often seen in life situations the analogy of a piece of playwriting. For instance, James sees the drama of his three relations, with Maria as heroine (*AU*, 107), conjoined with an artistic parallel, as Proust sees the town Combray emerge as a stage set.

Both have strong architectural infantile memories, Proust of the Combray church and the medieval character of the town, James, in his nurse's arms, aware of the neoclassic "great Greek temple" of the hotel at New Brighton (a hotel child as much as the older Proust would be in his later volumes). Neoclassicism was the historic architectural background for a young Ameri-can of the Atlantic seaboard in the late 1840s and 1850s (as it was also for the Dubliner Joyce). Both were theater-mad, though Proust, ill and carefully guarded by his parents, was limited to looking at the playbills advertising the plays and reading them in their printed form, whereas James, in America, with an unstructured life-style in which children and parents fed from the same pot, could see the play as well as focus on the posters. These printed advance notices of plays take on equal symbolic and aesthetic roles in both writers. For James, the Broadway poster for a few chapters acts as the "clue," the crumb of the madeleine, the "tiny particle" that stirs up the varied and almost extravagant experience of the lavish theatergoing of his childhood. In just this way the Morriss column with its playbill, with its special color and type, had to serve for Proust as the total playgoing experience of his early years. Peaches, plums, and smells of Albany are balanced by the smells of cooking that signify Combray for Proust. Smells "like a baked pie" and his "unconfessed gluttony" made Proust "bury himself in the fruity smell of the flowered quilt." James is likewise made happy by feeling the mounds of coconut candy stickily placed in his coat pockets. As the death of James's Aunt Wyckoff marked off his childhood, so the death of Proust's Aunt Léonie marked off his early youth. Jean-Jacques Rousseau is suggested to both little boys as fitting for their years, but they both end up reading George Sand because Proust's grandmother and James's mother (both contemporaries though there was a generation between them) loved Sand's pastoral and sentimental novels (Proust and James both mention *François le Champi* as part of their youth).

There is another small point that unites the sensibility and taste of both James and Proust. The taste for Vermeer, which did not burgeon until the 1920s, was developed by a few connoisseurs after Theophile Thoré-Bürger's article in the 1860s and spread more widely after the dispersal of his collection in 1902, when the National Gallery acquired its Vermeers and Mrs. Gardner acquired one. Bergotte's death occurs after his visit to see the *View of Delft,* a fictional detail that masks Proust's own visit to the Jeu de Paume to see the picture on loan from The Hague shortly before his own death. The appreciation of Vermeer, a taste that separated the man of feeling from the Philistine, had been fictionally used by James in *The Outcry,* when the sensitive young art historian recognizes the Lord Theign's collection a "Vandermeer" (the earlier spelling), which the others all had confused with a Cuyp.

A very important coincidence seems to indicate that, given the kind of creative autobiography both were striving for (to which Proust gave the name "novel" and which James himself saw was a new form of fiction), they were both bound to discover that the most dramatic form of self-history was the dream-within-the-novel. In Proust it acts as the climax of "Swann in Love," when Swann has a dream in which he has been divided into two people, a strong "I" and a suffering young man with a fez. They both climb a mountain and watch Odette retreat with Napoleon III, presumably to make love

(P, 412). According to Proust, "like certain novelists," Swann had "distributed his own personality between two characters, the one who was dreaming the dream, and another whom he saw in front of him sporting a fez" (P, 413). The dream is Swann's unwritten piece of literature. The "first person" in the dream tells his alter ego that Odette has become the mistress of Napoleon III because he, the "I," has "advised her to do it," indicating his control over Odette. Her image, which Swann remembers upon awakening, reminds him of how he has "wasted years of [his] life . . . for a woman who didn't appeal to [him], who wasn't even [his] type!," at which point his story ends (P, 415).

James's dream, in contrast, is the apogee of the education of his early consciousness, when his knowledge of glory, power, and art comes through his experience of the Galerie d'Apollon, the importance of which surfaces years later in "the most appalling yet most admirable nightmare of [his] life," which he tells in A Small Boy (AU, 196). In the dream he also has divided himself into two: the self who is not an artist and the self who is, the latter routing the other, the intruder, the time-waster. We may interpret this dream to mean that in the Galerie d'Apollon James recognized his vocation and routed the alter ego that would stand in the way of his artistic commitment. Leon Edel has figured out that the dream took place in July, 1910 (MA, 444), which would make "The Jolly Corner" (a story in which one part of a man attempts to rout another part of him that is threatening him) come into being (1908 publication) just two years before the dream. It was a drama that operated both consciously in a story and unconsciously in a dream. It is the great climax of A Small Boy. The recognition of his vocation and the acceptance of the standards of the best art and also the glory by which to measure it became, in a dream, James's only unconscious work of art.

The dream's significance as a strategic ploy and as a psychological truth becomes a bigger thing yet in Joyce's Finnegans Wake, where the dream surrounds the entire story and where consciousness belongs no longer to the individual but to the race. The language is that not of an "I" but of all mankind. With this novel finally finished, though "in Progress" for so many years, the autobiographical novel of the twentieth century, which in Proust and James had been wedded to psychology, becomes hitched to anthropology, philology, and semiotics and more or less explodes itself, having had other manifestations in the 1920s in the novels of Virginia Woolf and Dorothy Richardson.

The relation between James's autobiography and Joyce's *Portrait of the Artist* is different. We do not see a spontaneous evolution from the sensibilities of two writers reviewing their youthful experiences, as in the case of Proust and James, one young and one old. The evidence suggests that Joyce had the advantage of reading James and using him as a model. He was forty years James's junior and respected James's work. With him, it is more a question of learning from James than of hitting on the same format of narrative technique independently. However, the James who formed the model was the James who wrote after 1900. We find traces of *The Sacred Fount* in chapter 5 in *Portrait of the Artist*. We find evidence in letters that Joyce was reading James as early as 1905, inaugurating the decade in which he worked on *Portrait of the Artist*. His comments on James were alternately irritable and laudatory, but the facts remain that he read him and that imbedded in this novel are both the lesson of Balzac and the lesson of James.

There are certain similarities between the relation of James and his father and that of Joyce and his father. Both small boys were taken by their worldly fathers into their urban group of friends. Joyce's revolved around the saloon, James's around the salon. However, Joyce's identification with and repetition of his father's unfortunate patterns of behavior did not characterize James, whose father was not a failure and did not dissipate the family fortune. Yeats called *Portrait of the Artist* a disguised autobiography, and in the same vein we could call James's *A Small Boy* a disguised novel. In chapter 5, Stephen Dedalus uses a metaphor that is very similar to the "torch of analogy" that James introduces in *The Sacred Fount* (by which the painter tries to figure out the relationships between a couple at an Edwardian house party, an image that is repeated and developed in much the same manner as Joyce's image). Stephen says, "I can work on at present by the light of one or two ideas of Aristotle and Aquinas. . . . If the lamp smokes or smells I shall try to trim it. If it does not give light enough I shall sell it" (*PY*, 218). He continues the image in a Jamesian fashion, though in his own poetic and phonetic use of language: "A smell of molten tallow came up from the dean's candle butts and fused itself in Stephen's consciousness with the jingle of the words, bucket and lamp and lamp and bucket" (*PY*, 218). James's metaphoric method is used by Stephen and ridiculed by MacCann. When Stephen reprimands MacCann for flourishing his "wooden sword," MacCann answers, "Metaphors! . . . Come to facts" (*PY*, 231). The imposition of classical icons on Catholic imagery suggests the similar effect of neoclassicism on James through the Louvre and through the American Greek revival hotels of his youth. Both men grew up in neoclassical provincial cities built up during neoclassical revivals.

The counterpoint of myth and fact in essence comes from James, in whom the myth varied from time to time. But the fact that Joyce, after he had finished *Portrait of the Artist,* was able to plunge into *Ulysses* indicates that the finding of the Greek myth was a heuristic aspect of neoclassicism that he well may have hit upon from James's late work. One of *The Finer Grain* stories so praised by Ezra Pound, "The Velvet Glove," is a mock-epic forged out of the facts of contemporary Paris and the myth of Artemis (Diana) and Endymion. *Ulysses* was much easier for Joyce to write than *Portrait of the Artist.* He had the example of Balzac's mock-heroic reference in *Père Goriot* to the Calypso episode from Homer before him, as well as the James story. (Evidence for the Balzac influence lies in the imitation Joyce makes in the word game at the Dedalus tea table, of the dinner table of the Maison Vauquer.)

Although Joyce begins his novel with the tastes and sensations of a small boy as James had done, there are certain sensations, those of sight and those provoked by painting, which never involve him at all. In that sense Proust and James are closer in their natural equipment. Actually, Proust's receptivity to music as well as to the visual arts made him a more comprehensive sensory receptor than either of the other two writers.

What separates James's "novel" from those of Joyce and Proust is the absence of sexuality. His "usurping consciousness" eliminated any attention to personal considerations. He concentrates on his consciousness as Monet did on his particular faculty of sight. When coming to do a late self-portrait, Monet painted only his eye, just as James focused on the development of his particular gift, his consciousness. The method is avant-garde, but James's repressed personality is definitely nineteenth century. Joyce and Proust were twentieth-century men. Each of the three novelists was completely involved with the history of his own life-material, and it was not surprising that when Proust and Joyce met they had nothing to say to each other.

When James answered Henry Adams's gloomy letter in response to having received a copy of *Notes of a Son and Brother,* he made a point of stating that his book was a "proof" of his "reactions" "in [the] presence of life": "I still find my consciousness interesting—under *cultivation* of the interest. Cultivate it *with* me, dear Henry—that's what I hoped to make you do; to cultivate yours for all that it has in common with mine. *Why* mine yields an interest I don't know that I can tell you. . . . It's, I suppose, because I am that queer monster the artist, an obstinate finality, an inexhaustible sensibility" (*HJL*, IV, 706).

The labyrinthian form of Proust's novel demonstrates his entrapment with his mother and consequently with those he loved up to the very end of his work, when he realizes that, used for art, his enslavement can become a liberty. Joyce's labyrinth, when read in the light of his biography, shows his love-hate relation with his father and his desire to duplicate his father's magical gifts as well as his awful faults. "Old father, old artificer, stand me now and ever in good stead" (*PY*, 299) has to be taken literally as a plea not only to Dedalus but to his own father. In fact, *Finnegans Wake* ends in total capitulation. James Joyce the son curls up in his father's "womb," as it were, and thus by getting back into his father, he gets back into the whole history of the human race.[17]

James's labyrinth is not, like the others, an analogue either of a submission to his parental environment or even of an engagement in a struggle against it. As a small boy, he is on his way, by saving those pebbles, those impressions for the creative life, to a personal and independent success. The only thing he seems to have sacrificed through suppression is sexual fulfillment, and for him, as far as we know, and we really know only what we read in his fiction and perhaps in his letters, this does not seem to have been too great a loss. After all, James preferred to see himself as "le petit poucet," a character who even in adult life had enthralled James by his "enchanting heroism" (*BL*, 50). Dr. Joseph Collins had seen in him "many of the characteristics of adult infantilism," as Leon Edel quotes from *The Doctor Looks at Biography* (*MA*, 453).

For James, his autobiography was the pushing to its conclusion of a tendency to "convert" his novels into a limited, personalized, single point of view, and the "experimental" nature of his work was that the point of view

17. See Daniel Mark Fogel, *Covert Relations: James Joyce, Virginia Woolf, and Henry James* (Charlottesville, Va., 1990) for the most complete study of the relationships between James Joyce, Virginia Woolf, and Henry James.

stemmed from a narrator who was unreliable in terms of textual accuracy but totally reliable in terms of detecting the growth and education of his own consciousness, totally responsible to his own truth. For who should know his hero better than the hero himself telling his own story, and what story should be more appropriate for the artist to tell than the story of his own genius? James felt that "objectivity" was what would save his book from the absurdity of the "usurping consciousness," which he demonstrated in his little monologue for Ruth Draper, written right after he had finished *Notes of a Son and Brother*. Cora Tuff (a pun on hard heart), its heroine, demonstrates the usurpation by monologue of a consciousness that is frivolous, selfish, arrogant, and without distinction or talent. She makes the parody that justifies the proper functioning of the "usurping consciousness" in James's tripartite autobiography.

James's "Monologue for Ruth Draper": A Parody of
"The Usurping Consciousness"

As we have already seen, James had written in his preface to *The Tragic Muse* that the only place in a play one can get the "usurping consciousness" was in "a mere monologue." About two weeks after he presented his defense of his notion of truth in *Notes of a Son and Brother* to his nephew, he wrote his "Monologue for Ruth Draper." It was never acted by her, since she preferred to do her own material. The monologue is a parody of "the usurping consciousness" of an American woman who thinks she is a queen. It is fitting in light of James's concerns at this time that "the usurping consciousness" should be most fully represented by an American woman as she waits to be presented at the British court; she is an absurdity of total self-absorption and self-expression. The untitled monologue exists as a kind of apology made by James, who had had the luxury of making his own "usurping" consciousness the hero of two installments of his autobiography. (*A Small Boy and Others* and *Notes of a Son and Brother* had already been finished by the fall of 1913. He died before he could complete the third part.)

The unsolicited monologue (*CP*, 811–16) that Henry James wrote for Ruth Draper in December, 1913, the authorship of which he preferred remain anonymous, is a slight, amusing, yet skillfully managed addendum that, however, holds serious interest for the student of James's work. In addition to its being the last completed, though unacknowledged, creative work by James on the international theme, thereby deserving a passing salute, and in addition to its being the most entertaining of his plays for the modern reader because of its "stand-up comic" character and its merciful brevity, it relates in a significant way to *The Tragic Muse*, James's novel of the theater written twenty years before.

Ruth Draper and Henry James knew each other because of close familial and social connections. Ruth's grandfather, Charles A. Dana, had been a friend of James's father, and her sister was to marry his nephew, Henry.[18] During the years 1912 through 1915, she and Henry James saw each other frequently, especially since they both had been sitting for John Singer Sargent, like characters in *The Reverberator*.[19] At that time, Ruth, a young woman nearly thirty, was performing her monologues in "a few private salons" in London and in her brother Paul's house, where Henry James heard her.[20] It was then that she consulted James as to "whether she should go on the stage in plays, devote herself to writing, or do the unique type of sketch she later made famous" (*CP*, 811). It was in this role as a young actress seeking his advice that she may have recalled to him his fictional actress, Miriam Rooth, the heroine of *The Tragic Muse*, especially in the scene in which Nick Dormer, Peter Sherringham, and Madame Carré all give their views as to the turn Miriam's acting career should take, Madame Carré insisting, "You're pure tragedy . . . or you're nothing." As Miriam decided that her own talent would determine her choice, "I shall have to work it out, what I shall be" (*TM*, I, 346), so James felt that Ruth Draper should take advantage of her own personal contribution to the drama, her monologues: "My dear child, you . . . have woven . . . your own . . . very beautiful . . . little Persian carpet. . . . Stand on it" (*CP*, 811). To help her stand on it, he felt moved to write a piece, his monologue without title, directed to her special gift.

In a two-thousand-word monologue one-third the length of his shortest story, James sets out to expose "the fatuous but innocently fatuous female compatriot of ours let loose upon a world and a whole order of things . . .

18. *The Art of Ruth Draper,* with a memoir by Morton D. Zabel (Garden City, N.Y., 1960), 41.

19. *Ibid.,* 42.

20. *Ibid.,* 41.

which she takes so serenely for granted" (*UL, 495*). Cora Tuff, as stout-hearted as her name, is shown scolding the poor secretary of the American Embassy in London for not finalizing the arrangement for her presentation at Court according to her "imperial" demands. The monologue consists of her exhortations to this exasperated gentleman and of her explanations of her position to her British admirer, Sir Robin Adair, "the two supposititious presences with which she is in relation" (*UL, 496*). This is couched in the all-encompassing form of the metaphor through which the lady presents herself, that of a queen or empress, titles that she claims have been bestowed on all American women by their men, "who . . . keep us on the pedestal where we belong," and which even Sir Robert continues to supply so she doesn't "miss our native pedestal." She explains to the two men that "the effect on us of being treated as Queens is that we have the grace and dignity and outlook of a class *expected* to receive homage sweetly." The "plot" of the monologue involves a cable from the lady's husband, Alvin Tuff, which instead of containing "a remittance . . . laid then, with his compliments, at the foot of [her] Throne," states his decision to join her as "a change," allowing for a pun made indirectly through Mrs. Tuff by Sir Robert, indicating that Mr. Tuff should *make* change, not *take* change (*CP, 814*). After cabling him to stay, Mrs. Tuff resumes her exposition of American queenhood. "We're queens . . . because . . . we do know how to take it, you see—and that's why we reign! Why, I'd be just as ashamed to abdicate . . . as Queen Victoria would have been; who was about the only one of your women, anyway, who has *had* our position." After Mr. Lynch, the secretary, leaves in desperation, she tells Sir Robin, "your old monarchs over here want looking after; and if they don't take care I'll just go for them. Perfectly—as you say—one regular Royalty is as good as another; when Royalty is what we claim!" (*CP, 815*). Finally Mr. Lynch (with whose boring task James must have sympathized, since in 1878 he himself was almost appointed secretary of the American Legation in Spain under James Russell Lowell [*CQ, 315*]) quite emphatically makes her understand that her presentation depends solely on her husband's presence. After she has cabled to Alvin, "King wants us both," she adapts herself to the snub without relinquishing her self-image as queen. James, in his covering letter to Ruth Draper, makes a big point of her rising to meet her crisis. "The little scene represents her being pulled up in due measure; but there is truth . . . in the small climax of her not being too stupid to recognize things when they are really put to her . . . this is a little case of it. She rises to that—by a certain shrewdness in her which seems almost to make a sort of new chance for her to glimmer out—so that she doesn't feel snubbed so very much, or pushed off her pedestal (*UL*, 495). On her pedestal she remains as queen, from her introduction of the figure just after she sketches in the situation and brings into being her two imagined gentlemen ("one off at the right and the other at the left of her" [*UL*, 496]) to her last readjustment to the arrival of her husband, who luckily, in her eyes, will make a presentable consort.

The "germ" for this vision of an actress doing a monologue or imitation of a woman who fancies herself a queen has not been divulged to us by the author. However, the careful reader of James may recognize that the spectacle has been lifted right out of James's own novel of the theater, *The Tragic Muse*. It occurs with its basic elements unambiguously presented in the scene in which Miriam Rooth rejects Peter Sherringham's offer of marriage. In this way the monologue can be considered a revision of *The Tragic Muse*. Suggested first in the description of the young star after her opening night success as "really like a young queen on her accession" (*TM*, II, 325), and then again, while she is being painted by Nick Dormer, in her comical rendition of a girl who gets a pretender to a throne to marry her by following her mother's advice to "tenir bon" (*TM*, II, 317), it culminates in Miriam's speech of renunciation of an "ambassadresship," which her marriage to Peter would entail. We heard her often in the novel give recitations as Clorinde from *L'Aventurière*, as Constance from *King John*, as Juliet, and others, but they were trial runs for the renunciation speech, the analogue for the later monologue. She orates a denunciation of the "nasty prim 'official' woman" whom Peter asks her to become as his wife, "who's perched on her little local pedestal and thinks she's a queen for ever because she's ridiculous for an hour! Oh you needn't tell me. I've seen them abroad—the dreariest females—and could imitate them here. I could do one for you on the spot if I weren't so tired" (*TM*, II, 347). Thus it appears that, like the real life Miss Ruth, the fictive Miss Rooth also did monologues, and this particular one, if she "weren't so tired," would be about a woman who "thinks she's a queen," who is "perched on her little pedestal," and although she is not someone about to be presented at Court, she is someone closely connected with that procedure. The same kind of scene is mounted on the same props;

the same kind of figure is invoked. Even Peter Sherringham's staff position as secretary to the embassy resembles that of Mr. Lynch of the monologue, and like him, he is responsible for arousing the heroine to an angry soliloquy. However, once James has fleshed out his domineering heroine, a close relation to Pandora Day and Mrs. Headway, he delights in her triumph by converting her rebuff to an advantage for herself, and she resembles Miriam Rooth, the triumphant actress, rather than the drab she refuses to become.

In September, 1913, three months before he wrote the monologue, he was thinking of *The Tragic Muse* when he listed it in his second and more sophisticated reading list of five preferred novels for Stark Young, the young Texan (LU, II, 333). But it was in 1909, when he wrote its preface, that his reconsideration of the novel stimulated him to make certain observations that seem to justify our taking the monologue so seriously. In the preface James places Miriam's consciousness on the same footing as Hamlet's, "the most capacious and crowded in the whole range of fiction" because, in a similar fashion, it "only takes its turn with that of the other agents of the story," for "no character in a play (any play not a mere monologue) has, for the right expression of the thing, a *usurping* consciousness" (AN, 90); the tendency of James's heroes and heroines to develop a "usurping consciousness" marks the progress of his work. In the preface to *The Princess Casamassima* he mentions those characters, from Rowland Mallet to the Prince and Princess, who are "intense perceivers" and whose "mortal consciousness," like that of George Eliot's characters, becomes "our own very adventure" (AN, 70). Although such characters as the governess in *The Turn of the Screw*, Maisie, and Strether are the prime consciousness in the stories that evolve from their perceptions, the extent to which they can really "usurp" is limited by the other "agents" in the action. Therefore, it can only be in "*a mere monologue*" (italics added) that James's "rooted vice" (AN, 71) can demonstrate itself so uninhibitedly.

As a parody of James's contribution to the modern novel, the enveloping personal consciousness in its most extreme form, the monologue has its own place. The price it pays is that it is only as a parody or as an extended joke that it can "usurp," and so it remains a literary curiosity rather than a work of art. The "usurping consciousness" of Cora Tuff is the reductio ad absurdum of James's experiments in perception and, as such, is worthy of attention. When it was recently presented as a public performance at the Morgan Library in New York City by Irene Worth, that attention was justified.

4

James's Twentieth-Century Concepts of Time

The early twentieth century was concerned with time. Physicists were measuring the speed of light and finding out that nothing in the universe moved faster than light. Albert Einstein's theory of relativity grew out of the same concern, and he noted how time alters with the observer. Wyndham Lewis's book *Time and Western Man*, published in 1927, showed how important time was in forming the consciousness of Western man's mentality. H. G. Wells invented the "time machine." In a quite new context, Jules-Henri Poincaré is echoing St. Augustine's *Confessions* when he is credited with saying, "If you ask me about time, I do not know what it is, but if you do not ask me, I know what it is." At the close of the nineteenth century, Henri-Louis Bergson was the philosopher who devoted himself to the study of this baffling entity as he clarified and segregated the different elements of time as we live through them.

Bergsonian Time in "The Great Condition": Time Endured and Time Measured

Although the first important appearance in literature of Bergsonian time is thought to have taken place in Marcel Proust's *Remembrance of Things Past*, Henry James's "The Great Condition," published more than ten years earlier, in 1899, seems to have paralleled Bergson's spectacularly important formulations of two kinds of time. In *Time and Free Will*, published in 1899, the English translation of his 1888 doctoral thesis at the

University of Paris, the French philosopher first distinguished between real, experienced, concrete time, known as *durée*, or duration (the time in which we actually live), and scientific or abstract time, measured by clocks and calendars and known to us as hours, days, months, and years. William James, who had a professional interest in the subject, incorporated a long essay on the French philosopher's notion of time in section 6 of *A Pluralistic Universe*, published in 1909. Although William had read Bergson's *Matière et Mémoire*, published in 1896, and hailed Bergson as a "magician," he confessed he was unable to understand it until four years later.[1]

There is no evidence that Henry James ever read any of Bergson's books, let alone his first, or that he discussed Bergson with his brother. We must assume that Henry's highly sensitive artist's nature intuited these philosophical distinctions of time at the same moment that Bergson was formulating them. The story was written before William "understood" what Bergson meant. Yet the experience of the duration of time and the measurement of time as two opposed attitudes maintained by two men of different temperaments comes through clearly in the tale, if we follow the careful clues that James offers. In fact, the very ignoring of these clues is probably the reason the tale has remained invisible to the critical eye, for there has been no criticism at all devoted to it. The summary way it is mentioned in the handbooks on James's fictions shows that no one has been able to make anything coherent out of it.[2]

Perhaps it was through his French friends, as well as his brother William, that James was aware of the ideas of Bergson, which in a few years would become so fashionable. Bergsonism in the social world of Proust, whose

1. William James to Henri Bergson, June 13, 1907, and December 14, 1902, in *The Letters of William James,* ed. Henry James, Jr. (Boston, 1920), II, pp. 290, 178. In the December 14, 1902 letter, he wrote: "My dear Sir, I read the copy of your 'Matière et Mémoire' which you so kindly sent me, immediately upon receiving it, four years ago or more. I saw its great originality, but found your ideas so new and vast that I could not be sure that I fully understood them, although *the style,* Heaven knows, was lucid enough."

2. "James reveals the seamy side of Victorian pruderies about female virtue" is the story's description in S. Gorley Putt, *Henry James: A Reader's Guide* (Ithaca, 1966), 289–90. Edel still considers it "a variant on his earlier stories about women with a past" (Leon Edel, *Henry James: The Treacherous Years* (Philadelphia, 1978), 285. In *Who's Who in Henry James* by Glenda Leeming (New York, 1976), the story and its characters are not even listed. Robert L. Gale mentions the tale in *A Henry James Encyclopedia* (New York, 1989).

cousin he was by marriage, would also become a catchword for both social conversationalists and artists. Bergson himself was to furnish more than an example of an aesthetic philosopher for the formation of the character of Bergotte in *Remembrance of Things Past*. Surely, by the turn of the century, Bergson had become the man associated with the invention, as it were, of the term *durée* for the meaning of time as real and experienced. Henry James in his tale intuited the popular form of philosophy it would become by following through the distinction between two kinds of time. James's story presents in a narrative form the difference between *durée* and scientific or abstract time, also known as "laboratory time." James had already censored George Gissing for his failure to give "the sense of duration, of the lapse and accumulation of time" (*NN*, 441).

What makes the story original and significant is the important part that the aspects of time play in the decisions characters make about one another. This distinguishes "The Great Condition" from the other tales James wrote about the kind of man who distrusts women, the heroes, for instance, of "The Diary of a Man of Fifty" and "The Given Case." A careful examination of the system of repetitive words that measure and divide time in "The Great Condition" shows the reader that James is calling our attention to measured time, which is translated into action, as well as to time that is not measured abstractly but lived through in experience (Bergson's *durée*). James allots the first to Bertram Braddle, the unsuccessful suitor of the desirable woman Mrs. Damerel, and the second to Henry Chilver, the man who does succeed in becoming her husband.

By this contrast of attitudes toward time, what did Henry James mean to tell us in his short story? Reprinted in the collection *The Soft Side* in 1900 but not in the New York Edition, it was based on an anecdote George Meredith told James in February, 1899:

> Some woman was marrying a man who knew very little about her. He was in love—intensely: but something came up about her "past." "What *is* it? Is there anything . . . ? Anything I ought to know?" "Give me 6 months," she answers. "If you want to know it *then*—I promise you I will tell you." That was all his allusion—but it made me, on the spot, tie a knot in my handkerchief. There *is* a little subject—but what is it? I seem to see different possibilities. (*CN*, 172)

James then works out the tale the way he sketched it above. It is the story of two men faced by the possibility of an "awkward page" in the obscure "past" of Mrs. Damerel, the lady one of them, at the story's beginning, is prepared to marry. The rich, young, and favored Bertram Braddle, who has proposed to her, expresses his concern that some "queer suppressed chapter" (X, 397) in her life may have sullied her reputation for him. Knowing his reluctance to marry a woman with an ambiguous past, she then sets a "condition": If after six months of waiting "from the date of [their] marriage" he still wants to know, she will tell him. Since he suspects her even more after she sets her "great condition," he decides not to meet it and breaks off their engagement. The other suitor, Henry Chilver, also in love with her, meets her "condition," marries her, and never asks her about her past, even after a year has gone by. Explaining that there never was anything at all unmentionable in her past, she binds her first suitor, still trying to find out her hidden phase, to secrecy so as not to deprive her husband of the happiness of enjoying his attitude of simply trusting her.

What gives this sophisticated contribution to Lady Churchill's *Anglo-Saxon Review* (written in the luxurious Palazzo Barbaro in Venice, the home of James's friends, the Curtises) its particular originality seems to have been encoded for James in three words from Meredith's germ: "past" and "six months." For *time* itself is the dominating icon of the tale, and the way each of the three characters acts in time reveals to the reader the author's attitude to his characters. This James does through a concentration on terms that define time and action in time. Each of his trio of characters has a different relation to time, which determines his or her behavior. How they handle time determines the happiness of each.

If, as R. W. Stallman has written, time is the important dominating theme in *The Ambassadors,* James's first exercise in dealing with time took place in this short tale written just before he plunged into the opening chapters of *The Ambassadors.*[3] There is no question that time, its action and its effect and the way people move in time, is the "little law of composition" of the tale. The vocabulary, the issue at hand, and the plot's resolution depend on time, and every word in the story builds up the case. The first few paragraphs are studded with "instants," "minutes," and many repetitions of "day," "second," and "hour." In addition, there are four time-pieces in the

3. R. W. Stallman, " 'The Sacred Rage': The Time-Theme in *The Ambassadors,*" *Modern Fiction Studies,* III (Spring, 1957), 41–56.

tale: the clock in the Liverpool hotel that makes its presence felt at the beginning of the story, the watches the two men in the story wear and consult, and the clock at the club. The word *time* itself appears twenty-eight times in a tale of forty-five pages. There are almost all the possible divisions of time as we measure it. "Year" appears five times; "day" appears more than a dozen times, as do "minute" and "month." Also mentioned are other divisions of time, like "interval," a word to measure spaces in time, occurring three times. Such phrases as "six days" or "six months" appear like calendar notations. Time is concentrated, as are its divisions, into those sections in which Braddle is moving, for he is the man always in a hurry to check on his fiancée, to travel by rapid transit, and, indeed, to exit from the story (X, 426).

One is impressed by Braddle's nervousness, jerkiness, and lack of patience. He will not accept the condition laid down by Mrs. Damerel. In contrast is the ability of Henry Chilver to be willing to wait, to endure, to live through not only six months but twice that period, and even then he never asks the question that so bothers his friend. His patience is met by the patience of the lady in question. There is no need to hurry in either of their cases, and time seems to stop when they are on the scene. The inability of Bertram Braddle to accept concrete time contrasts with the success of Henry Chilver in his courtship of Mrs. Damerel—a courtship that consists of waiting for the opportune moment. The one continuous action in the story is the clock watching by the time-conscious Bertram Braddle. He has no sense of *durée*. He is a man who transfers his anxieties to "the aggravating face of his watch" (X, 381). He knows only how to relate to abstractions of time. Always "positively in such a hurry" (X, 383), he hurries away in a cab at the end of section one.

The rushing quality of the first section seems to infect for a moment the first part of the second section, in which Chilver, usually quiet, also "jump[s] up" and "consult[s] his watch," but he gets over it (X, 385). He thinks about the "rapid voyage" on "the great hurrying ship" that made its way in "six days," during which time Braddle had cultivated Mrs. Damerel, after the "ten bustling weeks" both men had spent in America (X, 386–87). In the third section, which takes place "ten days later," time and its divisions stuff the pages, as Braddle begins to wonder about Mrs. Damerel's past. Her "past" is, of course, that part of her time the men cannot experience and about which she herself tells them very little.

In section four, "two full months" have elapsed. Braddle has "dashed off once more to America" (X, 396). It is now winter, for each seasonable passage of time is also noted in this tale. Braddle writes that he is engaged to Mrs. Damerel, and Chilver visits him at Brighton. In the "ten minutes to spare" Braddle has they discuss the problem, for even though engaged, Mrs. Damerel has not told Braddle of her past. However, she has set "the great condition" under which she will marry him: "Six months" after that marriage she'll tell him all if he wants to know it.

Section five takes place in the spring, during which Braddle still tries to find out about his fiancée's past (X, 405). But he has lost his chance with Mrs. Damerel. References to time in the dialogue between Chilver and Mrs. Damerel are minimal because neither of these two is obsessed by abstract time, though the phrases "several days" and "a tolerable short time" continue to make the reader aware of the time it takes for Chilver to realize Braddle has failed to meet Mrs. Damerel's "test," a test *he* has passed with distinction. Section six opens on "one day of the following year" when the two men meet "in time" (X, 409). They keep up their conversation "with pauses—pauses during which . . . the loud tick of the clock gave their position almost as much an air of awkward penance" (X, 411). Braddle continues to look "at his watch" as he had in the first section of the story. When Chilver tells him *he* has married Mrs. Damerel with her "great condition" and that *he* "waited," Braddle receives this information only by looking "at the clock and at his watch" and then "restlessly" giving it "a second glare" (X, 416).

Chilver tells his friend that he has even chosen to "double the time" of his wife's "great condition." When he says "give me time," time in which to learn her secret, the time he refers to is of a different order. On that note, once more the chapter ends with Braddle's "going off" (X, 418) to return at "the end of your year" (X, 418). Section seven begins when Braddle comes "back punctually." With his arrival, all temporal words, exiled while Chilver and Mrs. Damerel are relating to each other, now come back with a rush.

The happiness of the hero and heroine depends upon two things. One is *his* ability to "wait" and to experience time as a continuous reality. The second is *her* "patience" and her confidence that if either of her suitors would experience real or concrete time in living with her, he would no longer be concerned with her abstract past. The relation of these two characters with time is an easy one, and they work well within it. Braddle, in his rushing, restless fight against time, cannot use time; time uses him, and thus he departs from every scene frustrated and in a hurry. He is a "type-A" personality: so time-bound that he is fixated on his fiancée's past, that part of her lifetime about which he knows nothing. He is always in a kind of random action characterized by "brusque" movements and by a pervasive "unrest" (X, 391). Always in and out of trains and ships, clubs and hotels, departing soon after he arrives, he represents the waste of time. Mrs. Damerel and Henry Chilver prosper, for they accept the duration of time as the condition of their happiness.

Henry James was no philosopher, not even a literary philosopher like Bergson, yet he seems to have intuited the Bergsonian distinction between time as duration concretely experienced and time abstractly recorded in "The Great Condition." It is an extraordinary proof of James's observation of human behavior that the direction that Bergson believed philosophy would take was the direction James realized concretely in his art. For Bergson's originality as a philosopher consisted in his beliefs that the true nature of things is apprehended by intuition and that philosophy, instead of projecting general theories, should devote itself to concrete problems, "each of which demands its own point of view."[4] The evidence that Proust read James or James, Proust is scanty enough, but there seems to be a link between them through Bergson. James in his intuitive way grasped the essentials of Bergonian time and placed them in his story, whereas Proust, a student at Bergson's lectures at the Sorbonne, through a conscious intellectual experience made the philosopher's time concepts the formative idea for his multivolume *Remembrance of Things Past*, the greatest continental novel of the twentieth century.

James wrote *The Ambassadors* at the same time as "The Great Condition," and in it the passage of time is mourned because of lost opportunities for experience. Since there may be a relationship between the naming of

4. Albert Thibaudet, "Henri Bergson," *Encyclopedia Britannica*, Fourteenth Edition (1932). This material first appeared in: Adeline R. Tintner, " 'The Great Condition': Henry James and Bergsonian Time," *Studies in Short Fiction*, XXI, No. 2 (1984), 111–15.

The Ambassadors and Hans Holbein the Younger's *The Ambassadors* in the National Gallery, this may account for a relation in their themes (*LE*, 87–95). Death is the hidden symbol in the picture as it is in James's novel, in which the idea of *memento mori*, a reminder that death is the end of all things, dominates. James says it in the first sentence in the proposal for the novel, he writes it in his *Notebooks* (*CN*, 225), and he declares that it is the theme of his book in his letters. Behind the idea of *carpe diem*, live all you can for it will be too late if you don't, is death. R. W. Stallman has shown the emphasis on time in this novel and suggested the small object that Strether refuses to name is a clock or some kind of time indicator. James's shaving off his beard at this time shows that he was aware of time as he was preparing to write *The Ambassadors*, as Edel has told us. The Spanish clock that Strether remembers has a motto, *Omnes vulnerant, ultima necat*, "All wound; the last kills" (*AM*, 67), and Madame de Vionnet, who is ten years older than Chad, is constantly aware of time as contributing to her tragedy. Chad has gray hair, and Jeanne de Vionnet, Madame de Vionnet's daughter, reminds Strether of a "small old-time princess of whom nothing was known but that she had died young" (*AM*, 67). But these are all more traditional concepts of the meaning of the passage of time, unlike the contrasting ideas of time endured and time measured in "The Great Condition." For the James of this story, their distinction is "the great condition" of human life.

The Sense of the Past and Some Twentieth-Century Fictions of the Past Recaptured

Whatever James's actual contact was with Proust's work, the awareness of a new century made writers turn to a concern with the passage of time, especially the resurrection of the past, especially at the time Proust was writing his *The Past Recaptured*. However, the passage of time was also being investigated in the other direction, the future, especially by H. G. Wells, a close friend of James until their rupture in 1915. The two writers looked at history differently. One of Wells's characters said that he flung himself into futurity, and this is just what Wells himself did. He sent James a copy of his *Tales of Space and Time* and by November 20, 1899, a period during which James was beginning to write *The Sense of the Past*, he wrote

to Wells that he had already "absorbed" and "assimilated" these tales
(*HGW*, 62). As James wrote to Wells, "I rewrite you, much, as I read"
(*HGW*, 63). Wells's stories, which really invented science fiction and which
were concerned with the future in space and time, may have created the
impulse for James (who always wanted to rewrite the fiction that interested
him) to do exactly the opposite, that is, to investigate the past. There is also
a tribute to the future in *The Sense of the Past* when he exchanges his personality with that of the ancestor who comes out of the portrait. This ancestor is as interested in examining the future (which is Pendrel's present) as
Ralph Pendrel is interested in experiencing the past in feeling his way into
1820 as opposed to 1910 (*PW*, 281–82).

However, we know of at least two books that are close to the general plot
of James's *The Sense of the Past*, where a man of the turn of the nineteenth
century, who enters through an old house, a part of the historical past, falls
in love with a young woman of that earlier time but one who cannot accompany him into his own time because of the reality of history.

Lucas Malet's *The Gateless Barrier*, 1900

The first of the two similar novels is by Lucas Malet, a pseudonym for Mary
St. Leger (Kingsley) Harrison, daughter of Charles Kingsley. One of her
novels, *The Gateless Barrier*, published in 1900, fits into the genre of fin-
de-siècle excursions and concerns itself with the interaction between real
people and ghosts in the past, a situation stimulating to many writers at the
turn of the century. Then, if ever, thoughts turned to looking back over the
achieved century and to testing whether or not such communication makes
for interesting fiction.

Talia Schaffer reads *The Gateless Barrier* as the source of James's *The
Sense of the Past* because of what seems to be certain resemblances in the
location of both novels. In them, the heroes enter a house to which they
have become heir, though in the Malet novel Laurence Rivers' uncle does
not die until way past the middle of the book. There is a part of the house
in this novel in which the hero, at the turn of the nineteenth century, enters
the world of the beginning of the twentieth century, just as James's hero
in *The Sense of the Past* does. Here, though, it is a leather tapestry showing
lascivious and erotic scenes that separates the main house from the room in

which a woman, who lies buried under the ground abutting on the walls, lives in the novel and becomes the love of the hero's life.

There is also a miniature that portrays the young man as the same person as the hero, just as the painting in *The Sense of the Past* shows Ralph Pendrel, but there the stories' resemblance stops, and what is absolutely lacking in the novel by Malet is anything indicating "a sense of the past." Laurence Rivers has no such thing. Since he does not like his own wife, he is ready to fall in love with a "fairy-woman," a ghost from the time of Horatio Nelson. Although Schaffer insists that James was a friend of Malet's, no evidence has remained of such a tie.

What makes Schaffer so sure that this book influenced *The Sense of the Past* since we have no evidence except certain few elements of the plot, such as a room remaining in the early nineteenth century while the rest of the house is late Victorian? There is no reason to believe that James read this very wordy novel in which there is an intrusion into a room by a ghostly woman who entrances Laurence. Schaffer assumes that the novel "inspired him and from which and with which he disagreed" (TS, 121). She ignores James's notes for the end of his unfinished novel, and she sees *The Sense of the Past* as being a "document obsessed with loss and failure and anger" (TS, 126), whereas actually it is not such a document, but it does show the success with which a finally happy Pendrel is pulled out of his obsession with the past by the reality of his American fiancée, Aurora Coyne. Schaffer claims it is an "unfinished tale that warns against the past" (TS, 126), whereas *The Gateless Barrier* is an "optimistic" story. Yet its hero Laurence, after the room is burned and his ghost lost, returns to his wife as a bitter man who does not love her. He waits to die to join the ghostly community and his "fairy-woman." Malet makes Laurence think, "Reality, as we know it, is precisely the biggest illusion of all" (*GB*, 58). For James, reality is the truth, and it is the basis for Pendrel's return to his own time and place. According to Patricia Lorrimer Lundberg, Malet is the author of at least three ghost novels (DFS, 390), and one can be sure that James would have steered clear of her pretentious style.

A tradition of fairy-people in a school of painting and illustration during the Victorian and Edwardian periods in England seems to be behind the world of *The Gateless Barrier* and gives the name "fairy-woman" to the heroine of Malet's novel. She is the unreal vision of happiness for an unhappily married man. Even though James has used as a metaphor the seven classic fairy tales by Charles Perrault in many of his tales, they have lost any fairies they may have had. For instance, his Mrs. Temperly, in the eponymous short story, is a real life *non*-fairy godmother who brings, not fulfillment, but disaster for her daughter's marriage hopes.

The genre depicting an old house with a section closed off that belongs to the world of the ghosts of a past time must have produced many such novels, if we could disinter them from the oblivion of time, and James may have known about any of them. They represent the nostalgia for the past centuries, beginning with *A Connecticut Yankee in King Arthur's Court* of 1889 by Mark Twain, which represents an interest in the very far past, before the year 1000, and takes place in one of the earliest and darkest ages in England, which is presented as a dream from which the hero awakens at the end. But at the very end of the nineteenth century, writers' thoughts tended to become occupied with the immediate past, the previous eighty years, as a subject for fiction. The ghostly "fairy-lady" cannot cross the barrier marked by the leather-lined tapestry: "To cross this threshold is to force some barrier," Laurence says, and "barriers are made to be forced" (*GB*, 290). She encourages him to go back to his own world, for she is only a ghost. Later he learns that the room has been burnt down and that her body has been found in a coffin close to the room.

Laurence has no use for reality, but James's Ralph Pendrel has, and he soon finds out in *The Sense of the Past* that he cannot communicate intelligibly with the past, nor can he erase the historical fact that Nan has been buried and that his relation to her must not be continued. None of this appears in Malet's work, and the characters of her hero and heroine bear no relation to those in Henry James's novel. Schaffer might say this is where James changes Malet's novel and rewrites it for himself. However, there is another novel with other elements closer to James's book by an author who knew James well and who has written his case for being the first to write a story like *The Sense of the Past*. He claimed that James took from him much of his material.

That novel is *The Old Country* by Henry Newbolt, published in 1906, and it poses certain problems of who wrote first, though the closeness in time shows that James, as well as Newbolt, was alert to ideas preoccupying other twentieth-century writers at the end of the century. A more interesting problem is whether *The Sense of the Past* was a matter of independent origin or had been influenced by Newbolt's novel already in print.

Henry Newbolt's *The Old Country*, 1906

It will help if we now gather all the information we have in reference to *The Sense of the Past* and Henry Newbolt's *The Old Country*. This information starts off with a reference in *The Legend of the Master* by Simon Nowell-Smith to a meeting in 1914 between James and Newbolt, recorded by the latter in the introduction to *The Old Country*.

> ### The Sense of the Past
> In the early months of the War I was invited suddenly, and a little peremptorily, by Edmund Gosse to dine with him at the National Club (in Whitehall Gardens)—to meet the Prime Minister and Henry James. . . . The party numbered eight in all, but when I had greeted my host in front of the fire I was at once button-holed—or more literally "lapel-held"—by Henry James, who spun for me so rapid and flattering and bewildering a thread that I lost consciousness of everything else that was going on, and we at last awoke to the fact that the rest of the company had gone into dinner without us. . . .
> [After dinner James] to my surprise turned to me with a renewal of his complimentary remarks on my prose work, which showed me that he had *The Old Country* still freshly in mind though it was by this time eight years old. The meaning of this remained obscure to me until 1917, when I read after Henry James's death his unfinished volume called *The Sense of the Past*. In that I found the evidences of an analysis, to me at any rate most interesting, of the motifs and situations devised by me for my story and afterwards used or adapted by him for his own book.
> HENRY NEWBOLT (*LM*, 129)

In footnote 1 to this passage we read Simon Nowell-Smith's comment: "Newbolt goes on to analyze the differences between his own and James's treatment of the same theme—that of 'passing back from the life of to-day to scenes and actions in the life of a past generation.' There is no reason either to question Newbolt's conclusions or to suspect James of unoriginality. *The Sense of the Past* had been begun in 1900, six years before the publication of *The Old Country*—but had been laid aside and was only resumed about the time of the meeting with Newbolt" (*LM*, 129). We find a confirmation that

Henry James attended this dinner at which he met Newbolt from *The Complete Notebooks of Henry James*. For December 8, 1914, Tuesday, we read,

> E. Bigelow 1.30
> To Mrs. Yates Thompson 5.40
> Dine Edmund Gosse 8. One Whitehall Gdns. (*CN*, 410)

From the dates that have been published concerning the two published sets of notes of *The Sense of the Past*, we know that Henry James's "First Statement for *The Sense of the Past*," a typescript of thirteen pages, was done on November 1 and 2, 1914 (*CN*, 509), and that the notes for *The Sense of the Past*, which appeared in Lubbock's 1917 edition of the novel, were completed. A second statement for *The Sense of the Past*, presented to his agent, J. B. Pinker, by Miss Bosanquet and at present at Harvard University, a typescript of nineteen pages, was written by James after he had the opportunity of rereading the manuscript that she had brought back from Rye.

We are told by Miss Bosanquet that by November 2, 1914, James had finished all of part three except the last six paragraphs, which involved Pendrel's conversation with the ambassador well before he closes the door on the present and moves into the past. We are told by Leon Edel and Lyall Powers that Miss Bosanquet was sent down to Lamb House in November, 1914 (*CN*, 502), to pick up the manuscript, and James writes to Edith Wharton on December 1, 1914, from 21 Carlyle Mansions, "I have got back trying to work—on one of the three books begun and abandoned—at the end of some '30,000 words'—fifteen years ago, and fished out of the depths of an old drawer at Lamb House (I sent Miss Bosanquet down to hunt it up) . . . but I must rally now before getting back to it" (*LU*, II, 425).

Newbolt writes in his introduction to *The Old Country*:

> The generating idea in both is one in which no inventor can claim exclusive rights—it is simply the imagination of a power passing from the light of today to scenes and actions in the life of the past generation. I chose the fourteenth century for my past; James chose a nearer one—the eighteenth and early nineteenth century—because it enabled him to use America as a starting point of his Time-traveler. . . . The method of the traveling is the same in both books: when the door of the Old House is reached. . . . Another element common to both stories is the misgiving which each Traveler feels as to his own return— "the horror of not being saved, of being lost—to stay in the Past." These are

the echoes of a passage in my dialogue. "I have often thought that perhaps some day I may lose my Cap of Darkness once and for all and have to stay at the other side of the valley altogether." (*OC,* 44)

In addition to that, Newbolt notices that "James's heroine breaks off her engagement, just as mine had refused to leave her century and her home duty, and go away with Stephen to the life to which he belonged." Newbolt feels that "the main general characteristics" of both novels are the same, though they are "followed out with an elaborate subtely of which none but Henry James was capable. He overrules me at two points only. . . . My story lies within the compass of a dream. . . . But James . . . says also that 'the hard little analogy of the dream is to be avoided.' " The second point of difference is that Newbolt's hero, Stephen, wishes to follow Aubrey, the girl from the medieval period and "to share the life of the past with her," but "James's Ralph, on the contrary, is *forbidden* by his Aurora, Mrs. Coyne of New York—to spend his time in the Old World, dallying with Europe, the 'Circe of our day'—that is, the bewitching influence which debases the truly American mind" (*OC,* 44).

We know that by 1900 James had written the part of *The Sense of the Past* that ends when Ralph Pendrel, the young historian who has been given the London house of the English branch of his family because of his fine essay on history, enters the house and closes the door on the present. Since it was not until 1914 that he took up the novel once more and wrote several further chapters and part of a scenario (*CN,* 502), it was possible for James to have read and learned from *The Old Country,* about which he had greeted Henry Newbolt with so much unreserved enthusiasm. We know that works of fiction he admired he "always wanted to rewrite in [his] own way" and often actually did. Since Pendrel's communication with the past was not written until 1914, it would be plausible to Newbolt that his version of the past in his *The Old Country* could be a source for James's novel. However, Newbolt was not aware of the fact, since he had no access to James's notebooks, that James had already written the first part of his book by 1900, eight years before *The Old Country* appeared. As far as Newbolt was concerned, James's book was published three years after he met him and nine years after the publication of his own book. Surely it would be natural for him to think that James had received many of his ideas from *The*

Old Country. We have the advantage of hindsight and can see that the main lines of James's story had been written down in his notebooks before Newbolt's book came out. However, the part that *was* written by James took place before his hero enters the past, and it is very possible that after James's meeting with Newbolt when he resumed writing *The Sense of the Past*, he could have made use of many of the details of Newbolt's book in his notes for that novel (*SP*, 185–351). We really have no way of knowing, except to compare both books in more detail.

In *The Old Country*, Stephen Bulmer, a young man of English descent but colonial upbringing, settles in England after twenty years of wandering as "a fearless spirit-adventurer" and a "student in the history of the future." As the author of books on the past and the future, he knew that "there were no light words, no hollow abstractions standing on each side of this small Present" (*OC*, 23). He thus resembles Ralph Pendrel, who is also a historian, and, because of the brilliance of his "Essay in Aid of the Reading of History," earns his 1820 London house. Stephen enters the past, in this case the fourteenth century, through the door of the church in Gardenleigh, "a really perfect door, like a private entrance to the Middle Ages" (*OC*, 44), just as Ralph enters through his front door with an expression of "the determined diver about to plunge . . . before the closing of the door again placed him on the right side and the whole world as he had known it on the wrong" (*SP*, 113). This is unlike entering by means of a tapestry in Malet's *The Gateless Barrier*.

Stephen, like James's Ralph, finds that the Middle Ages are unintelligible. When he tells the fourteenth-century girl Aubrey that he failed as a historian since he found no use in the future, she answers, "It is too bare" of "possibilities." He finds himself involved with Ralph Tremur, a Protestant and apostate who questions the Church's authority (*OC*, 142). (It is interesting that there is a Ralph in each book.)

Unlike James's Ralph, Stephen finds that when he mentions Napoleon, a nineteenth-century figure, his audience ignores the solecism. When Stephen predicts to Newbolt's Ralph some historical events of the future, "Ralph looks at him curiously" (*OC*, 237), but his reaction is to consider Stephen one of those men of second sight. This Ralph is "a man of the fourteenth century whose soul is out of the nineteenth" (*OC*, 315), just as

Nan Midmore in James's novel is "modern, modern!" This cannot be found in *The Gateless Barrier.*

Stephen enters the past because of Aubrey, but he cannot stay there because it is only a dream. Not so with James's Ralph, who is saved by Aurora's coming to London. It is through her concern and anxiety for his welfare and through the drive of her consciousness to contact him that he is brought out of his past. Malet differs since she shows that Laurence Rivers wishes to remain in his past.

The point of this discussion is not whether James derived some details of his material from Newbolt's novel. He certainly could have. His enthusiasm for *The Old Country* arose undoubtedly from the recognition or cognition of their mutual concentration on the same theme. The historian heroes of both novels discover to their chagrin and great anxiety—a mood that entered even into Twain's humorous account of the past recaptured in *A Connecticut Yankee in King Arthur's Court*—their inability to understand and to be understood in the past and their need to escape from the locked room of history. These elements do not in any way appear in Malet's *The Gateless Barrier.* However, in all of these fantasies in which modern man tries to tamper with what has actually happened, the time travellers are finally conquered by the sheer ineluctability of past events.

J. L. Balderston and J. C. Squire: *Berkeley Square,* 1926

James's *The Sense of the Past,* left incomplete until 1917, was too subtle and too complicated in its language to arouse public interest by itself. But the story intrigued another American who extracted the interesting theme at its core and made it popular. *Berkeley Square,* a stage version done in 1926, is one of the many ways in which the writers of this century were to feed on James.

It was fitting that John Balderston, living mostly in Europe and of British descent but born in Pennsylvania, should have taken up *The Sense of the Past* seven years after it appeared in print and attempted to modify James's fantasy for contemporary theater audiences. Thought of in 1925, finished in 1926, the play didn't take on its continuing popularity until it appeared in America in 1929 with Leslie Howard as the hero. Balderston renamed the characters and placed them in 1928, alternating the scenes between that present and 1784, which allowed him to costume his characters in a more attractive style. James had placed his past in 1820 because it was a link with his own lifetime, for he had known people who had been alive during the period.

In the play, Ralph Pendrel, James's hero, has become Peter Standish, an architect whose interest in Queen Anne buildings, which he presented in an essay admired by his transatlantic cousin, has made him the recipient of a house in Berkeley Square that has taken over his imagination. He is possessed by the Queen Anne period house he has inherited and in which he now lives.

Balderston changes James's first scene, which is laid in New York, and also the dialogue betwen Pendrel and his fiancée, Aurora Coyne. He opens his play in 1784 when we meet the former, impoverished owners of the house, the Midmore family in *The Sense of the Past* but here called Pettigrew. They await their transatlantic cousin almost officially affianced to Kate, the older of the two Pettigrew daughters, Helen being the younger and the equivalent of Nan, the younger of the two daughters in *The Sense of the Past*. Peter, like Ralph, however, is already engaged in real life to a rich, young, American woman who wants, unlike Aurora Coyne, to live in England, but we do not meet these two Americans until we have first been introduced to the original family. The entrance of the twentieth-century man as his ancestor of the eighteenth century takes place with a storm raging outside the house, and he is seen with his back facing the audience, a position that converts the back-turned portrait in James's house into the back-turned transatlantic visitor.

The next scene takes place in the house in the 1920s where a very nervous Peter, pacing up and down, is very anxious to get into the past. The Ambassador, a character also taken from James's play, is now sitting in the living room and trying to figure out whether Peter is a sick man, since he is acting in a peculiar fashion, or perfectly normal. Peter gives him a talk about "real Time" being "nothing but an idea in the mind of God!" One wonders whether this Berkelean metaphysical idea is meant to resonate with the concept of *Berkeley Square*. We notice that the portrait of the ancestor is face front in the living room of the house, and Sir Joshua Reynolds is the painter who has made it, not like the back-turned portrait of Pendrel's ancestor by an unknown artist in *The Sense of the Past*.

When we get back to the scene in which Peter Standish attempts to communicate with the eighteenth-century family, we see that he makes a bad mess of it, creating all kinds of slips, just the way, only more dramatically, that Pendrel had anticipated certain bits of information in a miraculous fashion, suggesting that he may have "second sight" or even infernal powers. When the presumed Colonial from America is challenged to be witty and entertaining, Balderston has his hero use some quips from Oscar Wilde in certain social situations. He gradually gets into more trouble. Meanwhile, Kate (the equivalent of Molly Midmore in James's novel), to whom he is engaged, feels repelled by him, while Helen, the modern equivalent of Nan in James's story, is drawn to him as he is to her. What Balderston has done is to make two members of temporally disparate societies fall deeply in love with each other. In this version, Peter wants to stay in the eighteenth-century time warp, but his beloved Helen tells him how unhappy he would be, for he has come to reject the eighteenth century, which he had earlier romanticized to himself. Tom, his future brother-in-law, is a brutal man from a brutal society. Peter reveals his true attitude in a public diatribe in which he shouts that there is "no warmth in your blood, no soul in your art, God! what a period," ending with "and God, how the eighteenth century stinks!" (BS, 680).

The big interest is in the love between Helen and Peter, between the woman of the eighteenth century and the man of the twentieth. Their love, Helen says, "is more real . . . than if you had been born in my world or I in yours, because—it is a miracle" (BS, 682), but she convinces him that he cannot live in her world. She gives him the Crux Ansata, the symbol of life and eternity her father had brought her from Egypt (BS, 682); "this little saint has crossed the great darkness between us" (BS, 683). He leaves, and the next scene is back in 1928 as his substitute reenters, just as in The Sense of the Past the ancestor of 1820 acts as Ralph's substitute. In Balderston's denouement, Marjorie, his American fiancée, resolves to devote herself to taking care of him while the broken Peter Standish decides to live secluded and unmarried as he reads out loud the copy he had made of the epitaph of Helen's tombstone. Apparently she had died unmarried three years after he left her in 1787, aged twenty-three (BS, 685).

Henry James had summoned his hero back through the love of Aurora Coyne and her desire to play a more active role in his life, and Ralph gladly returns to the twentieth century. Peter Standish, on the other hand, regrets the ineluctable and unchangeable part that history plays in human lives: that he cannot marry the past and it cannot join him in the twentieth century. Here he approaches Malet's hero. However, the fact that the young woman has died, unmarried, three years after he has made his visitation into her time warp indicates that he made no change in her life and he was not able to change the date of her early death.

James resumed his writing and planning of *The Sense of the Past* when, faced with the awful agonies of the onset of World War I, he could no longer go on with the realistic cruelties of *The Ivory Tower*, yet neither he nor his contemporaries Henry Newbolt and Lucas Malet could have their students of history evade the iron unalterability of the past; even Balderston, in his postwar fantasy on James's theme (which he freely acknowledges as being the basis of his play), had his architectural historian broken and defeated by his encounter with the stubborn facts of history. Given the notes James made to his unfinished novel, he, more than Newbolt and Malet, foresaw a happy finale to his version of entrapment in the past.

This playing with futurity and the past in the almost infinitely developed science-fiction genre continues up to the present day to fascinate writers of the 1990s. *Doomsday Book* by Connie Willis has both the middle of the twenty-first century, the future for the writer and reader in 1992, and the past, here the Middle Ages, join hands using this double material. It has won a number of prizes for being a distinguished book.

Although there must be countless excursions into both future and past, this particular one has been extremely popular and well thought of. The future here is the time of the story, 2054, fifty years after our present, and the "drop" into the medieval time of 1320 during a two-week Christmas vacation (*DB*, 12) involves a young Oxford University historian, Kivrin Engle. Her intellectual interest in the past is like that of the heroes of *The Sense of the Past* and *The Old Country*, but her misfortune is to arrive when a case of the flu is rampant at Oxford in her time, and because of an error in the set-up, she arrives in the Middle Ages with a "slippage" of time. Because of this error, she arrives not in 1320 but in 1348, when the Black Death, or the plague, began to kill thousands of people starting at Bath and Oxford. Computers are a help in executing the "drop" and creating a "net," which protects the historian and which arranges for her usually easy re-entry. But things go wrong, and Kivrin's new friends in the medieval world all suffer from the dreaded plague. Finally, she is rescued, though she would like to stay and help the sufferers of the 1348 plague. However, in most examples of this genre, if they "attempted to revise events that already happened, the net wouldn't open" (*DB*, 213). Unlike the books we have described (those written at the turn of the last century), this book does not have the young woman historian fall in love, either with the fourteenth century or with any person of that period. She is simply heartbroken and frustrated that the nonexistence of medical enlightenment had destroyed so many lives. Her rescue from this disease-ridden past, involving the difficulty of finding the location at which she had been dropped and the delayed discovery of the time slippage by a flu-infected member of her crew back at Oxford, makes the quest for a return home the chief focus of this science-fiction novel of our own time, using chiefly space-travel for its metaphor. Like in *The Sense of the Past* and *The Old Country*, there are difficulties in making oneself understood by people living in an earlier time; here the problems are multiplied by the seven-hundred-year difference, since the sounds of the English spoken then and of that spoken now differ so radically. But the genre is still alive and kicking. It shows signs of being even more interesting and more complicated because of the explosion of scientific methods of communication. Now the historian takes with her a recorder so she can bring back with her the material directly from the past.

The dictates of the genre are the factors that really create the similarities among the examples given here. The realization of this must make the effect on James of Malet's and Newbolt's time-travel novels less convincing to the investigator. What remains is the knowledge that James, as well as the others, was on to a literary genre that has blossomed fully in the twentieth century and produced such an impressive flower as *Doomsday Book* at the century's end.

5

Attitudes Toward Sexuality in James's Text and Subtext

Surely in the later novels of Henry James one detects a freedom and loosening up of the author's attitude toward sex. Densher's sexual blackmail of Kate Croy, who, though really a bad heroine, elicits our sympathy in the situation, is an unusual event not explicitly delineated in James's earlier novels. In contrast, we see that Madame de Vionnet, who is an adulteress, is presented as a totally good heroine, and it is now generally conceded that James loosened up in regard to the inclusion of sexual references after the turn of the century. In the New York Edition, the changes that James made in *The American* reveal Madame de Bellegarde as an adulteress, and she is explicitly so recognized ("Go on the same" with her lover), as well as a murderess. And sexual references lose their ambiguity when James revises "The Siege of London."

We arrive now at two examples of jokes involving hitherto unsuspected sexual motifs. They occur in two pieces of James's fiction that have always presented problems to the reader and have remained puzzles from the moment they appeared. The first one, "The Figure in the Carpet," appears as early as 1897, and the second one, *The Sacred Fount,* in 1901. My conclusion in both cases, that James has instituted a whole system of references to sexuality, is an attempt on my part to present an argument that explains the stories. From my analyses I also take into account that at the turn of the century the interest in sex per se, sex as adultery, and alternate sex was not expressed but was understood to be in the minds of the upper middle classes and the aristocracy. My interpretations may not be acceptable to all readers, but my motivation for making them, and tending to pose the questions that

I have tried to answer, is based on my inability, like that of most readers, to know what really happens in both "The Figure in the Carpet" and *The Sacred Fount*. My method of finding out is to extract from the text clues that suggest a subtext, and this methodology has helped me to explain to myself what happens in each piece of fiction.

In my interpretations, I insist on the fact that in each narrative James is having his little joke. In fact, James calls *The Sacred Fount* a "consistent joke," and my reading of "The Figure in the Carpet" sees that tale as an equally consistent one.

"Some Safe Secret for Enjoyment": Autoeroticism in "The Figure in the Carpet"

"Phrenology" is the concept in "The Figure in the Carpet" that acts as a possible key to directing the reader's attention to the "secret" of a writer's work that every critic has ignored. On the manifest level the story concerns a noted writer, Hugh Vereker, who complains to a young critic that the overall intention of his work has never been guessed by the countless analysts who have attempted to explain it, and the introduction of phrenology in the tale implies that it is so classifiable.

There is a marked epidemic of words starting with the letter *P*, beginning on the first page and climaxing at the point where "the preference for the letter P" gives the repetition its rationale. The writer Vereker tells the narrator that what "nobody has ever mentioned in [his] work is the organ of life" (IX, 284). The young critic answers him, "[It's] some kind of game you're up to with your style, something you're after in the language. Perhaps it's a preference for the letter P! . . . Papa, potatoes, prunes—that sort of thing?" (IX, 284). The contiguity of the "organ of life" with the letter *P* suggests to the modern reader a physiological organ, the penis. But the modern reader, until now, has been stopped by the fact that the genteel tradition in Henry James's writings is strong; it would be preferable if possible to see whether one might not square the treasure hunt and its clues with some other interpretation. Hence phrenology is introduced in connection with Mrs. Corvick's very intellectual second husband, Drayton Deane, so that the reader can translate "organ of life" into phrenological terms, for the various "organs" are mapped out on a plaster replica of the human head and mentioned in the tale. Deane looks "like a dim phrenological bust" (IX, 313), and there apparently is the clue to the "secret." "The numbers on his bumps," we are told, began "to come out" (IX, 313). But this turns out to be a red herring, for this is a story in which James hides behind himself, and close attention to "The Figure in the Carpet" will reveal that James sees to be doing just that to conceal his subtext, which actually describes the autoerotic act.

There is, however, no place on the phrenological chart for "the organ of life." The only one that corresponds to it is "the organ of amativeness," which is number one, situated low in the back of the head near the neck. "Next to it, number two," is the "organ of progenitiveness" (the organ Deane can satisfy since he has given Gwendolen two children). But he was not worthy of learning the secret of "the organ of life." What are we to make of that? Vereker had said that the secret *might* be learned from husbands and wives given "time" or from "lovers supremely united," which might mean two men or two women as well as a man and a woman.

"The secret" is discovered by one of the young men, Corvick, while he is in India. He passes it on to his wife but dies before he can publish it. She refuses to tell it to anyone, including her second husband, who, after her death in childbirth, continues his search with the narrator. It is on one level a simple tale of an unsuccessful quest. However, although the secret remains so for the survivors, the reader should be able to "conclude" something from "the evidence" presented on the various levels of systematic meanings (as James wished him to do in the preface he wrote to the story). The conditions of the search are stated in a kind of twenty-question game, so that "once you see," the element in question soon becomes "practically all you'd see" (IX, 282), as Vereker assures the narrator.

Although the "organ of life" is set within the terminology of phrenology, which acts as a metaphor for the rather dim Drayton Deane, phrenology had lost its popularity at the end of the century: William James downgraded its scientific status in his *Principles of Psychology;* we don't, then, expect his brother to take it seriously. Deane is an intellectual, and the "bumps on his head" on which "the numbers" began to show indicate that the amative organ is not strong in him. Therefore, he didn't deserve to hear the "secret" from Gwendolen.

That human passionate love might be the first system of meanings in the tale is supported by the root of "heart," *cor,* in Corvick's name, so he is the successful detector of the secret. This is supported by words such as "infatuation" and "intoxication" and the reference to Venus, the goddess of love, in the line quoted by Gwendolen from the *Aeneid* when the secret suddenly appears to Corvick. That it helps to be married to learn the secret helps the reader to conclude that that is what the secret is. But there are certain things in the tale that militate against the impression that it is about heterosexual love. If sexual love between men and women is meant, why are the four women who appear so unpleasantly presented? Everyone wants Gwendolen's mother to die, and she annoyingly takes her time doing so. Lady Jane, at whose house the narrator meets Vereker, is treated to a demeaning pun. "She was . . . so good as to make me a sign, an invitation to her beautiful seat" (IX, 294). Vereker himself is contemptuous of women. "A woman will never find out" (IX, 288), he says of his "secret." Corvick doesn't think Gwendolen Erme, his fiancée, pretty, and she appears to the narrator as having "no sense of humour" and as being someone you want "to shake." Her book, *Deep Down,* appears to be an obvious reference to her sexual zones, especially since the narrator uses the title in a pun, "Deep Down, as Miss Erme would have said, I was uneasy, I was expectant" (IX, 292), the last word acting as prologue to her two pregnancies, another unpleasant pun on conception. Miss Poyle, the unattractive lady at the country house weekend, has a name that in French indicates bodily hair, and its customary use is in the phrase *poil pubique.*

A phrase occurs that utilizes Gwendolen's first book's title to show how normal sexual intercourse is something Corvick is weaning Gwendolen away from. *Deep Down* was a "desert in which she had lost herself, but in which too she had dug a wonderful hole in the sand—a cavity out of which Corvick had still more remarkably pulled her" (IX, 296). This seems to mean that her husband had directed her away from normal coital experience. We read that he had discovered the "very mouth of the cave" (IX, 313), an obvious metaphor for the clitoris, not the vagina. Although Gwendolen is anxious, Corvick decidedly wishes to postpone the marriage.

That he discovers the secret without her suggests that the sexuality he finds has to do not with his fiancée but with something more general. The repeated Ps in the tale, the opening line with the word *pence,* repeated a few lines later, the introduction on the first page of the word *organ* as it refers to a journal, all point to the word *penis* through word games. Since the first word among the *P* words the narrator tries out on Vereker is "Papa," one sees that the idea of the progenitor in penis is presented first. The word *pen* follows twice in that paragraph. ("Pence" and "pen" suggest the word *penis.*)

From the verbal evidence, the reader concludes that there is a concentration on the penis per se and its pleasurable capacities. The repeated term "buried treasure" (the penis hidden in modern clothes), which has "a beauty so rare, so great," seems to mean sexual pleasure either by itself or only in relation to the penis, without consideration of a partner. We cannot relate the pleasure even to homosexuality, though Vereker puts his arm on the narrator, and Corvick claims that Vereker's words give him a "rare pleasure." Discounting both homosexual and heterosexual love, we must leap, it seems, to what can only be onanistic love: the autoerotic act.

Even certain figures of speech concentrate either on the appearance or on the sexual function of the penis. "He had hold of the tail of something; he would pull hard, pull it right out. He pumped me dry on Vereker's strange confidence" (IX, 287). Gwendolen is told by her fiancé in a telegram written in French, *"Tellement envie de voir ta tête!"* (IX, 299). Why in French? The French method? The word *head* can be used for the penis, rather than "face," which is the way it would usually be translated into English. Corvick's description of the pleasure he had in the secret he has discovered sounds like the pleasure of an orgasm: "Now that it was there it seemed to grow and grow before him; it was in all time, in all tongues, one of the most wonderful flowers of art. . . . The desire to drain it, in its freshness, to the last drop, was what kept him there close to the source" (IX, 300).

Since Corvick did not want to get married, there is room for the inference that he had discovered in Vereker's work a sexual pleasure that does not depend on a partner and is not experienced in normal intercourse with a woman. Since he only gets the "secret" when he goes to India, the sexual experience suggested is fellatio. The next few lines seem to confirm this, for Gwendolen's mother's resistance to her daughter's marriage to Corvick elicits this response from her daughter: " 'Poor dear, she may swallow the dose. In fact, you know . . . she really *must*!'—a proposition of which, on behalf of every one concerned, I fully acknowledged the force." To "swallow the dose" is referred to twice (IX, 301, 303).

By all these somewhat cryptic, though finally classifiable, elements we are finally brought to the conclusion that Vereker's secret consists of the joy of having a penis whose pleasure-giving powers go beyond the pleasure of heterosexual experiences and do not apply either to amativeness or to progeniture, organs number one and two on the phrenological chart situated on the phrenological bust suggested by poor Deane to the narrator in James's tale. In fact, Deane's tie-in with phrenology would eliminate him from autoeroticism, for Orson Fowler, the leading phrenologist, had written a large sex manual in which self-abuse had been severely castigated.

The last paragraph of the story shows the narrator and Deane engaged in the preparatory stages of an erection that achieves tumescence but not a climax. It begins with the word *ejaculations*, used in its linguistic rather than its sexual sense. This mounting spasm is disguised as Deane's reaction to his wife's want of trust in him: "But I saw that immediate shock throb away little by little and then gather again into waves of wonder and curiosity—waves that promised . . . to break in the end with the fury of my own highest tides. I may say that to-day as victims of unappeased desire there isn't a pin to choose between us" (IX, 315). Vereker had told the narrator that once he had a glimpse of his "secret," "the element in question would soon have become practically all you'd see."

This is finally all we as readers do see, and we realize, at last, why the secret had to be kept. It is only now that it can be seen. For the secret in human sexual experience that is most likely to be kept is the onanistic experience, that of solitary pleasure. With no partner and no witness, there is little risk of being found out. In such a way and by such an analysis, which disposes of heterosexual or even homosexual experiences in this story, the reader concludes with this answer to what James called the "fascinating case . . . of Hugh Vereker and his undiscovered, not to say undiscoverable secret" (AN, 228). James was having his ingenious fun with little danger of having his secret guessed. Naturally, it would be absurd to assume that James meant us to think that Hugh Vereker wrote twenty volumes devoted to onanism. What he did mean us to see was that the intent of a writer could be as private as the most private sexual act. Not sex but secret sex here parallels the secret of a man's literary style. In this way a covert analogy becomes the heart of a theme seemingly remote from it. The distinguished English critic S. Gorley Putt stopped just short of discovery when he called this story an "*almost* auto-erotic parable" (italics added).[1] I believe it really

1. S. Gorley Putt, *Henry James: A Reader's Guide* (Ithaca, 1966), 232.

is one, and "The Figure in the Carpet" read in this way shows that James could be very funny.

The more we know about the society in which James moved at the turn of the century, the more we realize that James was *au courant* with certain concerns of the literary milieu of his day. A relatively open topic of conversation among intellectuals was the autoerotic act and the extent to which one should indulge in it. We know that in Cambridge in 1899 at one of the meetings of the Apostles, the philosopher G. E. Moore read a paper, now lost, called "Is Self-Abuse Bad as an End?" (and the majority said no).[2] Indeed, it was "in the air" among the university avant-garde, and James might count on some of his close friends (such as Edmund Gosse or Arthur Christopher Benson, who relished ingeniously turned private jokes) to see what he was driving at. When the story was published, he wrote to Gosse some hint of his intention when he described "The Figure in the Carpet" as a "simple, (but I won't affectedly say artless) little tale."[3] One guesses that James, too, was "a man with some safe secret for enjoyment" (IX, 290).

When this material was first published as an article in 1982, it met with almost universal skepticism. Now nearly twenty years later the climate has changed in regard to the sexual content of James's fiction. No longer viewed as one of the last practitioners of the genteel tradition, James is now seen as the first of the moderns who has included subtexts of radically advanced sexual freedom. Robert White has erected on my thesis a further extension of the phallic content of "The Figure in the Carpet," finding in the oriental carpet on which Verver stands the design of the sacred phallus, or the *lingam*, itself.[4] This probably is not the last word on the sexuality of "The Figure in the Carpet."

A Precedent for James's *The Sacred Fount*: Rhoda Broughton's *Dear Faustina*, 1897

The first lesbian novel in English literature appears to have been Rhoda Broughton's *Dear Faustina*, which had been published in 1897 and is impor-

2. Paul Levy, *Moore: G. E. Moore and the Cambridge Apostles* (Oxford, 1981), 208.

3. Communication from Leon Edel to the author, 1995.

4. Robert White, "The Figure in the Carpet of James's Temple of Delight," *Henry James Review*, XIII, No. 1 (1992), 27–50.

tant to Jamesians in that it may have contributed to *The Turn of the Screw* of the next year. The suggestion of sexual deviation and corruption is found in the fact that Miles attempted "to contaminate. . . . To corrupt" (X, 30) and to be an "injury to the others" (X, 29). This might mean sexual activity among the boys, as well as an encouragement of autoeroticism. That a year before *Dear Faustina* James wrote "The Figure in the Carpet," in which such a theme is deeply inserted in analogic figures of speech and rhythms of climactic resolution, I have just discussed. That it was possible for James to write a darkly veiled novel about homosexuality in *The Sacred Fount*, too, may be related to the precedent his longtime friend Rhoda Broughton set in *Dear Faustina*. Richard Ellmann has noted its pioneering place in this genre.[5]

In her book, where the situation she describes seems clear to us today, Broughton was careful to declare its lesbianism not in actual words but only in an ambiguously represented threat. Here is her story. Young Althea Vane and her three siblings, after the death of their father, are summoned by their mother, who is dressed in "austerely masculine" clothing, with "thick short hair parted on one side," looking like a "slender man." She tells her children that she is leaving them, selling their house to lead a life of good works on her own, which, while her children were growing and her husband was alive, she was unable to do. Althea, therefore, has to room in with her friend, Faustina, who is overly affectionate and addresses her as "Darling" and "Beloved" and by the pet words that a young man in love with a girl would use. Like Olive Chancellor in *The Bostonians*, she brings Althea into her own uncomfortable flat so that they can both engage in living and helping the poor. Her behavior all along to Althea is clearly that of a masculine lover, yet it is expressed not in overt fondling, only in hand-holding. When the aristocratic Miss Cressida Delafield also shows great interest in the missionary work among the poor that Faustina and Althea are doing, Faustina turns Althea out of her house and brings in the new young lady, her brother's fiancée, and her brother Edward insists that his sister should refrain from airing her "peculiar" views to her.

Faustina clearly is using both these girls for her own personal ends. For instance, she wants Althea to use her influence in society to get the present

5. Richard Ellmann, *Along the riverrun* (New York, 1989), 10.

home secretary on their side, but he refuses. Faustina wants to replace Althea with Cressida because the latter is socially superior and can be more
useful to her. In response, Lady Lanington, Cressida's mother, asks Althea
to get her away from Faustina, an intimacy of which Althea was ignorant. In
this predicament, Drake, a young man also involved with this philanthropic
movement who has rejected his father's millions because they were made
in an industry that caused physical harm to the workers, says he knows how
to get Faustina to relinquish Cressida. He meets with Faustina and says that
if she doesn't give up the girl, he will go to the lengths that she knows he
can go to. She claims that he really is on her side, since they "had both been
turned out of doors" for "fidelity to [their] opinions." He says, "Was it for
your opinions that you were turned out of doors?" He looks at her pierc-
ingly, in the eyes, and hers, after trying to brazen it out for an instant, drop.
"It was for carrying, or trying to carry, them to their logical conclusion," she
answers (*DF,* 272–73). He answers her, "I have no wish to stir up that old
mud." He claims that he had believed at first that her convictions "*were*
convictions, although they had led [her] into extravagant and immoral action" (*DF,* 273). She answers, "*Extravagant and immoral?* Give me time to
enjoy this new strain. Since when has this admiring loyalty to the Marriage
Laws blossomed out in you?" She claims she doesn't care, but that's not the
case: "As he continues to hold her with the quiet determination of his eye,
she changes her tone: 'It would be more to the purpose if . . . you were to
treat me to a practical statement of what it is you wish me to do' " (*DF,* 274).
He says he wants to dictate to her a note she will write to Miss Delafield, to
which she answers, "You have used a lever which no generous mind would
have employed; and now, will you please tell me what I am to say?" (*DF,*
275). These are the only words accompanied by significant silences that
imply the presence of lesbianism, for what else could they possibly imply?
What kind of hold has Drake got on Faustina other than his significant
glances and certain words that are underlined? Why does the steely look he
gives her make her tremble and give in? There is nothing but the issue of
lesbianism, which could not be expressed in direct terms. However, the
message is clear to those who understand it, and those who do not understand it just will not have gotten the point.

Such a climate of opinion, in which a popular novelist like Rhoda
Broughton could make such suggestions perhaps encouraged James to sug-

gest in *The Sacred Fount* a similar, homosexual situation, only in his case even more concealed and veiled but capable of being interpreted by the most careful and sophisticated reader. Viewing it in this way, one can understand why James never wished to reprint the novel and why, when people referred to it, he tossed it off as a "little concetto." An analysis of *The Sacred Fount* with this possibility in view shows that a case can be made for it as a novel of homosexuality.

A Gay Reading of *The Sacred Fount*: The Reader as Detective

> *The Sacred Fount* is a detective story without a crime—and without a detective. The detective, indeed, is the reader.
>
> —Leon Edel, preface to *The Sacred Fount*

> Eliminate all other factors and that which remains must be the truth.
>
> —Arthur Conan Doyle, *The Sign of Four*

A few years after the subtext of autoeroticism in "The Figure in the Carpet," we come across a possible concealed love relation between two men and two women, hidden not in a subtext but in the narrator's unsuccessful attempt to detect a heterosexual concealed relationship. This reader seems to have been urged to follow clues leading rather to homosexual couples. This interpretation follows the suggestion of sexual activity, if only onanism, in "The Figure in the Carpet" in 1896 and follows the publication of Broughton's *Dear Faustina* in 1897.

What was bound to come, sooner or later, was a reading of *The Sacred Fount* as a text of homosexual love; if Henry James did not write it, we will write it for him and underline his *jeu d'esprit* by our own reading. Meanwhile, I try here to show how a reader-response to this puzzling book can be based on some elements intended by James to reveal yet conceal the unexpected gender of the partner sought for Gilbert Long by the narrator. Reading *The Sacred Fount* can be a maddening task, especially so if we read it in the light of "the torch of analogy" of the nameless narrator with his "ridiculous obsession" (*SF*, 89). Based upon his "articulate axiom" (*SF*, 107) that in an emotional relationship one partner grows at the expense of the other (crystallized by Mrs. Grace Brissenden's apparent thriving upon the wastage of her husband, "Poor Briss"), he erects his "working hypothesis"

(*SF*, 95): "The thing we're looking for ought logically to be the person, of the opposite sex, giving us the maximum sense of depletion for his benefit" (*SF*, 38). Using this law, the narrator infers that "stupid" Long's improvement from bore to marvel must be matched by his correspondingly depleted woman lover (*SF*, 81). The narrator is convinced by the painter Ford Obert that by "psychologic signs alone" (*SF*, 66), rather than by the method of "the detective and the keyhole" (*SF*, 66), "we shall find the right woman— our friend's mystic Egeria" (*SF*, 37). As Mrs. Briss puts it, "There had so, by your theory, to be a woman" (*SF*, 300), for she snatches at the phrase "of the opposite sex" in his proposition (38) to divert the narrator from the truth that it is not a woman to be sought for but a man and that the man is her own husband, Guy Brissenden!

This is a speculative attempt to read the novel that James, in his serious letter to Mrs. Ward, called "a *consistent* joke" (*HJL*, IV, 186), filled with "nothing *but* screens" (*SF*, 38), displaying "the perfection of a red herring" (*SF*, 146), even boasting of "*two* red herrings" (*SF*, 87), if not more. Yet it is consistent with "its own little law of composition" (*HJL*, IV, 186).

The main point is that when the narrator believes "that the thing we are looking for ought logically to be the person, *of the opposite sex*, giving us the maximum sense of depletion for [Long's] benefit" (italics added), he falls into a basic logical fallacy through his naïveté and through the fault of a mind "for which the vision of life is an obsession" (*SF*, 23). I propose that the lover to be sought for is of the *same* sex and that *The Sacred Fount* is a homoerotic, homosexual novel. The point of this demonstration is to show that the gender *concealed* within the words of the proposition formed by the narrating character is the key to the puzzle *The Sacred Fount* seems to be. The word *concealment* is the magic word itself, and to understand its importance in *The Sacred Fount*, one must know that in 1899, the year before James began to write the novel, he had written an important essay called "The Present Literary Situation in France." In it he complained about the overriding taste of the French fin-de-siècle writers for adultery and the "concealed attachments" that constituted it. "There *are* others, after all, than those of the eternal triangle of the husband, the wife and the lover, or of that variation of this to which we are too much condemned as an only alternative—the mistress, the first and the second, or the second and the third, the third and the fourth, lovers. What we continue to have, for the most part, is the *paraphernalia of concealment*—the drama of alarm and exposure; on which, with prodigious ingenuity, all the changes have been rung" (*EL,* 120; italics added). Especially had those changes been rung by Paul Bourget, whose twenty-nine novels and thirty-four collections of short stories and *nouvelles,* containing over two hundred tales, were sent regularly to James (whom Bourget idolized) over the years—tales that James had to read because his friendship with the French writer, though wearying, was very close.[6]

In this sense, *The Sacred Fount* can be considered a parody of Bourget's novels of psychological analysis, which he felt he had invented for the French and which Proust followed, carrying the method even further. One novel, *La Terre promise,* whose proofs James read in 1892 when he visited the Bourgets in Siena, he described to a friend as "perhaps 'psychology' gone mad" (*HJL,* III, 388), and that is what *The Sacred Fount* is. But if the technique of "psychologic signs" is applied, which Obert says is acceptable (since it is not the action of a "detective" nor does it involve "the keyhole"), it is to be applied to two couples involved in the "paraphernalia of conceal-ment." However, it is *not* to be "the eternal triangle," *not* to be an attach-ment of the opposite sex, which obsesses the French writers, but one of the same sex in James's parodic novel.

It is not a question of whether Henry James was homoerotic, though his attraction to such young men as Arthur Christopher Benson, Morton Fullerton, Hugh Walpole, and Jocelyn Persse is now granted by most schol-ars. Nor is it a question of whether the narrator, with his paranoid fear of "possible enemies" (*SF,* 1) and his obsessions, is a repressed homosexual himself. Rather it is simply that the novel makes more sense if we see that James's *"consistent"* joke depends on our discovering that the observer was off on a wild goose chase when he committed his "psychologic" error, for the lovers are really two men and two women, a situation that, on the surface of the novel, is well concealed. Otherwise, the tale remains a "mystery of mysteries" (*SF,* 17). Searching for a woman to pair off with Gilbert Long, the narrator had missed what he was looking for; he was not "on the track of a law, a law that would fit" (*SF,* 23). This is because he limited his law to

6. Adeline R. Tintner, *The Cosmopolitan World of Henry James* (Baton Rouge, 1991), 159–232.

its operation only on those of "the opposite sex." He has made an error of gender, and for this reason, he never noses out the truth.

James always required a second reading of his fiction, for, as Mrs. Briss said, "When one knows it, it's all there. But what's that vulgar song?— 'You've got to know it first!' " (SF, 70), and as she repeated, "When one has had the 'tip' one looks back and sees things in a new light" (SF, 74). Thus, we get our clue from the text itself. What is at issue is not even Henry James's sexuality, or his friendship with a long list of well-known homosexuals, which involved Morton Fullerton, clearly bisexual; Robbie Ross, Wilde's original seducer at Oxford; and André Raffalovich, patron of the poet and Catholic priest, John Gray ("Immorality on stone floors" [MA, 408]). It is not even James's interest in the darker aspects of human behavior (an interest he had, as Walpole wrote in The Apple Trees). We know his fascination with the Wilde trials and his continuing interest in J. A. Symonds, as well as his reading of Otto Weininger's Sex and Society with its chapters on homosexuality (PW, 87).

More pertinent is his literary use of homosexuality. One ought to remember the fact cited above that his friend's, the novelist Rhoda Broughton's, Dear Faustina was "the first lesbian novel in English," according to Richard Ellmann.[7] From Edmund Gosse's suggestion, James felt he perhaps had "divined" Symonds' problem in his short tale "The Author of Beltraffio," and in "The Death of the Lion," James had touched on the "larger latitude," which Guy Walsingham, a pretty but manishly gotten-up girl writer, surely suggesting the lesbian, professes.

In his essay "The Uses of Decadence: Wilde, Yeats, Joyce," Ellmann has shown us convincingly that Wilde's trials had stirred up a literary interest in homosexuality (witness A. E. Housman's A Shropshire Lad, published a year after the trials). Ellmann holds that even Henry James wrote a series of works that "took advantage of the freedom that Wilde had won for art even while losing his own freedom."[8] Ellmann then cites The Turn of the Screw with its suggestion of the lesbian effect the governess has on Flora and the homosexual "corruption" by Quint of the boy Miles. He points out that James there saw homosexuality in terms of the corruption of children by

7. Ellmann, 10.
8. Ibid.

adults, resulting in "bad conduct." In "The Figure in the Carpet," I have suggested, a subtext involving autoeroticism is contained within a concealed parallel. Let us say that once the frontier of the new century has been crossed, James allows himself to write certain things that he had not dared to write before, even in *The Turn of the Screw.* (In 1900, he wrote to his friend Fullerton, "I have told you before that the imposition of hands in a certain tender way 'finishes' me," and, he continued, "you are dazzling, my dear Fullerton; you are beautiful; you are more than tactful, you are tenderly, magically *tactile.*")[9] Ellmann argues, "It is in large part thanks to Wilde, then, both to his books and to his trial testimony, that the taboo against writing about homosexual behavior or other forms of sexuality began to be lifted in England. Opening our eyes has been the principal labor of modern literature."[10]

Going beyond the pairing of the children in *The Turn of the Screw* with their corrupters of the same gender (Miles and Quint, Flora and Miss Jessel), James of the twentieth century makes the same kind of pairing in *The Sacred Fount,* his first novel of the new century: Gilbert Long with Guy Briss and Mrs. Briss with May Server. However, the real pairing is concealed in the manner of the continental "concealed attachments," criticized by James two years before in his essay, but it is a concealment so completely under the surface of the novel that only a web of subterranean clues can reveal it, for it *had* to be concealed. If the autoerotic act had to be concealed and could only be suggested in the metaphors of excitement and ecstasy in "The Figure in the Carpet," how much more would "the love that dare not tell its name" have to be concealed in *The Sacred Fount,* since it carried with it the stigma of criminality? The narrator fails as detective since he failed to look for the real crime at that time, which was sodomy.

The clues are to be discovered through a process of ratiocination, which is the inverse of that presented by the narrator and abetted by Mrs. Briss as a cover-up. We are able to place our foot in the doorway of the solution because of the logical fallacy in those four words, "of the opposite sex," in the narrator's proposition. Since he is to fail in his search, as we are told at

---

9. Henry James to Morton Fullerton, September 26, 1900, in *Henry James, Selected Letters,* ed. Leon Edel (Cambridge, Mass., 1987), 325.

10. Ellmann, 10.

the end of the book, the failure is due not to Mrs. Briss's obvious counter-lie, in which she matches Gilbert Long with Lady John, but in the narrator's failure to see what really is going on.

The question is: What is there in *The Sacred Fount* that raises the possibility that the clue points to a homosexual pairing off of the lovers? In the light of the interesting analyses done in the last couple of decades on *The Sacred Fount* beginning with Jean Blackall's in 1965, followed by John Carlos Rowe's analysis of 1976, and, in 1977, Shlomith Rimmon's application of the concept of ambiguity, it may seem too simple-minded for me to suggest another reading that does not partake of the linguistic and postmodern systems of literary analysis but that might be considered as belonging to the reader's response school.

The reason I can avoid this postmodern territory and still promulgate a new reading is that I have examined certain elements that are there. In my reading, I see the existence of a secret, but a secret the narrator is not on to. By avoiding the "red herrings" (a phrase, as we have seen, encountered in the novel), today's reader, in the light of a certain wider knowledge of the period and of the circles in which James moved, as well as with recent revelations of the details of his personality, can decipher a state of affairs existing at Newmarch different from the state presented by the narrator and Mrs. Briss.

Certain aspects of James's life and friends are pertinent at this point. From Mrs. Ward's reminiscences of James's trip with her to Ariccia in 1899 to see the home of Egeria, "the sacred fount," it is clear that James was very much taken with a beautiful young boy named Aristodemo, "encountered among the strawberry beds." He exclaimed about the boy and his name, "What a name! What a place!" James wrote after the excursion to Mrs. Ward, "For me, the Nemi lake, and the walk down and up (the latter perhaps most), and the strawberries and Aristodemo were the cream. . . . I am clear about that" (*TR*, 297–98). James's experience with "the sacred fount" (the germ of his novel) is bound up with his response to a beautiful boy and created the mood of the novel he wrote. A few weeks after the excursion, back home for the late summer months of 1899, he enjoyed a visit from the handsome young sculptor Hendrik Andersen. Edel reviews the young man's effect on James in terms that suggest the transfer of vitality and youth onto another person, such as we see in *The Sacred Fount*. James "bestowed on

Andersen his own taste, his own high standards, his own feeling for beauty. He looked into the mirror and saw smiling and healthy youth instead of his obese and aging self. The image charmed—one might say it enchanted" (*TR*, 309). However, Edel did not see how this could constitute a support for an interpretation of *The Sacred Fount* as a "gay novel," whereas the passage of twenty years since Edel wrote *Henry James: The Master* and the revelation of the special feelings James had for his male friends allows us to consider these speculations. Throughout James's letters to his friends, he uses figures of speech of physical embracings. He wrote to Andersen after the death of Andersen's brother, telling him: "Lean on me as on a brother and a lover. . . . I embrace you with almost a passion of pity" (*TR*, 313).

Fred Kaplan's more recent biography of James puts more emphasis on James's homoeroticism.[11] During the period just before James wrote *The Sacred Fount,* his sick brother William spent the winter months of 1899 and 1900 with him at Lamb House. Henry was worried about his brother, and he wrote to Miss Reubell how "to see him down" while he himself was up "bewilder[ed] and disorientate[d]" him (*TR*, 324). This figure of speech also describes the relation between Gilbert Long, the tall handsome man who is "up," and "poor Briss," the young man still under thirty, who is "down." If, in *The Sacred Fount,* "we enter a maze at the book's beginning and are still in a labyrinth at its close,"[12] the thread that can lead us out of the labyrinth, I suggest, is to follow from certain suggestions in the novel the theme of homosexual, not heterosexual, love. The basis for our consideration of what may seem at first to be an outlandish suggestion is that there is a fallacy in the proposition propounded by the narrator that the narrator has created for himself in order to detect which lovers are feeding off others. When we first read it, we don't notice it. It is only after we begin to get suspicious at the end of the novel that we realize that that particular phrase ("of the opposite sex") is what is making him fail in his search.

In the sophisticated house-party society of this period, those who engaged in adultery were usually known to the hostess and carefully placed near each other. In this novel, Lord Lutley and Mrs. Froome are an open example of this habit. However, there existed also those relationships that were neces-

11. Fred Kaplan, *Henry James: The Imagination of Genius* (New York, 1992), *passim.*
12. Pelham Edgar, *Henry James: Man and Author* (New York, 1927), 147.

sarily secret, even though the homoerotic ones in more restrictive circles were well known. Lady Lovelace's house parties were known to cater to those practicing the "larger latitude." James's friends, as I have pointed out, were homoerotic in their tastes, even though a few were married, and James's attachments to the young men he knew are now also accepted as homoerotic. Just before *The Sacred Fount* was written, James wrote a letter to Morton Fullerton, which I have quoted above, a letter extraordinarily candid about his special physical feeling about Fullerton, then a young man of thirty-three compared to James's fifty-seven years. I find that I can make a case for the two people feeding off each other in this novel not to be Gilbert Long and May Server (the narrator's opinion) or Gilbert Long and Lady John (Mrs. Briss's final revelation) but the over-forty Gilbert Long and the under-thirty Guy Brissenden. Long has depleted Brissenden. Balancing that relationship, Mrs. Briss can, in turn, be seen as depleting Mrs. Server, and the two couples can be seen in cahoots with each other. In fact, Mrs. Briss's strategy is to conceal this all from the narrator by her double lie. First, she pretends to suggest and to encourage the narrator to think of Mrs. Server (in specific heterosexual terms) for the discovery of the guilty pair. Then she retreats and names the true couple as Gilbert Long and Lady John, still heterosexual. This pairing destroys the cannibalistic proposition simply because neither Long nor Lady John has been depleted in any way. It also denies Mrs. Briss's previous pairing off, when she agreed with the narrator, with "an ironic *exposure* of her own false plausibility," as James wrote in his explanatory letter about his novel to Mrs. Ward (*HJL*, IV, 186).

James gives us another clue as to the unmentionable aspects—"the unnameable" aspects—of this novel in another letter he wrote to Fullerton after the book was published. He called *The Sacred Fount* "an incident of technics, pure and simple—brought about by—well, if you were here I could tell you" (IV, 198). This suggests a revelation dangerous to put into writing. In his important letter to Mrs. Ward, cited above, he insisted that the novel was a "joke" but a "*consistent*" one. The joke I think resides in the fallacy in the proposition, something that would be easily overlooked because the one thing that James did not want was to have too many people dig out his secret. Yet those who could dig it out were entitled to it. The elements that may encourage a homosexual reading of the book, once one gets the idea, are detectable, but, as Mrs. Briss says, one has to get the "tip."

The important scene that gives us "the tip" is the art gallery scene. The clue resides in the fact that the young man in the important picture they are looking at resembles Briss, a fact they all agree on. He has in his hand a mask that could be "fantastically fitted and worn" (*SF*, 55). Equally important, maybe even more important, is the fact that the mask is that of a woman. The narrator tries to influence the others to see the face in the mask as that of Mrs. Server. Since the figure that resembles Mr. Briss holds in his hand the disguise of a woman, we can reasonably infer that he therefore *becomes* a woman whenever he puts the mask on. This transformation raises the androgynous notion that Briss can *be* a woman for somebody else in this group. It is significant that Long takes an unfriendly attitude to the whole discussion of this picture and the mask, even though he has given a lecture on it before the narrator and the painter Obert arrive on the scene. We never know what Long said, but since he seems to want to keep out of the discussion, we suspect him of trying to avoid betraying some kind of emotional relation to the subject.

It is this gender change attributed to a painted simulacrum of young Briss that gives us the "evidential" material. We can check on this from James's letter to Mrs. Ward:

> As I give but the phantasmagoric I have, for clearness, to make it *evidential*, and the Ford Obert evidence all bears (indirectly) upon Brissenden, supplies the motive for Mrs. B.'s terror and her re-nailing down of the coffin. I had to testify to Mrs. S.'s sense of a common fate with B. and the only way I could do so was by making O. see her as temporarily pacified. I had to give a meaning to the vision of Gilbert L. out on the terrace in the darkness, and the *appearance* of a sensible detachment on her part was my imposed way of giving it. (*HJL*, IV, 186)

I read this as Mrs. Briss's appearing not to know that her husband is to meet Long on the terrace, and therefore she is concealing the homosexual attachment Briss has with Long.

Everybody at Newmarch agrees that the portrait reminds them of and, in consequence, stands for Briss, but what Obert gives evidence for is that the mask "looks like a lovely lady" (*SF*, 56). The sex of the mask is female, on which all agree. (It is only the narrator who thinks the mask resembles Mrs. Server.) James seems to corroborate the importance of Obert's testimony when he wrote to Mrs. Ward that Obert's evidence supplies "the motive for Mrs. B.'s terror." It is Obert's word not only that the mask is that of a woman but that the young man *is* Briss. Once Long names Briss, Obert realizes that is the name he has been looking for (*SF*, 56–58). This identification of a man with a woman's mask terrifies Mrs. B., for she fears the narrator will zero in on her husband's illicit emotional relationship to Long. Therefore, she stresses Mrs. Server's connection with Long.

The next bit of evidence that James attributes to Obert is when he notices that Mrs. Server flirts with all the men ("she darts from flower to flower" [*SF*, 61]) and that, therefore, "the real man must be one she doesn't markedly collar" (*SF*, 64). The "real" man, if it *were* a man, is not there, but suppose it was a woman? The woman in this context could only be Mrs. Brissenden herself, for May Server and Grace Brissenden are the only women at the party who have no conversation of any kind with each other. They conceal their relationship, as Long does with Briss, by *not* calling our attention to them. James connects them only through omission. Mrs. Server's hysterical interest in men makes James tell Mrs. Ward that "O." (Obert) sees her as "temporarily pacified" in her showing "her common fate with Briss." They are both "pacified" because Mrs. Server has used all the men as "screens" (*SF*, 39), just as Briss has used all the women, including his own wife, as "screens." It is after the gallery scene that Mrs. Briss's terror makes her re-nail the coffin, that is, makes her most effectually conceal the "love that dare not tell its name."

The second major scene that seems to give us evidence for a homosexual concealed relationship occurs later, on the second evening of the weekend as the guests prepare to go either to bed or to the smoking room. The narrator tells us that to get some fresh air he is leaning on the sill of the window that overlooks a terrace adjoining the smoking room. He notices that there is "the electric light" (*SF*, 201) behind him, which would make him visible, though he figures, wrongly I think, that nobody will really see him (*SF*, 202). As he looks out, he sees Gilbert Long smoking a cigarette and wandering on the terrace. Very clearly Long is there for a rendezvous, but since the narrator has told us that he himself is visible because of the light shining behind him, we know that the other partner of the rendezvous knows that Long is being watched and will, therefore, not show up (*SF*, 202). It is very possible that Long had indicated to Briss by a series of signals not to meet him on the terrace. Long, who was close to the smoking room and the place where they would meet, could, in some way, signal him in a manner that we cannot see to change their meeting place. (The sexual behavior of two homosexuals in a party like this would have to be extremely carefully concealed.) The next move is that Mrs. Briss retires to her bedchamber, since Briss, as we know, has been assigned to a room in the bachelor wing (*SF*, 21). We don't know at this point what Briss does. He probably had been on his way to a rendezvous with Long, which is now cancelled. When he comes down later to tell the narrator that his wife will meet him for a conversation, we are told, "He looked round the room—at the two or three clusters of men." The narrator thinks, "It was absolutely as if, for me, he were seeking such things—out of what was closing over him—for the last time." And the narrator adds to Briss that he will be leaving Newmarch "tomorrow before you show." Briss answers, "*What* do I show?" Here we see his fear (*SF*, 226–27). It seems as if he has been looking around for Long. (His interest could be nothing else but that.)

We have now gotten the idea that there is a secret relationship going on, not between members of the opposite sex, but between members of the same sex, because we are not convinced at the end by Mrs. Briss's decisive and final statement that it is Lady John who is Long's lover. In his letter to Mrs. Ward, James makes that quite clear when he describes the "ironic *exposure* of her false plausibility." If the narrator is wrong and if Mrs. Briss is lying about what has been taking place, one can decide that *nothing* has been taking place among these heterosexual couples, though before we read James's letter to Mrs. Ward, it looks as if Mrs. Briss, who seems to know the real story, has been protecting her friend and, since the weekend is over, tells the narrator what the true relationship is. But James's letter warns us against this interpretation.

Now, would James be spending all this time casting red herrings to come up with only two interpretations of what is going on, both of which are false? Something *is* going on. But what it has to be we can only read in a subtext. The educated reader who knows about the existence of a large homosexual society with which James was connected in terms of friendship must reread the novel. As soon as the reader looks once more at the first chapter, alerted to the possibility for clues to a homosexual relationship, he can see certain sentences that now, in the light of "the tip," can be interpreted in this way.

In the rereading, with our new idea in mind, certain things that seemed to have no particular meaning when we first read them now take on a different significance.

1. In the first few lines of description of the railway station, the narrator sees, in the entrance of the guests on the train, "possible friends and even possible enemies," that is, perhaps those at the party who are gay and those who are straight.

2. The narrator had met Long before at "Newmarch, a place of charm so special as to create a bond among its guests" (SF, 2). This suggests Lady Lovelace's house, well known to cater to homosexual couples, and where Henry James and Jocelyn Persse were known to have had "contiguous bedrooms" in the early years of the century.[13]

3. That ordinary adultery would not be a secret at this house is confirmed in the first few pages by the fact that Lord Lutley and Mrs. Froome were in "the wondrous new fashion . . . starting, travelling, arriving together" (SF, 4), openly.

4. Mrs. Briss thinks that Long should know that her husband and Lady John were coming together on another train, to which Long answers, "Why in the world should I know?," to which she answers, "Oh, it's only I thought you always did!," that is, since Long and Briss we are assuming now are lovers, he would know anything that Briss did. She adds, "You know why he should as well as I, don't you?" (SF, 4–5).

5. The narrator tells us on page 1 that he had "already more than once met Long at Newmarch" and that "he was a friend of the house" (SF, 1–2). If Newmarch was like Lady Lovelace's place, the same men and their friends were invited over and over again, yet not necessarily openly.[14] Even though Gilbert Long seems "stupid," Newmarch "always had to see something before it made a sign" (SF, 2). Long was at any rate very "good-looking" (SF, 3). The homoerotic note is thus sounded, only screened, in the first few pages of the book.

6. Mrs. Briss throws red herrings to the narrator. She says that Gilbert Long looks well because "a clever woman for some time past" has taken

---

13. Henry James to Jocelyn Persse, access to a carbon copy made possible by Leon Edel, 1992.

14. Rupert Hart-Davis, *Hugh Walpole* (New York, 1952), 92–93.

an interest in him. This is among her early lies to cover the homosexual truth about the quartet.

7. She also says, giving herself away in the subtext, that people cover up: "They cultivate, to cover their game, the appearance of other little friendships. It puts the outsiders off the scent, and the real thing meanwhile goes on" (*SF*, 10).

8. We are told that Guy Brissenden, though married and with his wife, "had been put by himself, for some reason, in the bachelor wing" (*SF*, 21).

The narrator, having noted certain things about these people, that is, that Mrs. Briss has gotten younger and Long has gotten more intelligent, wants to create a "law" about this human phenomenon. He is ignoring the fact, which we already have suspected, that Long has been living off Briss. On the primary level of reading this novel, one would have to say that Mrs. Briss at the end has broken down the whole proposition that people feed off each other. We know that James had previously suggested the theme in so many stories that we want to keep the proposition going, except for the phrase in it that makes it invalid for the present state of affairs. In the search for the "law," the narrator asks Long if he hasn't noticed how old Briss has become and whether he saw him often. Long replies, "No, why should I? . . . He's not an object of the smallest interest to me" (*SF*, 24). This protesting too much is another red herring. Long is now "uncomfortable" after his change (*SF*, 25). We also notice in the novel that the lovers are very rarely together. For instance, when Long approaches Briss with the narrator, Briss turns his back on them.

9. In the narrator's next discussion with Obert, the axiom is announced: "One of the pair . . . has to pay for the other" (*SF*, 29). He then notices that "the agents of the sacrifice are uncomfortable, I gather, when they suspect or fear that you see" (*SF*, 31). Long has just been declared "uncomfortable" because of the narrator's remarks about Briss (whom we now feel he has been draining). Then the law is formulated, with the fallacy in the phrase "of the opposite sex." However, the narrator says there must be "the evidence of relations." But in this there is an obvious contradiction: If the evidence has to be hidden, how can one from the outside *see* the evidence? I think James explains all this in his letter to Mrs. Ward, quoted above. But in the novel, the pieces of evi-

dence that Mrs. Briss and the narrator find turn out to be only "screens." The reader alone must detect and select the true evidence behind the narrator's back. Now, if this depends on the absence of any overt connection between the guilty parties, we the readers must recognize the details in the *lack* of connection, which is the necessary condition for their relation. We then become aware of those persons with the absolute *lack* of connection who take care, by *not* meeting and by *not* talking to each other, that they are not observed; it is they who are the guilty ones. When Long gives a lecture on the painting in the gallery, we are not told what he has said, and it is this omission that is significant. We remember the narrator saying that the two who are in relation "perhaps haven't spoken to each other," but "where he comes she does" (*SF,* 41). The only people who are there and who have not spoken to each other, if we carefully check the novel, are Mrs. Server and Mrs. Briss and Long and Mr. Briss. They are in the same environment. They may pass each other, but they do not speak to each other.

In the art gallery scene, Guy Briss looks like a "whitened old-world clown" (*SF,* 55) and carries in his hand "a complete mask" (*SF,* 55). We have to be concerned not with the alternate interpretations that the mask is one of death or of life but with the fact that the painted man is desiccated and the mask is blooming. When Briss puts on that mask, he becomes a different person of a different gender, and it is he who then blooms. Briss is, after all, the "man with the mask," the one whose real motive is concealed. We are to assume from these end-of-the-century symbols that Briss is happy when he becomes a woman even though he has been depleted. An amusing detail from Miss Theodora Bosanquet's diary while she was acting as secretary to James in the 1900s is pertinent here. At a Christmas dinner at Lamb House Henry James wore a mask, which was that of a "fat old lady with side curls . . . so hilarious that he had to send for a shaving-glass to see himself in. 'Why,' he propounded, 'don't we all wear masks and change them as we do our clothes?' Why not, indeed—it would be almost as good as changing one's personality."[15] In the case in *The Sacred Fount,* it is "as good as changing one's" sex.

15. Theodora Bosanquet, "Diary," December 26, 1909 (Ms. in Houghton Library, Harvard University).

As James had noticed in his letter to Mrs. Ward, Obert gives the evidence for most of my points. "She [Mrs. Server] is absolutely," says Obert, "not the same person I painted. "It's exactly like Mrs. Brissenden's having been for you yesterday not the same person you had last seen bearing her name" (*SF*, 65). In this way, Obert's eye sees the connection between the two women and we can see it as causative once we've got "the tip." *We* see the pairing there, but the narrator does not. Another statement by Mrs. Briss shows what we should be looking for. The attached pair "ignore each other in public; they foregather in private" (*SF*, 73).

10. At Newmarch "none of the stupid, none even of the votaries of the grossly obvious, need apply" (*SF*, 98). In other words, we are here alerted to the fact that whatever we are looking for must be very subtly concealed, not "grossly obvious." Another statement declares: "She had at once to cultivate contacts, so that people shouldn't guess her real concentration" (*SF*, 99). Long, at one time, does come together with Guy Briss, but Guy Briss is also then with Lady John. They seem to have no contact, for Briss and the narrator immediately leave when the three meet, and the narrator passes his "hand into his [Briss's] arm" (*SF*, 107). So far, Long and Briss have not said one word to each other, just the way Mrs. Briss and Mrs. Server say not one word to each other, though they talk freely to all the others. When the narrator gets to talk to Briss, the latter tells him that his wife tells him everything and that he's "not a fellow who goes about much after women" (*SF*, 120), which is, if we pay attention, a clue to his own homosexuality, and we are told by Howells to pay attention not to what the narrator says but to what the other people say. It is true that Guy and May Server "had the sense of a common fate," but they're not interested in each other. They both are the victims of this depleting process, only she experiences it with Mrs. Briss and he experiences it with Gilbert Long. Then there are sentences that act as a subtext, yoking the homosexual lovers. "The play of Long's mind struck me as more marked . . . as the march of poor Briss's age," remarks the narrator. Here he associates the two men in some fashion, though he doesn't realize why. (But James, one presumes, does.) He says about Guy that "his inexorable fate was to be an unname-

able climax" (*SF*, 171), which seems to be another way of saying "the love that dare not tell its name."

The important scene, which is very hard to figure out, even on a second reading, but which is helped by James's letter to Mrs. Ward, takes place just before the guests of the house go to bed for the last night that they are at Newmarch. Leaning on the sill of a window looking out on a terrace, the narrator says, "It would perhaps have been better still if I had gone straight to bed. In that case I *should* have broken off sharp—too sharp to become aware of something that kept me a minute longer at the window" (*SF*, 201). He thought of turning out "the electric light" behind him. "I resisted this impulse and, with the thought that my position was in no way compromising, chanced being myself observed." In other words, he does not conceal his position there, so anyone on the terrace could see him. Since he "leaned for refreshment on the sill," where he "thought of many things" (*SF*, 199–200), he definitely can be seen from the terrace, where Gilbert Long is "resting on the balustrade . . . with a cigarette in his lips" (*SF*, 202). When he sees Long "in such detachment, in such apparent concentration," the narrator notices that these things "marked and presented him more than any had yet done, and placed him more than any yet in relation to other matters." He saw his "situation as grave." He can't say what the other matters prove, but he "was as affected by them as if they proved everything" (*SF*, 202–203). In fact, they *do* prove everything, just what the narrator does not and never will see. What *we* have to see over the narrator's shoulder is that since he is seen, Long, who may have had the rendezvous with Briss, who did not go upstairs with his wife, realizes that the narrator has to be put off the scent. After his self-exposure on the window sill, the narrator goes back into the room and meets Obert, who asks whether everybody has gone to bed. Obert says perhaps the ladies who have retired left a "black plume as a token," and the narrator answers, "Not, I trust, of any 'lie' their 'soul hath spoken!' " (*SF*, 204). This is the clue as to the "false *plausibility*" of Mrs. Briss later. The narrator asks, "But not one of them lingers?" That is the point at which Briss comes down to him to give him his wife's message that she will meet him.

Certain words are exchanged between the narrator and Briss. "I shall be gone tomorrow before you show." And Briss answers, "Show? *What* do I show?" (*SF*, 227). From this we get the feeling, once we're on the track, that Briss is worried that he, revealing his gay inclination, may have shown some interest in Long (though he has been very careful) and that the narrator has seen it. James cleverly has made clear that only the reader can see it, though the narrator has described it. We are directed to this by the comment of the narrator: " 'You show nothing! You're magnificent!' He let me keep his hand while things unspoken and untouched, unspeakable and untouchable, everything that had been between us in the wood a few hours before, were between us again" (*SF*, 227). But the narrator has not made sense of what he has seen. This and the following scene seem to give away the secret, especially since James focused on them in his letter to Mrs. Ward. As Briss passes the smoking room, the narrator notices that "He looked round the room—at the two or three clusters of men." For this action, the narrator gives the wrong reason: "It was absolutely as if, for me, he were seeking such things . . . for the last time" (*SF*, 226). It is more likely that Briss is attempting to find out what had happened to make Long warn him off the terrace and that he wants to know where Long has disappeared to. Has he joined the clusters of smoking men? That's why he looks at them very carefully. The one opportunity for the lovers to meet had been ruined by the narrator's snooping. It is quite a feat for James to feed us the details through the narrator's description, which the narrator himself cannot interpret.

What Mrs. Briss at this late hour comes down to tell the narrator before they all leave the next day is that his proposition is completely wrong, that he is crazy, that no improvement has taken place in Long, who is just as stupid as he always was, and that his lover is Lady John, who is just as brash as she always was. Mrs. Briss tells the narrator that he has gotten the wrong characters together and that the only reason she encouraged him was out of protection for her friends. He thought of "the marvel of their exchange of signals," for "they both had their treasure to guard, and they had looked to each other with the instinct of help" (*SF*, 274). Of course, he is describing the wrong couple. He is describing Mrs. Briss's conversation near the end of the book with Gilbert Long. Mrs. Briss pooh-poohs the narrator's assumptions about the give-and-take of vitality and declares that "Lady John *is* the woman" (*SF*, 303) and Long is "the same ass" (*SF*, 305).

The pieces of evidence that support my arguments depend on three things chiefly. The first is the presentation of Guy Brissenden as a painted image holding the mask of a lady, which shows his androgyny. The second is the terrace scene where Long, clearly concentrating and waiting for somebody, must have seen the narrator gaping at him and therefore sends a message to Briss warning him off. This the reader has to infer for himself. Whatever concealed contact has taken place between Long and Guy has taken place in the bachelor quarters at a time when no one could see them. Since Mrs. Briss does not share a bedroom with her husband, and since Mrs. Server is a widow, they, too, have ample opportunity to meet each other in each other's rooms. Obert, who, James tells Mrs. Ward, gives the "evidential" elements, says that the ladies have gone upstairs "to high jinks—isn't that the idea?—in their own quarters. Don't they too, at these hours, practise sociabilities of sorts?" (SF, 204). On second reading, with our idea in mind, we see that the women lovers have their own opportunities, just as Briss and Long have theirs in the bachelor quarters.

The third piece of evidence we find in James's letter to Mrs. Ward, which says that "the Ford Obert evidence all bears (indirectly) upon Brissenden, supplies the motive for Mrs. B.'s terror and her re-nailing down of the coffin" (HJL, IV, 186). This bit of outside information is necessary, not only to support our reading, but to point out certain things in the novel that we would not have noticed without James's direction, namely, the amount of weight we should give to Obert's observations. When James writes to Mrs. Ward, "I had to testify to Mrs. S.'s sense of a common fate with B.," the common fate is that they are both victims and both partners in a lesbian and a homosexual relationship. What is important is the next part of James's sentence: "and the only way I could do so was by making Obert see her [Mrs. Server] as temporarily pacified"—a pacification that takes place by her making love to every man in the crowd but only as a screen. After we read James's comments in his letter to Mrs. Ward, we realize he is referring to the two scenes. I have also called attention to these two scenes, which are the only places where we can get a certain amount of evidence that this is homosexual love that is taking place at Newmarch, namely, the gallery scene and the terrace scene. It is the latter to which James specifically wants Mrs. Ward to pay attention. "I had to give a meaning to the vision of Gilbert L. out on the terrace in the darkness, and the *appearance* of a sensible detachment on her part. . . . [It] was my imposed way of giving it. Mrs. S. is back in the coffin at the end, by the same stroke by which Mrs. Briss is." By that sentence, we see that James sticks to his vampire theory and that his proposition as a whole does hold. It is here in the place where he connects the two women that we see it.

That everything is either a fantasy or a lie on the surface of the book is also confirmed by the last part of James's sentence in his letter: "Mrs. B.'s last interview with the narrator being all an ironic *exposure* of her own false plausibility, of course." Mrs. Briss's "terror," as James says, occurs because she is afraid the narrator will find out that her husband is having a relationship with Long, as she is with Mrs. Server, and because she wishes to protect them and is full of the terror of the narrator's discovery, she resorts to the most ridiculous answer to the narrator's proposition, that Lady John, the most unlikely candidate, is having an affair with Gilbert Long.

One feels totally defeated by this novel when it ends with all the couples heterosexual and when its statements are either pure fantasies of the narrator or the lies of one of the participants. Seen as a gay coupling, it all makes sense. Once one has a picture of the lively homoerotic male society James was part of, once we take into consideration his treatment in *The Bostonians* of a lesbian relationship and see in "The Death of the Lion" the introduction of the "larger latitude," *The Sacred Fount* is not so odd a Jamesian book. Broughton's *Dear Faustina* gave him an example of a novel already published that suggested a lesbian relationship without making any explicit statements about it and that directed the reader to it only through the reader's knowledge that such things exist. For instance, in Broughton's novel, the young hero uses his knowledge of her lesbianism as a means of blackmailing Faustina in order to break up her friendship with a young woman whose fiancé is objecting to it. He achieves his end by simply giving her significant looks and saying that the reason for his threatening her with legal action was *not* the philanthropy she engaged in with her young women friends but something that he need not spell out for her, at which point she immediately capitulates, since her behavior toward the young woman has been a mimicry of male lovemaking. The reader would have to know what is implied; otherwise there is absolutely no meaning to Faustina's instant capitulation.

In *The Sacred Fount,* James uses a similar technique. The elaborate system of observation and discussion is broken down finally by Mrs. Briss's statement that he has been on the wrong track. This opens up to the reader the possibility for a discovery of the right track. If we take the novel at the plot's face value, we cannot wonder at its being so unpopular and "maddening" to serious readers. It is only James's letter to Mrs. Ward that confirms a feeling that what is hidden in this book is something that *had* to be hidden, for it concealed a crime at that time punishable by law. What he had planned was "only to make the one thing it *could* be—a *consistent joke" (HJL,* IV, 186). The joke was that the narrator had the sexes wrong. If no reader got the joke because of the concealed way James wrote it, it still could not be written in a more obvious way. And so James regretted the whole attempt.

As I was finishing this analysis, I happened upon a clever parody called "The Sacred Front," in which its author, Veronica Geng, rewrites *The Sacred Fount,* keeping the plot and all the characters, but making the guests members of a "radical chic" coterie involved with the revolutionary politics of the 1930s and 1950s. Grace Brissenden is seen as a sadistic woman wielding Emma Goldman's horsewhip and threatening her husband, Guy, as well as everyone else. When the narrator tells her about his "theory, omitting . . . any unflattering reference to poor Guy's virtual senility," she answers, "I wonder who she [the woman involved] can be? I know that in principle we've no right to assume it's not a *he,* but I don't blame you for not thinking of it. If Long wasn't 'straight' before, I'll bank on my instinct that he is now. You must let me know the minute you flush her out."[16] Geng, as a late twentieth-century writer, notices that it could be a man and not a woman, but she throws such a possibility away as irrelevant. But it surely crossed her mind. I have, on my side, taken seriously such a reversal of gender relations among a couple of lovers in the hope that, by such a view, the reader may find at last a possible solution to the problems of meaning and interpretation in *The Sacred Fount.*

In spite of what Leon Edel said in his introduction to *The Sacred Fount,* there *is* a detective, albeit malfunctioning, in the novel. Why has he failed to solve the mystery at Newmarch? Because he has not been able to detect the possibility of an alternate kind of sexual relationship. He has limited his law by putting in the phrase "of the opposite sex." If James had become bored with the French version of "concealed relationships," as he demonstrated in his essay, he would here amuse himself with this "consistent joke" about "concealed relationships." But in this case the relationships would

16. Veronica Geng, *Partners* (New York, 1984), 123–35, esp. 123.

indeed be criminal if not concealed. Here the subtext does the concealing, and the detective no longer is the narrator; he is now the reader who gets his clues for his detection from the text.

Some Sexual Innuendo in the 1908 Revision of "The Siege of London"

In *The Golden Bowl* there are clearly signs of a greater relaxation about sexual matters without requiring a subtext. The adultery between Charlotte and Amerigo is presented as it is, an openness clearly influenced by French fin-de-siècle novels, especially those of Bourget.[17] The pun on Fanny Sitwell's name, which becomes Fanny Assingham in the novel, is another sign of comic sexual innuendo. Further, Maggie's physical feminine response to her husband's person is expressed in accurate physical terms.

Four years later in 1908, we see a further extension of sexual insinuations in a revision for an earlier tale. The New York Edition revisions that James made for "The Siege of London," his tale of 1883, were directed chiefly toward consolidating the relationship of the story to Thomas Couture's celebrated 1847 picture, *The Romans of the Decadence*, then in the Luxembourg Museum, later in the Louvre, and now in the Musée d'Orsay, a picture that represented "the grand manner" to both Henry and William James and to their coterie at Newport during their adolescence.

However, along with those changes, which emphasized the Roman "orgies" and the classical elements in the tale of the successful attempt of the American "barbarian" divorcée Mrs. Headway to marry into the English aristocracy, there is also definite evidence that James is now more outspoken about sexual matters and more relaxed about alluding to them than he had been in 1883. In 1908 he clearly shows that Mrs. Headway is a high-class prostitute, as we can see if we examine the changes made.

The behavior and even the language of Mrs. Headway has become more profane. Where she said, "for God's sake" in 1883 (V, 103), twenty-five years later she says, "for Christ's sake!" (NYE, XIV, 262). When Littlemore asks whether she is traveling with her lover, Sir Arthur, she answers in 1883, "Do people travel with their lovers?" (V, 34), but in 1908 she replies, "Do people travel—publicly—with their lovers?" (NYE, XIV, 121). This makes her definitely more knowledgeable about extramarital affairs.

17. Tintner, *Cosmopolitan World*, chap. 8, *passim.*

In 1883 Mrs. Headway reports on her social failure in New York and explains it. "They decided I was improper. . . . I'm very well-known in the West . . . if not personally (in all cases), at least by reputation" (V, 56). This is changed so radically in the 1908 version that there is absolutely no doubt as to what Mrs. Headway was before she came to England: "There are plenty of spicy old women, who settled I was a bad bold thing. They found out I was in the 'gay' line. They discovered I was known to the authorities. . . . I'm known to all classes" (NYE, XIV, 202). This is virtually a confession of prostitution, even though it is uttered in ironical contempt for the validity of the facts. The meaning of "gay" was, at that time, "in *slang* use, of a woman: Leading an immoral life, living by prostitution."[18] The *OED* then gives a quotation from the *Sunday Times* of 1868: "As soon as ever a woman has ostensibly lost her reputation, we, with a grim inappositeness, call her 'gay.' " James is, in no ambiguous terms, stating that in her past Mrs. Headway was a prostitute, which makes her immediately one with the central courtesan in *The Romans of the Decadence* (*LE*, chap. 1).

Another reference to Mrs. Headway as a meretricious woman who sold her body is clear in the addition made in section ten, the final part of the tale, when she pleads for Littlemore to clear her reputation. "She glared at him a little, at this; her face was no longer the face that smiled" (V, 102) becomes, in 1908, "She glared at him a little on this; her face was no longer the hospitable inn-front with the showy sign of the Smile. The sign had come down" (NYE, XIV, 261). The "headway" she makes is by foul as well as fair means. The last line in the story presses the insistence on the fact of her earlier prostitution. After her marriage to Sir Arthur, Waterville "heard from New York that people were beginning to ask who in the world was Mrs. Headway," as the 1883 version has it (V, 110); the 1908 text reads "he heard from New York that people were beginning to ask who in the world Lady Demesne 'had been' " (NYE, XIV, 271). The change of tense here has the force of driving the question back to the heroine's previous reputation, back to something that had taken place in the past, rather than to something taking place in the present. It is fitting that the words *had been,* the last of the story in its revised version, haunt Nancy's future.

18. *Oxford English Dictionary,* see "gay."

"A Kiss Such as They Would Never Receive from a Woman": Henry James's Markings in Zola's *La Débâcle*

From James's private world of his own library, one can gain additional information about his attitude to sex, information seemingly limited to his own eye. Yet books from personal libraries get dispersed, and the privileged person who gains possession of a volume may receive a message unintended for any eye other than that of the man who owned the book originally and who marked certain passages in it. Since James made very few markings in the books he owned, those he did make seem all the more significant.

Of the thirty-six volumes by Émile Zola in Henry James's library, there is only one that has markings by James. They occur in *La Débâcle,* published in 1892. James has written, in pencil in his characteristic handwriting, "178" and under that "478" on the back pasteboard of the volume, and on each of the indicated pages, there are pencil markings. On page 178, there is a vertical line indicating two printed lines of the text. On page 478, there are two crosses on the left margin, indicating the beginning and the end of the passage. The two markings are interesting because of James's appreciation of the main theme of the novel, the defeat of the French army in the Franco-Prussian War at Sedan. It is this particular novel that his 1903 article on Zola pays the most attention to in terms of his feelings about Zola as a novelist. He ends his essay with a long paragraph in praise of *La Débâcle,* though the rest of the essay is concerned with certain failings on the part of Zola.

There James writes about the circumstances in which he read the novel. "I recall the effect it then produced on me as a really luxurious act of submission. It was early in the summer; I was in an old Italian town; the heat was oppressive. . . . I remember that in the glow of my admiration there was not a reserve I had ever made that I was not ready to take back" (*NN,* 63–64). James spent the early summer in Siena visiting the Bourgets for a month after his arrival on June 5, 1892, during which time he probably read *La Débâcle* (*MY,* 321).

What he did not mention in this concluding passage of his essay on Zola is that the great subject of this novel set within the devastating picture of the defeat of the French was the growing love between two young men: one, Jean Macquart, a peasant, the corporal of the 106th squadron of the French army; the other, Maurice Levasseur, a young lawyer, well-educated, who had enlisted. But he makes up for the neglect in public print by mark-

ing privately the passage in which Zola expresses the emotional depths of
that relationship.

The two men begin by resenting each other: Maurice resents the fact that
the man who gives him orders is someone of peasant origin, and Jean resents
Maurice's spoiled and arrogant personality. However, their growing mutual
affection, their increasing interdependence, and their saving of each other's
lives until the unfortunate accident at the end are things that apparently
struck James so forcibly that he was moved to indicate a passage that particularly touched him.

The first marking is early in the book when starvation affects not only the
soldiers but their horses, so essential at that time for the engagement of
men in battle. Jean Macquart sees an African chasseur whose horse is
starved. "The horse's large teeth were making the sound of a grater against
the wood of the ammunition wagon while the African cavalry man wept"
(*LD*, 178; my translation). These lines call attention to the humanistic aspects of Zola's style rather than to his strict naturalism, for here that naturalism is connected with an intense feeling for the horse exhibited by the
horseman. It is Zola's understanding of emotion that James seems to be
calling attention to.

But the second set of markings, on page 478, draws attention to a passage
that exploits the brotherly feelings of the two friends who survive and help
each other in the battle scenes to which the book is devoted. This time the
markings seem to indicate James's homoerotic predispositions:

> In the wood, in the great dark silence of the motionless trees, where they
> heard no sound and where they believed they were saved, an extraordinary
> emotion threw them into each other's arms. Maurice wept violently, while slow
> tears ran down Jean's cheeks. It was the ceasing of their long torment, the joy
> of their telling each other that sorrow was perhaps going to take pity on them.
> They clasped each other in a violent embrace, in the brotherhood of all that
> they had suffered together; and the kiss that they then exchanged seemed the
> sweetest and the most powerful of their lives, a kiss such as they would never
> receive from a woman, immortal friendship, the absolute certainty that their
> two hearts would be only one, forever. (*LD*, 478; my translation)

Ironically, this kiss takes place just before Jean suffers a wound that separates the two friends for months and is responsible ultimately for Jean's
return to Paris after it heals. There, he unknowingly but fatally wounds
Maurice, who is now fighting on the opposite side on the Paris barricades as
a Communard. The novelist has built up his narrative on a succession of

horrors and deceits and on the hunger and the death of loved ones. Finally, after the accidental killing of Maurice by Jean, Paris itself burns. Yet Jean survives with "la grande et rude besogne de toute une France à refaire" (*LD*, 636), with "the great and difficult task of reconstructing all of France."

What we are not sure about is when James made his markings. Was it in 1892 when he first read the volume, presumably in Siena, or in 1903 when he wrote his commemorative essay on Zola? As for the kind of markings used for this passage, Leon Edel wrote that "By the time of Zola he tended to use the crosses on occasion," which might also argue for the 1903 date, later, possibly, than the vertical line marking on page 178.[19]

One thing we are sure of is that the marks are by James: The numbers are in his handwriting and the book was sold by Mrs. Henry James, Jr., to Fabes, a bookstore in Rye. The passage that James marked on page 478 is significant because it calls attention to James's interest in a kiss shared by two men that could never be equaled by a kiss a man shared with a woman. It therefore fits in with the picture we now have of Henry James as a man with strong homoerotic feelings. It also argues for 1903 as the year in which James may have made the marking of the long passage, rather than 1892, because by 1903 he had exhibited his homoerotic attachment to Hendrik Andersen. It was also the year during which he met Jocelyn Persse, someone he loved dearly.[20]

---

19. Communication from Leon Edel to the author, June, 1996.

20. My own curiosity in following through a possible subtext in "The Figure in the Carpet" began when I read Philip Roth's *Zuckerman Unbound* (1981). There, in a fictitious book titled *Carnofsky,* a disguise for his best seller *Portnoy's Complaint,* a book about autoeroticism, Roth refers indirectly to James's "The Figure in the Carpet" and includes a subtext like James's own by having words starting with *p* abounding in the text. Wondering why he did this, I concluded there might be a similarity between Roth's novel and James's story, so I reread the latter through what I thought was Roth's lens.

As for *The Sacred Fount,* its resistance to a meaningful interpretation made me question the narrator's axiom. Was there something wrong with it? Perhaps the phrase "of the opposite sex" was responsible for the narrator's failure to identify the correct couples. How might the omission of this phrase alter the relationships and make the new couplings, now within the same sex, more reasonable? After my article was published in 1995 in *Twentieth Century Literature,* I received an unpublished manuscript by Patrick J. Smith, titled "Gilbert Long's Gay Voice," which made an argument almost identical to mine but which, because my article had anticipated his, was no longer news. However, his work shows that I was not making unreasonable assumptions about what the narrator missed in his unsuccessful researches.

6

The Gissing Phase in Henry James: The Underclass and the "Essentially Unheroic"

In the midst of his immersion in the upper classes and swamped by the novels of adultery spawned by the continental writers, James met, read, and found George Gissing a refreshing reaction to such concerns a few years after the turn of the new century. Stimulated to write about a man deprived of European contemporary education, as Gissing himself had been and as most of his characters were, James, in his last story, "The Bench of Desolation," written in 1909, created the character of Herbert Dodd, a man who fails in his effort to maintain his intellectual gentility. Yet he is finally propped up by the woman who had made the most of his character deficiencies to provide him late in life with a missed cosmopolitan possibility—the kind of possibility that has become an actuality for millions of the same class today. The antihero made so much of in modern and postmodern literature makes a debut in James's twentieth-century prose.

Scholars know that Henry James read three novels by George Gissing (*New Grub Street*, *In the Year of Jubilee*, and *The Whirlpool*); that he wrote a six-page mini-essay on Gissing for *Harper's Weekly* in 1897 but never mentioned him again in his critical works; and that when he finally met him he was very impressed by him. In Henry James's library there were at his death three novels by George Gissing: *New Grub Street*, published in 1891, in three volumes, inscribed on the fly-leaf by Henry James, "George Gissing at Lamb House with H. G. Wells"; *In the Year of Jubilee*, published in 1894; and *By the Ionian Sea*, published in 1901, an autographed presentation copy given to him at the time he met George Gissing himself. The pages are all cut, so we may assume James read those very volumes, all of which are first editions.[1] As is also well known, Wells brought Gissing over to Lamb House to meet James in June, 1901 (*HGW,* 71). There is a letter from James to Wells asking him to post a letter of thanks he had written in gratitude for Gissing's present of "his beautiful book," undoubtedly *By the Ionian Sea.* James wrote that Gissing was "highly sympathetic. . . . But, by the same token, worn almost to the bone (of sadness)." James then asked, "Why *will* he do these things?"—a comment made apropos Gissing's habit of marrying prostitutes (*HGW,* 73). What is more important is that not only did James read him, write on him, meet him, and own his work, but he used him in his own fiction.

It is very striking that aside from *The Princess Casamassima,* where the hero (though brought up as a member of the lowest middle class) is still the son of a duke as well as of a prostitute, we see no tales or novels by James dealing with the lower middle class until after the publication of *New Grub Street* in 1891, which seems to have stimulated three stories. Following his reading of Gissing's novels as recorded in his "London Notes" of 1897, three stories seem to have been affected by the Gissing material. However, it was not until after his meeting with Gissing that he really began to pay attention to Gissing's world in stories of his own, written in 1902. Then, from 1904 to 1909 when he reinforced this influence by his desire to be another Balzac (who had also paid attention to this segment of lower middle-class society), there appear five stories that deal with the lower- and middle-class material, ranging from the suburbs of London, to New York City, to Switzerland, and finally to the invented town, Properley, a seaside resort for the middle classes. The struggle for money and the loss of class position are also implicated in these stories. James has attempted during his last period to borrow some of Gissing's "saturation" in his milieu and in the personalities of characters formed by the social conditions that Gissing knew so well and James did not.

There are therefore four different stages of Gissing stimulation. The first is after James read *New Grub Street* in 1891. Then, for the first time, he wrote three short stories about "grubbing" in London, two of which were published in the following year. "Sir Dominick Ferrand," from 1892, is

1. *The Library of Henry James,* ed. Leon Edel and Adeline R. Tintner (Ann Arbor, 1987), 34.

about a young man and a young woman who grub their way by writing lyrics and songs; they live in a lodging house, typically Gissing in setting. "Greville Fane," also from 1892, deals with a woman from the lower middle class who writes about the aristocracy only for the members of her own class in order to elevate the position of her children, which she does do and for which they do not thank her. In "The Next Time," published in 1895, the hero, Ray Limbert, resembles Reardon, the hero of *New Grub Street,* for he wants to write a book that will be a popular hit, but he can never do it, while his sister-in-law does so every time. The rigors of the living conditions for Limbert's family seem to have been influenced by those in *New Grub Street,* as well as by those of Robert Louis Stevenson's family.

There are other elements in Gissing's novel that would naturally interest James. In *New Grub Street* there is a discussion between Harold Biffen, another novelist, and Reardon on the "art of fiction." Reardon says, "There may surely exist such a thing as the *art* of fiction." Biffen responds, "It is worked out. We must have a rest from it" (*NGS,* 153). This exchange has a historical basis in fact. The entire contemporary literary controversy on the nature of fiction was started by Walter Besant on the occasion of his lecture "Fiction as One of the Fine Arts," delivered at the Royal Institution, on April 25, 1884, followed by a short essay called "The Art of Fiction" by Andrew Lang in the *Pall Mall Gazette.* This was followed by "The Art of Fiction," Henry James's response in *Longman's Magazine* for September, 1884. This, in turn, called forth Stevenson's "A Humble Remonstrance" in the same magazine for December, 1884. All this seems to have contributed to Gissing's manifesto of realism in *New Grub Street.* When Biffen's book is published, one of the "sages," or critics, writes that "a novelist's first duty is to tell a story." A few lines further it occurs again: " 'The first duty of a novelist is to tell a story': the perpetual repetition of this phrase is a warning to all men who propose drawing from the life" (*NGS,* 520). "This phrase" was the burden of Besant's lecture, and it was one of the statements that James, as well as Gissing, challenged in his answering essay.

In Biffen's exposition of his "art of fiction," he says: "What I really aim at is an absolute realism in the sphere of the ignobly decent. . . . I want to deal with the essentially unheroic, with the day-to-day life of that vast majority of people who are at the mercy of paltry circumstance. Dickens understood the possibility of such work, but his tendency to melodrama on the one hand, and his humour on the other, prevented him from thinking of it" (*NGS*, 150–51). He repeats it again: "Dickens goes down only with the best of them, and then solely because of his strength in farce and his melodrama" (*NGS*, 405). When James comes to touch on the problem of the dramatization of "the vulgar" in fiction in 1897 he uses the very concepts of Gissing: "But save under the immense pressure of Dickens we have never done anything so dreadful as to recognise the vulgar. We have at the very most recognised it as the extravagant, the grotesque. The case of Dickens was absolutely special; he dealt intensely with 'lower middle,' with 'lowest' middle, elements, but he escaped the predicament of showing them as vulgar by showing them only as prodigiously droll. When his people are not funny who shall dare to say what they are?" (*NN*, 440).

The second stage of Gissing's influence occurs just after James wrote his "London Notes" for July, 1897, when he had to counteract the hectic atmosphere of London during the Diamond Jubilee by reading a number of novels. These included Gissing's *In the Year of Jubilee* and *The Whirlpool*, from 1897, as well as recollections of *New Grub Street* once more. These "Notes" constitute James's only essay on Gissing. After reading *New Grub Street* he professes "a persistent taste" for Gissing's fiction, "a taste that triumphs even over the fact that he almost as persistently disappoints me." James finds it is "mainly his saturation that makes him interesting . . . in the sense of making him singular." Gissing "reeks with the savour . . . of contact with the . . . lowest middle-class, and that is sufficient to make him an authority— *the* authority in fact—on a region vast and unexplored" (*NN*, 438–39). But James would "wish" Gissing "to go further." Since he "overdoes the ostensible report of spoken words," unfortunately "it crowds out—the golden blocks themselves of the structure, the whole divine exercise and mystery of the exquisite art of presentation" (*NN*, 441). In other words, Gissing lacks form. Then James chides himself for not saying something more positive. "Mr. Gissing's feeling for his subject, a subject almost always distinctly remunerative to the ironic and even to the dramatic mind" must be praised. "He loves the real," which the realist in James liked, and "if he only had distinction he would make the suburbs 'hum.' " James's conclusion is generally positive: "He has the strongest deepest sense of common humanity, of the general struggle and the general grey grim comedy" (*NN*, 443).

We can infer that James was so under the spell of the Gissing novels he had just read and reread that the following month when he continued his "London Notes" for August, 1897, in *Harper's Weekly,* he perhaps unconsciously assimilated a Gissing image, the vision of London as a whirlpool, an image that gave the name to the novel *The Whirlpool,* which James had also mentioned he had read. He is writing not about Gissing but about Paul Bourget's trip to London on his way to deliver a lecture on Flaubert at Oxford just at the time of the Diamond Jubilee when London was jammed with visitors. James realizes that he expresses the situation "but feebly . . . for those at a distance from the edge of the whirlpool, the vast concentric eddies that sucked down all other life" (*NN,* 446).

But what seems to be the direct product of James's perhaps recent rereading of *New Grub Street* is his story "In the Cage," published first as if it were a novel, in book form, in 1898. There, the world of the grocery store with its telegraph dispatch office is investigated through the consciousness of a young woman of the lowest middle class. Her fiancé, Mr. Mudge, is a grocer, and the story probably was suggested by Biffen's novel, *Mr. Bailey, Grocer,* in *New Grub Street.* James measures this world against the upper-class world that impinges on it and examines the contrasts made by the telegraphist and her friend, Mrs. Jordan (who consorts with aristocrats by doing their flowers), with the privileged gentry.

By-products of the Gissing effect on James can be seen in a pair of stories entitled "The Great Condition" and "The Given Case." In "The Great Condition," from 1899, James has taken one of Gissing's characters from *In the Year of Jubilee,* the mysterious Mrs. Damerel. He has, in fact, used her very name and has made *his* Mrs. Damerel suspected of having the kind of equivocal past Gissing's Mrs. Damerel had; that is, she has either run away from her husband and children or has been involved in some domestic faux pas. Actually, in the James story, Mrs. Damerel's suitor, Bertram Braddle, refuses her "condition," namely, that he should marry her first and then she would tell him her secret. Braddle also suspects her of being poor, and he fears some "queer suppressed chapter" in her life. However, the other man who is enamored of her is willing to marry her on her "great condition," though it turns out that there had never been the slightest deviation on her part from normal behavior. She was using her "condition" as the test of both suitors' love. The other story, published in 1898, is "The Given Case," in which a problem Gissing deals with in *In the Year of Jubilee* (if one marries a woman and does not love her, can one leave her?), is made the tale's center but in reverse. The married woman, Mrs. Despard, stays with her husband, with whom she has ceased to have relations, but her friend, who is only engaged, leaves her fiancé and marries another man. Mrs. Despard is jealous of the freedom society gives her unmarried friend and tries to discourage her from using it.

There were things that were intimately involved with James's thoughts and feelings about the art of fiction in Gissing's book, but he seems to have ignored those possibilities for discussion. He went to Gissing only for the "savour" of his milieu and for the characters produced by it. James's use of Gissing material was very idiosyncratic, and his données are never to be confused with Gissing's. James's optimism in every case where he uses some of Gissing's material is in striking contrast to the pessimism of the original. Yet it is not the same kind of optimism that mars the novels of Walter Besant, for here it is based on the freedom of the imagination. For instance, it seems very curious that in James's one dream story, "The Great Good Place," published in 1900, George Dane, a writer harassed by interruptions in his creative work, quotes the children's hymn "There Is a Happy Land, Far, Far Away," so often referred to in Gissing's *Workers in the Dawn*, a hymn to which the child Arthur Golding, sick and "overcome with weariness . . . fell asleep" after his flight to London.[2] In James's story it appears in the same context, only metaphorically, to characterize a fatigued writer about to escape through sleep to a dream world. "Dane sat down to his table and started at his ragged phrase. 'There is a happy land—far, far away!' He chanted it like a sick child" (XI, 17).

The next and third period in which the Gissing influence seems to assert itself occurs just after Wells brought Gissing over to James's house in Rye in June, 1901, at which time Gissing most probably presented him with *By the Ionian Sea*. Two stories by James emerge from this period. The first, "The Papers," written from 1901 to 1902 and published in 1903 handles *New Grub Street* material in the Gissing manner. The opening page introduces us to the Fleet Street atmosphere of starvation, uncertainty, and the ensuing feelings of bitterness that are experienced by the young journalist, Howard Bight (the name repeats the initials of the novelist Harold Biffen),

2. Hymn No. 608, by Andrew Young, in *The English Hymnal* (London, 1973), 437.

who is truly a Gissing character. "The Papers" in one sense can be considered James's *New Grub Street*, with the desperation of an unsuccessful journalist somewhat modified. James makes it tolerable to himself by disguising it as a fable based on *As You Like It*, just as the Fleet Street atmosphere is a correction of or a variation on Gissing.[3] Although he does somewhat mimic the pessimism of Gissing's characters, the young people's "measure of their detachment, their contempt, their general irony," given "in respect to the conditions of their life" (XII, 13), they escape upward and outward, not downward. They don't starve, unlike Gissing's characters, for like the characters in *As You Like It*, they still can afford to be always eating. The connection with Shakespeare's play may even have been inspired by its performance featured in Gissing's *Our Friend the Charlatan*, a book that had just appeared in 1901. If James's hero is "sardonic," he is only "softly" so. He is more like Jacques than Biffen, "railing" against society but able to detach himself without self-destruction and, in addition, borrowing the romantic lineaments of Orlando.[4]

"The Papers" was written along with another story, "The Birthplace," whose hero, Morris Gedge, is even of a lower middle-class origin, but he is equipped with the sensibility of a "gentleman." The latter story was published during the same year, 1903. Morris Gedge is a small-town ex-librarian and inheritor of the curatorship of the museum of the great "Bard." His wife, of a somewhat lower-class origin, with fantasies of moving up a notch to the position of the housekeeper of a castle, causes him trouble, but she is the mere shadow of one of the lower-class wives in Gissing's life and stories. She phrases their advantage in getting the job of the care of the museum in terms of language ("We're refined. We know how to speak" [XI, 407]), the lack of which ability is the great drawback in the lower middle-class climb upward. One remembers in *New Grub Street* Mrs. Yule's defects in that direction and Alfred Yule's care that his daughter Marian will not make the same mistakes in the usage of language. Mrs. Gedge adds: "We know the difference between realities and shams. We hold to reality," which reminds us of Biffen's speech about telling the truth in writing. Here, however, Morris Gedge adds a Jamesian modification. "Allow that we hold also

3. Adeline R. Tintner, *The Book World of Henry James* (Ann Arbor, 1987), 28–33.
4. See *ibid.*, 32.

a little to the romance" (XI, 407). He would pay attention to his wife "if she were such a wife as you!," he tells lovely, upper-class, educated Mrs. Hayes, the wife of the rich young American who understands Gedge and his problems as the curator of a museum in which there are no real data to work with. In the crisis scene Gedge's wife appears "like a woman of the people" (XI, 461). Her husband is more or less like the men described at the beginning of chapter 8 in *New Grub Street*, "men with unpresentable wives" (*NGS*, 106). Morris's triumph depends on letting his art, his rhetorical skill, service a role that his sense of reality tells him is a sham. A Gissing character would not do this and still get the author's praise for it. Morris's compromise is redeemed in James's eyes because he has made it into art. When James wants to give a parallel in pictorial art to the situation Gedge finds himself in, he chooses a genre painting lithographed for mass distribution. "The three . . . had the effect of recalling to him . . . a sentimental print, seen and admired in his youth, a 'Waiting for the Verdict' . . . or something of that sort; humble respectability in suspense about humble innocence" (XI, 464), recalling the famous print by Abraham Solomon.

A fourth wave of Gissing influence came in James's final spurt of creativity when he returned to England in 1905 after his trip to the United States. His lecture "The Lesson of Balzac" had focused his great desire to go down in history as an American Balzac. But as he had not paid as much attention to the lowest rungs of the social ladder as his French model had, he was compelled to make up that deficiency if he wished to be another Balzac. It is not without interest that Mrs. Despard, in the earlier story "The Given Case," has the same name as a recurrent character in Balzac's *Comédie humaine*, Madame d'Espard, a woman of the world who tried to control the behavior of her women friends very much the way James's Mrs. Despard did hers. It is possible even in 1898 that James thought that a fusion of Gissing material with Balzac material would thicken his own data. He went now, therefore, again to Gissing, the one writer in English who was "saturated" with that material. The title character of "Julia Bride," the short story written soon after his return home, apes Constance Bride, of *Our Friend the Charlatan*, though unlike Gissing's finally independent heroine, Julia wants yet fails to get a husband to raise her to a position of social security and therefore fails in life completely. Money as a necessity for class location is as desperately sought for in James's story as in any tale by Gissing, and to the basic plot of a Dickens novel, he adds some flavor from Dickens' finest critic, George Gissing.

In *The Finer Grain* stories, published in 1910, James tells us in the publisher's blurb he wrote himself that "the series of illustrations" for the "predicaments" arising in each story "considerably ranges: from Paris to London and New York, and then back again, to ambiguous yet at the same time unmistakable English, and ultra-English, ground."[5] This proclaims his attempt at doing an *Étude de Moeurs*, or *Scènes de la vie de province* à la Balzac, a *Comédie humaine* in miniature. If we examine the stories, we note that there are merely two English tales in the suite, but they both tap the Gissing vein. "Mora Montravers" is James's conversion of *The Whirlpool*, where he substitutes Wimbledon for Pinner and where Mora Montravers finally avoids the suburban fate that destroys Alma Rolfe. The story, thoroughly Jamesian, is seen through the sensibility of Sidney Traffle, the suburban aesthete who counteracts "the sense of decency" of his wife Jane by "perfunctory aesthetic rites." The words *vulgar* and *refined* occur as often as they do in a Gissing novel. The location of the suburbs is a twentieth-century scenario.

Although James does not, as Biffen does, "aim at . . . an absolute realism in the sphere of the ignobly decent" (*NGS*, 150) but aims only at getting at the "savour," he gets closest to the Gissing type in "The Bench of Desolation." The basic plot structure of the tale is so close to that of the final episode in *Isabel Clarendon* from 1886 that it is difficult to think that James in this story involving an obviously Gissing character had not paid attention to the one Gissing novel that has struck some readers as an imitation made only five years after the publication of James's novel of *his* Isabel, *The Portrait of a Lady*. In the last chapters of *Isabel Clarendon*, Bernard Kingcote is saved by his friend Gabriel and put in charge of a bookstore in a small town. Mrs. Clarendon on a visit to him invites him to her room at the local hotel at the tea hour and offers him her fortune as restitution for what he had considered her failed love. This he rejects. In James's tale Herbert Dodd, a lower-class bookseller in a small resort town, is also visited by Kate Cookham, a woman who has caused him irrevocable tragedy and who has invited him to have tea with her at the local hotel. There she, too, offers

5. E. V. Lucas, *Reading, Writing, and Remembering* (London, 1932), 184–85.

him a fortune as restitution, only in this case the money, cleverly invested, had originally been legally extracted from him because of his breach of promise to marry her. Unlike Kingcote, James's hero accepts the woman and her money. In spite of the transposition in the plot, Herbert Dodd, the weak, ruined hero, is the out-and-out Gissing man. The word *vulgar* appears in Dodd's thoughts on the second line, and we come across it nine more times before we have finished the fifty-page story. The bitter fight between man and woman starts the tale. The "gage of battle" in the war between the sexes is thrown down in the first paragraph, and the question is of a breach of promise suit that this weak man could have challenged and probably would have won, had he not been a coward. The word *sordid,* a Gissing word, occurs here, too. Kate Cookham, the heroine of James's tale, is at heart a twentieth-century feminist.

Herbert Dodd was one of "five scattered and struggling children," living "in the back room above the shop," like Gissing himself. He is "over-re-fined," and "it would all have been because he was, comparatively, too aris-tocratic" (XII, 375–76). His instinctive taste in women is low, for the pretty girl whom he married, "had, it was true, forms of speech, familiar watch-words, that affected him as small scratchy perforations of the smooth surface from within." This sentence seems to show a sympathy with and an under-standing of Gissing's contradictory sexual drives. But Dodd rationalizes his choice. With "her regular God-given distinction of type, in fine, she couldn't abide vulgarity much more than he could" (XII, 379). However, Kate Cook-ham is the villainess who becomes a heroine, for she comes back as a "real lady"; she is now "refined" (XII, 393). The amount of money she has made for him from what she forced from him attracts him in his "pauperized state." She made money for him because of her "hatred" of what she should be doing to him. She adds, "It made me work" (XII, 424). Herbert Dodd is controlled by the contradictions between his refinement, his love of beauty, and his need to be bolstered by a strong woman, the typical Gissing double-bind.

In his "London Notes" James had criticized Gissing for an abuse of what he called "the blight of the colloquy," or dominant dialogue, which ends in a failure, using almost Bergsonian terms to give "the sense of duration, of the lapse and accumulation of time" (*NN*, 441), a fault, he adds, that Balzac never had. James himself would correct this flaw in Gissing in his own story of Herbert Dodd, a member of the lowest middle class who leads what seems to be an endlessly monotonous life. In this James is following Biffen's prescription for "honest reporting," and "the result will be something unutterably tedious": "Precisely. That is the stamp of the ignobly decent life." James, in "The Bench of Desolation," proves himself an apt pupil of Biffen in reproducing the tedium of Dodd's life. Herbert at first belongs to "the relatively poor (who are so much worse off than the poor absolutely)," a phrase from *New Grub Street* (*NGS*, 151) repeated again in the same book ("in poor homes, most of all where the poverty is relative" [*NGS*, 133]). Herbert had been able to ape the educated classes through his private reading, his selling of books, and his discussion of those books with customers of a more thorough education than his own. He has taken on the "grim grey comedy" of Gissing's novels.

These sudden late appearances in James's work of stories centering on the lower and lowest middle-class people must be considered a tribute to George Gissing, whom he saluted as "*the* authority . . . on a region vast and unexplored" (*NN*, 439), testifying to a refreshing new interest on the part of an author who had spent a lifetime of writing about the upper middle class. It is through the works of Gissing that James in the twentieth century was led back to the classics of lower middle-class English life by George Crabbe. It is in "The Bench of Desolation" that Gissing is put into that tradition of English literature that included Crabbe and Charles Lamb among its few numbers. They were the writers from and of the lower middle class whom James, using again his technique of cluing in the reader to his models, brings into his tale by a reminiscence of a sale Dodd had made to a woman of "a set of George Crabbe; largely, he flattered himself, under the artful persuasion of his acute remarks on that author, gracefully associated by him . . . with a glance at Charles Lamb as well" (XII, 395). It is to Crabbe that he directs the reader, and the set of Crabbe Dodd sold to his customer was like the set James himself owned, the collected works of eight small volumes containing all the author's poems of village life and death in the heart of England.[6] His interest in Crabbe is shown by the books about him James had in his library. They included the memoir by his son with annotations by

6. *The Life and Poems of the Reverend George Crabbe and His Letters and Journals and His Life by His Son* (8 vols.; London, 1836).

Edward Fitzgerald, as well as Alfred Ainger's *Crabbe* in *The English Men of Letters* series published in 1903 (close to the publication of "The Bench of Desolation").[7] Crabbe's home town was Aldeburgh (today spelled Aldeborough), "a pleasant and quiet watering place on the coast of Suffolk" that "began to be known for its fine air and sea-bathing about the middle of the last century," possibly the model for Properley, the sea resort in James's tale. Crabbe himself sent his poem *The Library* to a Mr. Dodsley, a bookseller, whose name is embedded in the name of James's bookseller Mr. Dodd, probably based on details he would have read in the books cited above. Crabbe's own life seemed as doomed as Herbert Dodd's, for his wife became deranged and died early. He was plagued by digestive troubles. His poem *The Borough*, a portrait of ruined people, is painted with closely observed psychological detail.

After Crabbe died in 1832, Fitzgerald championed him, and it is through his letters, in which he constantly refers to Crabbe, that James was at this time directed to Crabbe. James owned the volume of Fitzgerald's letters to Mrs. Kemble from which a quotation about "October Day" seems likely to have been the germ for a part of the relationship between Herbert Dodd and Kate Cookham. Fitzgerald writes: "I am positively looking over my everlasting Crabbe again: he naturally comes in about the Fall of the Year. Do you remember his wonderful 'October Day' "?[8] He is referring to part of "The Maid's Story," one of the *Tales of the Hall* about a young woman who is beloved by a younger son who has to make his fortune.[9] She has ideals about her lover. Years pass, and the lover comes back a middle-aged man, "A travell'd man, and as a merchant dress'd / . . . A head of gold his costly cane display'd / And all about him love of gold betray'd."[10] This encounter, like the encounter between Herbert Dodd and Kate Cookham, to whom he had been engaged many years before, is also set "On a certain October Saturday," the autumn mood repeating Crabbe's. Kate Cookham returns like the suitor in "A Maid's Story": She has become "a real lady: a middle-aged person, of good appearance and of the best condition," and the cane

7. *The Library of Henry James*, ed. Edel and Tintner, 19.
8. Edward Fitzgerald, *Letters to Fanny Kemble* (London, 1895), 55.
9. *The Life and Poems of Crabbe*, VI, pp. 284–86.
10. *Ibid.*, 286.

is replaced in James's version by "a small and shining umbrella" (XII, 390). Dodd's resistance to this transformed Kate Cookham corresponds to the young woman in Crabbe's poem. "They parted lovers, both distress'd to part! / They met as neighbours, heal'd, and whole of heart: / She in his absence look'd to heaven for bliss, / He was contented with a world like this." The girl is in a dilemma, for she "fear'd the love, and would the lover shun."[11] She explains to her sister, "This is a man the naughty world has made, / An eating, drinking, buying, bargaining man— / And can I love him? No! I never can." However, he soon "overpower'd her soft timidity; / Who, weak and vain, and grateful to behold / The man was hers, and hers would be the gold; / Thus sundry motives, more than I can name, / Leagued on his part, and she a wife became."[12]

If this poem be translated in reverse, we get some explanation for the plot-turn that takes place in James's tale. Allowing Kate Cookham to be the man in this case, she returns mature, worldly and rich, while Herbert Dodd, who is first revolted by her offers to take care of him after he and his family have so suffered, in his weakness and timidity in the end accepts her financial and psychological help. One feels that James adopted the psychology of these people of depressed lives to which he had been directed probably through Fitzgerald's correspondence and, most of all, through his recent reading of Gissing.

But in addition, the twentieth-century James has perhaps used Gissing the person in his characterization of Herbert Dodd in "The Bench of Desolation." Gissing's psychoneurotic attraction to prostitutes, evidenced in his stealing for one of them as an adolescent at school—an act that led him to marry not one but two prostitutes in succession, both drunkards and at least one an insane woman, who dragged him into penury and disadvantaged him as far as middle-class privileges and education were concerned—played into James's interest in abnormal human types. Herbert Dodd is not the same kind of masochist that George Gissing was, but masochist he nevertheless is. And his form of masochism works in beautifully with Kate Cookham's particular form of sadism. His lack of normal response to her breach of

11. *Ibid.*

12. *Ibid.*, 287. See Adeline R. Tintner, "Some Notes for a Study of the Gissing Phase in Henry James's Fiction," *Gissing Newsletter*, XVI, No. 3 (1980), 1–15.

promise suit and his passive acceptance of the conditions of life she imposed on him because of this suit pronounce him to be a man pathologically timid. But the final act of permitting himself to be gathered up by his oppressor and restored to the kind of life she had deprived him of by her original threats makes the reader aware that this man has been psychologically damaged and that his actions, such as they are, must be measured by the yardstick of abnormal behavior. The reader at the end of the story must ask himself the same question that James asked Wells about Gissing's consistently masochistic behavior: "WHY does he do such things?" As Herbert Dodd does these things, too, we are forced to think, after knowing about Gissing's life and James's reaction to the events in that life, that Gissing has been the source of the characterization of the fictive hero.

7

Crime and the Criminal as Artist

James's Pre-War Loosening Up: The Aristocracy of Crime

While the next chapter is mainly devoted to World War I and to James's release from repression, it is enlightening to see how his interest in crime and the criminous find their place in this part of his life just before and during World War I. His enthusiastic friendship with William Roughead, the historian of Scottish trials, needs to be seen from this perspective, not as a distraction or a relief from thinking about the daily agonies of the war, but as being integrally related to James's basic anxiety and concern for the future of European civilization. After 1900, his own interest in the criminous could be appeased by reading the collected crime trials by William Roughead, and his fourteen letters to Roughead show his intense interest and passion for such recountings.

The new century saw James write a tale in 1900, "The Third Person," about a lady who inherits a house lived in by one of her smuggling ancestors. She repeats his crime in miniature by smuggling in a Tauchnitz volume from Paris in order to lay his ghost to rest. He had "wanted some bold deed done, of the old wild kind; he wanted some big risk taken" (XI, 168), and she takes it. "Even the highwaymen of the same picturesque age were often gallant gentlemen" in spite of their crimes; "therefore a smuggler, by such a measure, fairly belonged to the aristocracy of crime" (XI, 152).

Interest in the criminal was shown in strange, surreptitious ways in the fiction James wrote after 1904. In "Julia Bride," his heroine, in a stressful period of her life that will end in disaster, is compared to Nancy from Dickens' *Oliver Twist,* engaging in thievery with Bill Sykes, and, like Nancy's fate, Julia's downfall is created by a bunch of liars. Her golden Basil French will never be won as a husband, and, like Nancy, she will die from the knife thrust, a metaphoric one it is true, by Murray Brush and his fiancée. The metaphor produces the atmosphere of Dickens' criminal world, which specializes in corrupting and training juveniles to be thieves and even murderers. James resurrects the Dreyfus case in "Mora Montravers," where Mora has created a similar case and a similar furor about her guilt or innocence. As in the Dreyfus case, it is here a case of resurrecting the scene of the murder of justice.

In "The Bench of Desolation," Kate Cookham is guilty of virtual murder when she reduces Herbert Dodd's wife and children to such a level of poverty by her financial demands on the faltering Dodd that they die. Yet she herself is a great success, and Herbert finally opts for allowing himself to be saved by the woman who ruined his life. Here the criminal is the heroine.

The princess of such beauty and high birth in "The Velvet Glove" is really nothing better than a prostitute, since she will bestow her favors on the narrator, John Berridge, if only he will praise her book. She is morally part of the underworld, the criminal, illegal classes. In "A Round of Visits," the story opens on thoughts about the cousin who has embezzled money from the main character, and it closes on the suicide who embezzled funds from so many others. Yet here the man who commits suicide, Newton Winch, has become refined by his criminality.

These characters created early in the century seem to anticipate the tremendous enthusiasm shown later in his letters written to William Roughead from 1914 to 1915, as well as the praise he bestowed on the murderers whose trials Roughead had sent him. The tales show his tendency in this direction, even before the war allowed him to release his repressed antagonisms. Although in *The Princess Casamassima,* Hyacinth's mother had murdered his father, the Duke, and in *The Other House,* Rose had murdered a small child, these murders were never condoned; the murderers were not praised, and as they were evildoers, their evil had to be punished. But after 1904 the murderer is praised. The criminal has seduced James's imagination.

The relation between James's interest in the violent crimes of murder, along with his extended correspondence and friendship with William Roughead in the early part of 1914, and his violent public patriotic activities during the early years of World War I can best be explained in terms of his mounting depression and ultimate release from repression. James seems to have been fascinated by criminals because they acted out their violent impulses. His were repressed, and when World War I broke out, his sense of violence expressed itself in his hatred of Germany, in his renouncing his United States citizenship, and in his love and care of so many soldiers. Through these activities, he was released from his own repression, and he no longer needed to read the history of such a cold-blooded criminal as Madeleine Smith, who, in getting away with her murder, satisfied James's need to punish society and not the criminal.

Yet criminous types and their crimes had appeared earlier in James's fiction. His very first story was about a murderer, a woman who mistakenly has her lover killed instead of her husband. In 1867, in "My Friend Bingham," the hero is a murderer through error, not intention. Because of his mistake he kills a child and tries to atone for it. Georgina, of "Georgina's Reasons" from 1884, is a criminal who allows her child to die of neglect after she commits the crime of bigamy, and we are not to admire her. Then there are the suicides of the 1880s: Agatha Chasemore, in "The Modern Warning" from 1888, who avoids her brother's anger by killing herself, and Hyacinth Robinson, the suicide in *The Princess Casamassima*, as well as Grace Mavis of "The Patagonia," who kills herself to avoid an unwanted marriage and to revenge herself on the lover who rejects her. These aggressive impulses make those who experience them turn against themselves. In regard to the suicide, Sigmund Freud tells us that the "murderous impulses against others are redirected upon himself."[1]

The close relationship between murder and Henry James seems to have been intuited by two modern murder mystery writers, Michael Innes (J. I. M. Stewart) and Amanda Cross (Carolyn Heilbrun), for James reappears in their mysteries frequently. Their familiarity with James and his work depends in their cases on their profession, that of the teaching of English literature. But even those like Agatha Christie, who had no such excuse, seem to have read carefully James's chapter in *The Whole Family*, the composite novel of 1907. When Christie has Hercule Poirot say in *The*

1. Sigmund Freud, *Collected Papers*, (4 vols.; London, 1942), IV, p. 162.

Mystery of the Blue Train, "To know when to stop. Ah! That is the art!," we recognize immediately the sensible advice of Charles' wife Lorraine to her difficult husband, "Stopping, that's art!" (*WF,* 167).[2]

James and the Criminous: "Not Guilty, but Don't Do It Again"

One cannot deny that James's intense interest in murder trials in his seventieth year, evidenced in the fourteen letters he wrote to William Roughead, the Scottish jurist and historian of crime, seems very peculiar. The crimes Roughead recorded took place in an earlier generation, yet Thomas Carlyle and George Eliot took a very different attitude toward the case of Madeleine Smith, which was contemporary with them. James's aesthetic attitude and delight in Madeleine as a person are expressed in the very intense figures of cannibalism that animate one of the letters he wrote to Roughead. But even as early as 1908, we find in Theodora Bosanquet's diary, while she was acting as typist for James, that James had an intense interest in crimes, specifically in the local Wood case:

> Mr. James made no remark this morning! I went to tea at the Bradley's and met several folks—a Mr. and Mrs. Fuller Maitland, and a Mr. Taylor—the latter told a rather nice story *re* Mr. James who has been immensely interested in the "Wood" murder case, and during a walk with Mr. Taylor went into all the details of it and convinced him that Wood *had* murdered the girl. Then they met old Mr. Dawes and Mr. James eagerly asked him what he thought of the verdict. "Well," said Mr. Dawes, "I never thought they'd *convict* him"— whereupon Mr. James fled away saying "I ought to have remembered that poor old Dawes has softening of the brain!"[3]

Note the curious fact that in February of 1905, during his American trip, James wrote to Henry Adams, "But I spent yesterday a.m. in Independence Hall with Weir Mitchell & the p.m. with 3 or 4 select murderers in the Penitentiary. Yet I *hadn't* murdered W. M."[4]

2. Agatha Christie, *The Mystery of the Blue Train* (1928; rpr. New York, 1940), 177.

3. Theodora Bosanquet, "Diary," January 7, 1908 (Ms. in Houghton Library, Harvard University).

4. Henry James to Henry Adams, February 1, 1905, Massachusetts Historical Society.

In his own fiction, James had a limited number of murders in relation to the large number of stories and novels he produced. It is true that his first story was a murder story, "A Tragedy of Error," written in 1864 when he was twenty-one, in which a woman has her lover, instead of her husband, killed by mistake. In 1877, in *The American,* the French noblewoman, Madame de Bellegarde, murders her husband. In addition to crime in *The American,* only in one novel, *The Other House,* is there a real murder, when a woman drowns a little girl. Two years later there is an equivocal murder, depending on acceptance of Freud's concept of unconscious murder, when the governess hounds poor Miles into a heart attack in *The Turn of the Screw* in her unconscious desire for him or his uncle. Unconscious aggression seems to be involved earlier in these murders or quasi-murders. But the kind of comments that James makes to William Roughead in the letters he wrote to him gives evidence of a very peculiar and special kind of reaction to the Scottish murder trials that took place earlier in the century. James's late epistolary style included certain exaggerations, but the type employed in these letters indicates an excess of terms of devouring and gorging on the criminal anecdotes and accounts. He refers to his "open appetite," in the very first letter, "for more such outstanding material in which you may be moved to bite or at least to make *us* bite" (RO, 251–56). He wants *"quantities,* handsome stores of crime," and more of "the strange twelve Scots trials" that Roughead had sent him. James is happy he has "earned [his] cake." This supports him in "crying for another slice or two" (RO, 251–56).

Four days after this letter, James immediately replies to Roughead's answer. He says that he prefers "comparatively modern crime stories, for there the *special* manners and morals become clearly disclosed." He wants more light on three of the murderers. He awaits the trial of Mary Blandy. He talks of the Arran murder he read in the book Roughead sent him and specifies what he admires in this case, "some strange unidentified element in the so prompt association, on a chance meeting, of the victim and the destroyer—as if the silly clerk had been somehow hypnotized" (RO, 252). Roughead's son, who edited the volume, quotes what Billy James wrote to him after reading these letters. "The special significance . . . lies for me, in the revelation of Uncle Henry's interest in the individual character or personality. His tales are constructed around and about the personalities of his 'people'—unlike those of some other eminent writers who sacrifice their people to their plot" (RO, 252). This does not, however, seem to explain the cannibalistic form or James's interest.

In letter three, James is aghast at the "unspeakable King's figure" (RO, 253). He prefers, instead of this historical tale, more modern trials, "the dear old human and sociable murders and adulteries and forgeries in which we are so agreeably at home" (RO, 254). In letter four he still awaits Mary Blandy. When in letter five he has received the material in which her trial is presented, he expresses his enthusiasm in cannibalistic terms once more:

> I devoured the tender Blandy in a single feast; I thank you most kindly for having anticipated so handsomely my appetite . . . History herself having put it together as with the best compositional method, a strong sense for sequence and the proper march, order and *time*. . . . one wants to know *more*, more than the mere evident supplies—and wants it even as in this case one feels that the people concerned were after all of so dire a simplicity, so primitive a state of soul and sense, that the exhibition they make tells or expresses about all there was of them. . . . the light would throw itself on the Taste, the sense of proportion of the time.

He claims he wants to hear more of Blandy and Dr. Pritchard: "*There*, perversely, I am all for knowledge. Do continue to feed in me that languishing need" (RO, 256). Every number of *The Juridical*, a periodical devoted to crime, he read with interest, and he continued to use the metaphors of eating up and devouring these tales. In relation to the Oscar Slater case, he writes, "But this is a loaf of bread on the shelf for you in the vivid hereafter! I shall probably then not be there to partake of it—which exactly makes me glad of every crumb at present!" (RO, 259).

After reading the *Report of the Trial of Madeleine Smith*, which Roughead presented to James (Figures 30 and 31), the latter wrote that his eyes were so "attached to the prodigious Madeleine" that he couldn't put it down: "I have read your volume straight through, with the extremest of interest and wonder. It represents indeed the *type* perfect case, with nothing to be taken from it or added, and with the beauty that she precisely *didn't* squalidly suffer, but lived on to admire with the rest of us, for so many years, the rare work of art with which she had been the means of enriching humanity" (RO, 260–61). The verdict in her case was the curious Scottish one of "Not Proven," which could be and was interpreted colloquially as "not guilty, *but don't do it again!*" This comparison of the perfect crime case with a rare work of art, expressed in this quasi-parodic form as well as quasi-criminal terminology, is not unique with James. Thomas De Quincey expressed it as well in "Murder Considered as One of the Fine Arts," and the sculptor Constantin Brancusi is quoted as saying, "A work of art ought to be made like a perfect crime," adding "without a spot, without a sign of the author."[5]

However, as Roughead points out, a true crime story has its rhythms controlled by a criminal act, and, after that takes place, by the apprehension of the criminal, either the right one or the wrong one. The art of the criminal investigation and its results intrigued James, as well as the art of the criminal, either in the execution of his crime or in his forensic skills.

"It is hard to account for the spell which even to this day Madeleine Smith unquestionably casts upon her votaries. Hers was an unlovely nature: false, self-centered, wholly regardless of the rights and feelings of others, so far as these conflicted with her own desires; and her treatment of her blameless suitor, Mr. Minnoch, was flagrantly perfidious." Her special "points" included her "amazing correspondence . . . her equally astounding courage, coolness, and seeming unconcern in a situation fraught with such danger and disgrace."[6] James wondered what Madeleine Smith thought of the sheer artistry of her case after her trial and when she lived as a married woman far from her native Scotland. For Henry James saw her as himself: he, too, had a secret, but his secret was not the kind that the criminal had. Freud has distinguished between the secret of the criminal, who has a secret that we don't know but that he knows, and the secret of the hysteric, who has a secret that we don't know and that he himself doesn't know either. Henry James saw the criminal as knowing his own secret, and so he was attracted to him and felt he could learn from him.

The Slater case was also one in which James was interested, for he mentions it twice in his letters to William Roughead. It is a case that would appeal to him because in a way it had many features that resembled the Dreyfus case. The apprehended murderer, Oscar Slater, was a German Jew who, on no evidence, was convicted by a jury of brutally murdering an old

5. Communication from Sidney Geist to the author, September, 1993.
6. William Roughead, *Classic Crimes* (London, 1951), 105–106.

woman without having robbed her of her many valuable jewels. When Trench, the policeman investigating the case who is interested in justice, tries to rectify the conviction, he is broken by his superiors, very much as Picquart had been victimized by his army superiors in the Dreyfus case. Trench also is arrested on trumped-up charges and dies. After eighteen years in prison, Slater gains the attention of Sir Arthur Conan Doyle, and in 1928 he is freed. But the criminal himself was not apprehended because the witnesses who lied at the beginning of the case would not come forward with the truth.

Roughead's collection of murderers exhibits men and women who have such an exaggerated sense of their own selves that they have no fear of death, neither when they impose death on their victims nor when they have to pay for their crimes with their lives. This conceit and enlargement of their egos may have meant to Henry James an extraordinary lack of fear of death, the facing of death without tremor, the almost complete denial that death exists, though these were not religious people.

James's twentieth-century interest, before he discovered Roughead's collections, in the criminous and in criminality shows itself in his "A Round of Visits," where Newton Winch becomes refined through having become a thief and a criminal. James's interest in crime and in those acting out crimes can also be seen in *The Ivory Tower,* in which Horton Vint (close in name to Winch) also will turn out to be a thief who steals from his best friend. "A Round of Visits" begins with a character portrait of a criminal, Phil Bloodgood, who "handsomely faced" the hero (XII, 429). "It was *because* he was so beautifully good-looking, because he was so charming and clever and frank . . . that one had abjectly trusted him" (XII, 429); and "it's the horror of *his* having done it, and done it to *me*" (XII, 430). The traitor and criminal thus enters the first round of the seven rounds of the tale. Newton Winch, a "pale, nervous, smiling, clean-shaven host had undergone since their last meeting some extraordinary process of refinement . . . some principle of intelligence, some art of life [that] would discernibly have worked in him." At college he had been "common . . . coarse" and now he appears "as if he had suddenly and mysteriously been educated." He now has "fine fingers" (XII, 444). Monteith asks, "what force had it turned on, what patented process, of the portentous New York order in which there were so many, had it skilfully applied?" (XII, 445). Mark Monteith enjoys here "the oddest intensity of apprehension, admiration, mystification" (XII, 445). Winch then asks Monteith about himself, and in doing so he "was simply writing himself at a stroke . . . the most distinguished of men" (XII, 446). And crime has been the cause of Winch's refinement.

Although the war was to mobilize James's pent-up feelings and energy, his fascination with Roughead's report on the trial of Dr. Pritchard was mixed with these feelings and continued through the war. In an introduction to "Dr. Pritchard Revisited," Roughead writes:

> I remember going to lunch with Mr. Henry James at his charming rooms in Cheyne Walk, Chelsea, on an April day of 1915. I recall the windows open to the river, the slow-passing barges, the soft spring sunshine; the gracious atmosphere of amenity that was the peculiar setting of his genius. He greeted me in friendly wise with one hand laid lightly on my shoulder while enveloping me in a flowing and embroidered robe of welcome; his other hand held a volume of an aspect to me painfully familiar. "I am reading, you see," he sociably observed, "one of your books—Pritchard." "I'm sorry it's that one," I ruefully protested, "for it was my first, and is, I hope, my worst." "Well," came the bland rejoinder, "perhaps it *is* . . . less mature than your later work." Thus, all genially, and generously, was I let off.[7]

Mary Blandy's cool behavior at her death takes second place. She prepared in her cell a false account to mislead future generations. Roughead sees her as a heroine by James. "If only she had been the creation of some great novelist's fancy . . . imagine her made visible in the exquisite medium of Henry James's incomparable art" (RO, 216).

James's nephew saw his uncle's interest in crime as evidence of his great interest in human personality. But James himself saw a work of crime, a successful crime, as a work of art, and this concern is repeated by Agatha Christie, a great reader of James, in one of her characters. Justice Wargrave in *And Then There Were None,* published in 1939, describes his desire to be an "artist in crime," even though he was a judge. "I have wanted—let me admit it frankly—*to commit a murder myself*. . . . I was, or could be, an artist in crime! My imagination, sternly checked by the exigencies of my profession, waxed secretly to colossal force. I must—I must—I *must*—

7. *Ibid.,* 240.

commit a murder! And what is more, it must be no ordinary murder! It must be a fantastical crime—something stupendous—out of the common!"[8]

The passionate involvement with crime as evidenced by these startling letters written to William Roughead would have interested Freud when he wrote about Fyodor Dostoyevsky's sympathy for the criminal, and his remarks might have shed some light on Henry James's deeper psychology.

> The criminal is to him [Dostoyevsky] almost a Redeemer, who has taken on himself the guilt which must else have been borne by others. There is no longer any need for one to murder, since *he* has already murdered and one must be grateful to him, for, except for him, one would have been obliged oneself to murder. That is not kindly pity alone, it is identification on the basis of similar murderous impulses—in fact, a slightly displaced narcissism. . . . This may perhaps be quite generally the mechanism of kindly sympathy with other people, a mechanism which one can discern with especial ease in this extreme case of a guilt-ridden novelist.[9]

Was James also guilt-ridden, and of what crime did he believe himself guilty? His avoidance of the Civil War, in which his two younger brothers served and suffered may be the secret of James's passionate outbursts in World War I and his identification with Walt Whitman with his activities of nursing and caring for the wounded young men of his own war.

8. Agatha Christie, *And Then There Were None* (New York, 1939), 186.

9. Sigmund Freud, "Dostoefsky and Parricide" (1927), in *The Standard Edition of the Complete Psychological Works of Sigmund Freud,* ed. James Strachey, with the cooperation of Anna Freud (24 vols.; London, 1961), XXI, p. 190.

8

Henry James and World War I: The Effect of the War on James's Writing

James the Propagandist: World War I and the Release from Repression

Few people know that James, the writer of fiction concerned with the private lives of civilized people, spent the last fourteen months of his life, from the fall of 1914 to December of 1915, when he became terminally ill, writing war propaganda. But this propaganda was written only as Henry James could write it, from deep convictions and in his customary complex style. What happened to this writer of the "unnewspaperized" elite (to use his term) to make him give his last energies to publicize the British war effort of World War I?

Two factors are probably responsible for this departure from James's usual terrain. The first contains two aspects, both connected with James's youth and the American Civil War fifty years before. The first part (of the first aspect) is connected with what James called his "horrid even if an obscure hurt," a mysterious back or groin injury sustained while the young James helped put out a fire just at the outbreak of the Civil War—an injury that eliminated him from military service. Because of it, he seems to have carried a burden of guilt, and his earliest stories, written in the 1860s and early 1870s, show how heroes who are not combatants lose their girls to active officers, colonels or doctors, in the Northern Army. As late as 1886, his novel *The Bostonians* presents a northern woman envying her southern cousin's active participation in the Civil War. She fights it over again for the love of a young woman whom she loses to the Southerner. It was only late in 1913, after almost forty years of living on English soil, that by writing his autobiographical volumes, *A Small Boy and Others* and *Notes of a Son and Brother*, James could, at the age of seventy, partially analyze himself and partially relieve himself of that guilt—a guilt that seems to have kept his back bothering him most of his life. Telling the reader that his "obscure hurt" had actually made him feel one with the Civil War soldiers who were wounded in battle, he says he could not decide "whether his ache came most from one's own poor organism . . . which had suffered particular wrong or from the enclosing social body, a body rent with a thousand wounds and that thus treated one to the honour of a sort of tragic fellowship" (*AU*, 145).

This writing out of his "hurt" in *Notes of a Son and Brother*, published a few months before the outbreak of World War I, helped rid him of many inhibitions, so that he was finally able to participate in another war as far as a man of seventy could. When the guns of August, 1914, boomed, Henry James was ready to enlist, and enlist he did in the only kind of war front that London could offer him. So excited was he by the rape of Belgium and France that his desire to become physically and actively involved made him, in the fall of 1914, the natural choice for the chairman of the American Volunteer Motor-Ambulance Corps. It was for this organization that he undertook his first propagandistic writing. His pamphlet published in 1914 was written as a letter to the editor of an American journal explaining the function of the corps. It urged Americans, in a fairly straightforward way, to send young men with resources on hand to help with the wounded at the front. But James's propaganda would always be couched in a Jamesian style. He wrote that the service offered by these American university men would represent "true social quality, sympathy, ingenuity, tact and taste." He asked for volunteers with cars to help with the removal of the wounded from the field of battle. "Carried mostly by rude arts, a mercy much hindered at the best, to the shelter, often hastily improvised, at which first aid becomes possible for them, they are there, as immediately and tenderly as possible, stowed in our waiting or arriving cars, each of which receives as large a number as may be consistent with the particular suffering state of the stricken individual" (*WR*, 66). This is a good sample of Jacobean propaganda, pointed at an elite readership.

James had shown signs of self-propaganda in 1910 in writing his own dust-jacket copy for his collection of late tales, *The Finer Grain,* for the English Methuen and Company publication in London—a blurb of fourteen lines and three sentences. James's *Notes on Novelists* (Figure 33), published after the war began in October, 1914, carries a dust jacket with a legend that reads like a James paragraph, also comprising three sentences but one line longer than the dust jacket for *The Finer Grain* (Figure 32). Following his pamphlet for the American Volunteer Motor-Ambulance Corps he "gave" his interview, published in the New York *Times* Sunday Magazine Section for March 21, 1915. With it, he broke his lifelong taboo against such personal exposure. He had briefly broken it for the New York *Herald,* on October 2, 1904, when a young woman armed with a letter from Scribner's arrived at Chocorua. "He stipulated, however, that she must send him no clippings." He told her that "one's art is his expression . . . not one's person" (*MA,* 241). But as he explains in the New York *Herald* interview, he reconciled his ethical standards by maintaining his aesthetic predispositions. He did this by writing the New York *Times* interview himself. His typist reported that he said to her, "no one would suspect that the interviewed dictated the whole interview."[1] The interview, recently republished in Pierre A. Walker's edition of *Henry James on Culture* in 1999, is a brilliant piece of James's late style, which, because it is propaganda with its object to attract contributions of men and money from our then-neutral country to the American Volunteer Motor-Ambulance Corps, is divested of the ornamentalism and obscurity usually encountered in James's later fiction. Although it is straightforward exposition, because it is a dialogue, it contains colorful colloquialisms and digressions as well as a candidly expressed attitude to interviews (Figures 34 and 35).

After a short introduction, the interview begins: " 'I can't put,' Mr. James said, speaking with much consideration and asking that his punctuation as well as his words should be noted, 'my devotion and sympathy for the cause of our corps more strongly than in permitting it thus to overcome my dread of the assault of the interviewer, whom I have deprecated, all these years, with all the force of my preference for saying myself and without superfluous aid, without interference in the guise of the encouragement and cheer,

---

1. Manuscript in author's collection; Leon Edel verified the corrections in ink as being by Henry James himself.

anything I may think worth my saying.' "[2] James speaks glowingly of the members of the corps:

[They are] moved . . . by that of the altogether exceptional chance opened to them of acting blessedly and savingly for others, though indeed if we come to that there is no such sport in the world as so acting when anything in the nature of risk or exposure is attached. . . .

The pretension to smashing world rule by a single people, in virtue of monopoly of every title, every gift and every right, ought perhaps to confound us more by its grotesqueness than to alarm us by its energy; but never do cherished possessions, whether of the hand or of the spirit, become so dear to us as when overshadowed by vociferous aggression. How can one help seeing that such aggression, if hideously successful in Europe, would, with as little of time as possible, proceed to apply itself to the American side of the world, and how can they therefore not feel that the Allies are fighting to the death for the soul and the purpose and the future that are in us for the defense of every ideal that has most guided our growth and that most assures our unity? . . .

English life, wound up to the heroic pitch, is at present most immediately before me, and I can scarcely tell you what a privilege I feel it to share the inspiration and see further revealed the character of this decent and dauntless people.

The last four words were quoted by Winston Churchill during World War II, and Ernest Hemingway, too, incorporated into *A Farewell to Arms* parts of the following passage where James comments on the horror of "enormous facts of destruction" in battle:

The war has used up words; they have weakened, they have deteriorated like motor car tires; they have, like millions of other things, been more overstrained and knocked about and voided of the happy semblance during the last six months than in all the long ages before and we are now confronted with a depreciation of all our terms, or, otherwise speaking, with a loss of expression through increase of limpness, that may well make us wonder what ghosts will be left to walk.

Sheldon Grebstein writes that in chapter 27 of *A Farewell to Arms*, Hemingway shows the influence, or "corroboration," of James's passage: "I was al-

2. Preston Lockwood, "Henry James First Interview," New York *Times*, Sunday Magazine Section, March 21, 1915, *passim;* recently republished in *HJC*, 138–45.

ways embarrassed by the words sacred, glorious, and sacrifice and the expression in vain . . . and the things that were glorious had no glory. . . . Abstract words such as glory, honor, courage, or hallow were obscene beside the concrete names of villages. . . ."[3]

During 1915, James wrote a dozen articles, a record for the last seventeen years of his life.[4] Among those, only three or four could be considered non-propaganda. Although certain of his war effort essays were gathered into a volume to be published after his death as *Within the Rim*, named after the title of the introductory essay, one sees in it no compromise between his ethical motivation and his vaunted interest in aesthetic form. Regardless of its propagandistic thrust, it stands on one's bookshelf chronologically next to *The Sense of the Past* and *The Ivory Tower*, both posthumously printed in 1917 and both works of fiction. James believed in the "sacred cause," but he also believed that everything he wrote should come up to the most stringent formal standards. The metaphors in these essays are as original and brilliant as any in *The Golden Bowl*, especially in the introductory essay.

Of the 1915 writings, James published the majority in American daily newspapers and two in London journals. Two days after he received his British citizenship on July 26, 1915, he sent a passage quoting a statement of his reason for so doing through his agent, J. B. Pinker, to the London *Times*. With the passage he included an unpublished letter, now in the Yale University library, from which I quote: "I not only haven't, as I say, any objection at all to its being made public, but quite desire that this should be the case—for the sake of what I feel as the good example!"[5] The war indeed made James throw over his previous stand on public statements. Now he, this essentially private person, exhibited himself for the great cause of the war.

Let us come to the second part of the first reason for his involvement in the war; the Civil War memories of James's youth that pushed him into his late war phase were connected with a visit he made at the beginning of the Civil War to wounded and depressed soldiers when he was eighteen years

3. Ernest Hemingway, *A Farewell to Arms* (New York, 1929), 184–85; Sheldon Norman Grebstein, *Hemingway's Craft* (Carbondale, Ill., 1973), 206–207.

4. *A Bibliography of Henry James*, ed. Leon Edel and Dan Laurence (3rd ed.; Oxford, 1982), 354, reprinted in *HJC*, 159–60.

5. Communication, Leon Edel, 1989.

old, a memory resurrected in *Notes of a Son and Brother.* This memory, as he wrote fifty years later in *Within the Rim,* came back as soon as he visited the Belgian refugees, who had penetrated even to Rye, his country house town, and with it came memories of Walt Whitman's visits to the wounded. This poet undoubtedly was his model for this behavior late in his life, and one feels sure that since the editions of Whitman's poetry, among them *The Wound-Dresser,* and other books about Whitman were on James's library shelves, they must have been reread by him at the time of his propaganda essays.

The second reason for James's exposing himself and his feelings to public scrutiny was his growing homoeroticism, which becomes apparent to anyone reading his letters to the young men he was attached to after 1897: the sculptor Hendrik Andersen, Jocelyn Persse (from 1903 on) and Hugh Walpole (from 1909 on), as well as earlier letters to Morton Fullerton and Arthur Christopher Benson. Whether or not James was conscious of his erotic focus is not a question to speculate on here, but we can say that his behavior as someone susceptible to male attraction became expressible and socially justified during this wartime situation. The ability to experience satisfaction in the sublimated level of visiting wounded soldiers in hospitals in London, his continual caring for them far beyond the call of duty, and the psychological satisfaction derived from this activity are apparent in his letters to his friends.

In addition, the young university men from Harvard, Yale, and Princeton who were active in the American Volunteer Motor-Ambulance Corps made his contacts with attractive young men permissible and valuable for a writer whose sexual tastes were finally asserting themselves through the layers of repression. The discipline of his writing had helped him keep such desires under control. For all writing, as Derrida has asserted in his articles on Freud, involves repression.

In his piece "The Long Wards" James speaks of "the high average of the beauty and modesty" of the British private soldier, which affects him "as probably the very flower of the human race" (*WR,* 109). In his letters he tells of taking a soldier, "a young attractive person whom I fished out of a hospital" to see "my dentist." He puts up for the night a young postman from Rye. He writes to Wilfred Sheridan on August 7, 1915, that "the town simply bristles with soldiers and for the most part extremely good-looking ones" (LU, II, 513). Given this evidence of James's luxuriating in the company of multitudes of attractive young men, it is interesting that at the outbreak of the war James stopped writing fiction. His repression was gone. Although he did try to work on his novel *The Sense of the Past,* it remained unfinished. With that stoppage, he no longer paid attention to meditation and to luxuriating in his consciousness. He was "acting out." His visits to the wounded and his chairmanship of the ambulance committee finally culminated in his naturalization as a British citizen. The real climax, however, was his receiving the Order of Merit medal bestowed on him while he lay dying after his final strokes in December and January. These acts show that in his last years of life his satisfactions were very different from the ones that we would have expected he had had throughout his life. The war, apparently, acted as a successful catharsis or self-analysis, which he had begun in his confessions in *Notes of a Son and Brother.*

The sense of power he achieved from these wartime activities may explain his last dictations to his typist while he was delirious, dictations in which he presented himself as a general and as none other than the greatest, Napoleon. One of these dictations involves an actual battle scene. Perhaps the one writer who understood this part of James was Gertrude Stein, who wrote of him as if he had been a general in her *Four Americans.*[6] She sensed his desire for power, to which for one thrilling last year of his life he could get closer by wielding his pen as if it were a sword.

His desires in this direction can be easily seen in the fifty-seven remarkable letters written during this war year collected by Percy Lubbock in Volume II of *The Letters of Henry James,* published in 1920, themselves a body of personally expressed war propaganda that have been supplemented by an additional twenty-three letters in Volume IV of James's letters edited by Leon Edel, brought out in 1984. These eighty letters are a record of James's actions and reactions to the terrible, yet at the same time for him thrilling, adventure of the war. Almost every letter reveals this duality of feeling: his response, on the one hand, to the awful threat that the war posed to the civilized world he had been writing for and, on the other hand, to the great release it was giving to his repressed homoerotic instincts and his yearnings for "risk" in life. He was proving Freud's thesis that war makes

6. Gertrude Stein, *Four in America* (New Haven, 1947), 119–59.

man to a certain extent regress back to his primitive instincts. A premonition of this came after James's initiating self-analysis in his autobiographical books of 1913 and 1914, for he developed an appetite for crime stories, a taste we have already seen in the letters he wrote to William Roughead, the criminologist and editor of murder trials—letters that extended through June, 1915, and exhibited an enthusiasm that astonished even Roughead himself for its unusual intensity. That primitive love for violence was now satisfied by the horrors of war. James was no longer merely a spectator at the murder trials of Mary Blandy and Madeleine Smith; he was a participant in mass murders.

The letters after August 10, 1914, combine this interest with his horror of war as if his primitive and his civilized natures were coexisting in a kind of pleasurable harmony, a harmony facilitated by his ability to "act out" his instincts through his war activities. In them he sees the pleasure in the adventure of war as well as the horror that the writer of civilized society par excellence could feel, both operating simultaneously. He writes to Edith Wharton, "And most thrilling & uplifting are you . . . to my imaginative sense."[7] The word *thrilling* occurs often in James's wartime letters. He writes to Mrs. Thomas Sergeant Perry, "Not, however, that there isn't a thrilling and uplifting side to it . . . which makes unspeakably for interest, makes one at hours forget all the dreadfulness and cling to what it means in another way" (LU, II, 422).

Again on October 25, 1914, James writes, "I at least feel and take such an interest in the present activity . . . that the whole effect is uplifting and thrilling and consoling enough to carry one through whatever darkness, whatever dismals" (LU, II, 432). He writes to his friend Edmund Gosse, "I don't think . . . I only feel and feel and *toujours* feel about the war—feeling so in Wordsworth's terms of exaltations, agonies, & loves."[8] Freud's analysis was that war is palatable and enjoyable because it brings back the sense of adventure to life—a sense that is lost when there is no risk. James writes to Edith Wharton, who was working on the French front, "I myself have no

7. Henry James to Edith Wharton, October 2, 1914, in *Henry James and Edith Wharton: Letters, 1900–1915*, ed. Lyall H. Powers (New York, 1990), 305.

8. Henry James to Edmund Gosse, December 17, 1914, in *Selected Letters of Henry James to Edmund Gosse, 1882–1915*, ed. Rayburn S. Moore (Baton Rouge, 1988), 305.

adventure of any sort equal to just hearing from you of yours—apart I mean from the unspeakable adventure of being alive in these days."[9]

The "Front" in London was not the "Front" in France, and James had to savor and enjoy the real battle-sense through his friends. He confesses to another friend, "How the sense of your impressions . . . excites my poor little private eye. I can live too, thank God, by my friends' experience, when I hang about them in imagination" (HJL, IV, 713). One tale current at the time is the anecdote about James meeting Mrs. Wharton for lunch. Bursting into her room, with "his great eyes ablaze," he cries, "My hands, I must wash them!" He continues: "My hands are dripping with blood, all the way from Chelsea to Grosvenor Place I have been bayoneting, my dear Edith, and hurling bombs and ravishing and raping. It is my daydream to squat down with King George of England, with the President of the French Republic and the Czar of Russia on the Emperor William's belly, until we squeeze out of it the last irrevocable drops of bitter retribution."[10]

He sees the loss of the beautiful young men in nature itself and engages in the pathetic fallacy when he writes to a friend about the loss of a tree, broken by a storm. He refers to the tree as a "him," as if it were also a male war casualty. His interest in society wanes. "I can't . . . look at a solitary new face save that of the wounded soldiers in hospital whom . . . I find of great and touching interest" (LU, II, 451).

One is reminded of Walt Whitman's The Wound-Dresser when James writes of "the irreparable loss of what is most precious, the inestimable seed of the future" (LU, II, 451). As an antidote against despair, he cultivated his feelings, for he wrote to a friend that that way is the only way to live "at this terrible pressure." Yet again, the great adventure of the war, the thrill of it, finds him advising Hugh Walpole in Russia to play "the immense adventure . . . up to the very notch. . . . Return in fine reeking with an experience" (HJL, IV, 751). It was an occasion to put into real motion what his hero in The Ambassadors, Strether, had told Little Bilham, "live all you can." He also sees the war as "the most prodigious affirmation of the energy and ingenuity of man ('however misplaced'!) that surely can ever have been in

9. Henry James to Edith Wharton, May 23, 1915, in James and Wharton Letters, ed. Powers, 342.

10. Simon Nowell-Smith, The Legend of the Master (New York, 1948), 166–67.

the world," and he thanks his friend, the Honorable Evan Charteris for his impressions of "that night visit to the trenches" and for giving him "more of the sense and the smell and the fantastic grimness, the general ordered and methodised horror" than anyone else (LU, II, 452).

His sense of living *now* is something he writes about repeatedly at this time. To his sister-in-law, Alice James, he writes, "It is a great experience. I mean the whole process of life here is now—even if it does so abound in tragedy and pity, such as one can often scarcely face" (LU, II, 466). To Mrs. Wharton he writes, "I unutterably envy you these sights and suffered assaults of the *maxima*—condemned as I am by doddering age" (LU, II, 468).

James's last piece of writing was his preface to Rupert Brooke's *Letters from America*. It took the form of a memorial to the young poet, who had just died as a war casualty, and it took its place next to James's recently published tribute, in 1915, to Alan D. Loney (an American volunteer for the Motor-Ambulance Corps who perished on the *Lusitania*), which appeared in September, 1915, in the New York *Times*, written to encourage Americans to volunteer.[11] The memorial to Rupert Brooke, published one month before James's death, epitomizes all the aspects of Henry James's wartime personality.

Although he wrote a serious tribute to the young poet, he also showed how this praise could be converted into a piece of propaganda. In war propaganda everything is exaggerated to the end of the reader's being inflamed to patriotic action. James's late tendency to hyperbole in his fiction makes this propaganda seem genuinely sincere. It is the result of James's desire for an all-out effort for the war cause, accentuated and motivated by his feelings for the young Rupert Brooke. In fact, this exaggeration tends to make him give too much praise to a young poet who was perhaps more gifted in his personal beauty and in the way he died than in what he contributed to the tradition of poetry.

The preface itself is a kind of poem to a beautiful dead poet as surely as Whitman's *Drum-Taps* is a poetic tribute to the dead soldiers of the Civil War. In a sense, James's death was to echo Brooke's as he describes it, for though Rupert Brooke had been "young, happy, radiant, extraordinarily

11. *A Bibliography of Henry James,* ed. Leon Edel and Dan H. Laurence (Oxford, 1982), 354.

endowed," he had "met a soldier's death, met it in the stress of action and the all but immediate presence of the enemy" (*LA*, xiii), yet he did not die on the battlefield. What chiefly attached James to Brooke and allowed him to make him a symbol useful for wartime propaganda is that "Rupert expressed us *all*, at the highest tide of our actuality" (*LA*, xiii).

James's sublimated homoeroticism now engages in a nostalgic view of the time at Cambridge when he first met Brooke among the group of undergraduates who had invited him to speak. "If one liked him . . . one liked absolutely everything about him, without the smallest exception." There enters a mythic quality about this memoralizing phrase. Sketching the blessed and lucky life that the young Brooke had led, James summarizes: "It was into these conditions . . . that the War came smashing down" (*LA*, xxxi).

But the climax of James's tribute to the dead young poet is when he puts him even above Byron, for Byron was the poet and person whom James had said he would rather have met than anyone else who had distinguished himself in the history of the civilized world from 1760 to 1830. Brooke was even superior to Byron, James tells us in this preface, because he had not "quarreled with the temper and the accent of the age" (*LA*, xiii). Yet he is linked with Byron, for he is connected in "the final romance," with "the isles of Greece," where both were buried. Rupert now "rests at the heart of all that was once noblest in history" (*LA*, xiii), and James's propaganda, in which he mythologizes the young poet whose beauty had so stirred him, exists as James's final word on the war, on the beauty of young men, and on his own climactic service as a soldier in his own terms. The emotional intensity of James's last piece of prose owes a great deal to its propagandistic aim and should be judged in the light of its role as propaganda.

In 1886 James had put into the mouth of Olive Chancellor of *The Bostonians* words that probably expressed his own deepest feelings. She felt for her southern cousin, Basil Ransom, "a kind of tenderness of envy for one who had fought and offered his own life even if on the wrong side, for the most sacred hope of her nature was that she might someday have such a chance, that she might be a martyr and die for something."[12] This, too, must have been Henry James's "most sacred hope," and in a way it came true. During the tightly packed last year of his life, he lived the way he never had

---

12. Henry James, *The Bostonians* (London, 1886), 13.

before and died as if on the battlefield, decorated with the Order of Merit virtually on his deathbed and acknowledged by his adopted country as a hero.

The Effect of the War on James's Writing

Henry James's two wars affected his literature. His earliest signed tale, "The Story of a Year," is the story about the Civil War, and in another earlier but unsigned story the young suitor who does not go to war loses the girl to an army officer. In a third tale, a wounded officer loses the girl to a doctor. The struggle for a girl in *The Bostonians* is between a Northerner, Olive Chancellor, and her southern cousin, Ransom, and this time the Northerner loses to the South. So, too, World War I affects the few creative pieces James wrote during that period. The unfinished *Middle Years*, the third volume of the autobiographical trilogy, dictated during the autumn of 1914, includes the war in its opening metaphor: "Youth is an army, the whole battalion of our faculties and our freshnesses, our passions and our illusions, on a considerably reluctant march into the enemy's country, the country of the general lost freshness; and I think it throws out at least as many stragglers behind as skirmishers ahead—stragglers who often catch up but belatedly with the main body, and even in many occasions never catch up at all" (*AU,* 547).

In an essay that James wrote called "The Founding of the 'Nation,' " recollections of the "fairies" that attended the birth of the periodical, published in the July 8, 1915, issue of *The Nation* in commemoration of its fiftieth anniversary, he writes that he has a certain amount of difficulty in writing about the situation because his "difficulty comes from the sense that to turn from our distracted world of to-day to the world of the questions surrounding . . . the cradle of the most promising scion of the newspaper stock . . . is to sink into a social lap of such soft, sweet material as to suggest comparatively a generally beatific state" (*EL,* 177). In the essay on Mr. and Mrs. Fields in both the *Cornhill* and the *Atlantic Monthly* of July, 1915, we find that the essay starts as follows:

> If at such a time as this a man of my generation finds himself on occasion revert
> to our ancient peace in some soreness of confusion between envy and pity, I

know well how best to clear up the matter for myself at least and to recover a workable relation with the blessing in eclipse. I recover it in some degree of pity by reason of the deep illusion and fallacies in which the great glare of the present seems to show us as then steeped. . . . We really, we nobly, we insanely (as it only can now strike us) held ourselves comfortably clear of the worst horror that in the past had attended the life of nations and to the grounds of this conviction we could point with lively assurance. (*EL,* 160)

The invasive content of the war appears also in the revision James made of his article "The Art of Coquelin," which appeared in the January, 1887, issue of *Century Magazine.* Brander Matthews, the professor of drama at Columbia University, wanted James to reprint it as a preface to one of the small series of books printed by the dramatic museum of Columbia. On February 2, 1915, James wrote to him that he shouldn't think James has a more continued interest in the theater than he is conscious of: "I am only now, and in a deeply obscured and discouraged way, interested in the drama—which is in our conditions so very different a thing."[13] He, of course, is referring to the drama of the war, which was going on on his side of the Atlantic. Actually, he does revise the text, and in it (which has nothing to do with the war at all), he could not help but include the present war and his feelings about it in a figure of speech. He discusses the quality of Coquelin's voice which "by so intimately connecting him with his characters, connects them inevitably with each other and shuts them up together as prisoners of war, so to speak . . . shut up in their ring fence."[14] His metaphors derive from the war. The war determines his matter and his point of view; it is the substance of life that shows itself in every bit of writing after August 10, 1914. Another invasion of the spirit of the war, though indirect, occurs in the same essay. James is talking about the fact that Coquelin is sometimes criticized for being "always the same Coquelin." He adds, "what it really points to, I suppose, is the infallibility and punctuality of the great artist's method, the fact of its always reporting his observation and his experience; just as the postman always delivers his letters he starts out his round with. The letters are various, but the postman remains the postman."[15]

13. Allan Wade, *The Scenic Art* (New Brunswick, N.J., 1948), 218.
14. *Ibid.,* 205.
15. *Ibid.*

James brings in this image of the postman because the postman was an important part of his wartime experience. He clearly sat waiting for letters from the young men at the front or from someone like Hugh Walpole, who was in Russia, or from any of the young men to whom he was bound in affection.

In addition to these appearances of references to the war made in his letter writing, James allows himself to produce types of essays written for the newspapers, which was an activity he never could condone in his pre-war years. He writes a letter to *The Observer*, he writes an obituary in the *Times* for a young man who was part of his ambulance corps in his capacity as chairman of the corps. He allows himself to be interviewed for the first and only time and takes upon himself, just in case he would be misrepresented, the writing of the entire interview as we have Miss Bosanquet's report of it.

The obituary, in memory of Alan Loney, who perished on the *Lusitania*, includes some very colorful, well-written paragraphs describing this heroic young man who gave his life in the service of Britain, an American who was, as James wrote, "a recruit to the wonderful modern band of those who swing from America to Europe and back, as the liveliest of matters of course, on any suggestion of the hunting field or the regatta . . . his fondest exercise was the chase, toward which pursuit he maintained in Northamptonshire one of the best known heavyweight stables in England."[16]

Although Henry James in 1913, in his first letter to William Roughead, complained about the fact that his library held too little of the kind of crime literature that Roughead was now supplying him with, there were on his shelves plenty of books about war and revolution. First, there were many volumes on the French Revolution, including Gabriel Lenôtre's four volumes on the revolution and Empire, including *Les Massacres de septembre*, published in 1907, which means James was buying these books a few years before World War I broke out. He paid attention to the novels on war, especially *La Débâcle* by Zola, on which I have commented earlier; it echoes his interest in the comradeship among men. There are certain volumes in James's library by Pierre Loti that concentrate on war, such as *Les Derniers*

16. Henry James, "Allen D. Loney—In Memoriam," New York *Times*, September 12, 1915, Sec. 1, p. 2; reprinted in *HJC*, 159–60.

Jours de Pékin, which tells about the sadness of the results of war. It is interesting that certain works written from about 1892 to the end of the century came late into James's library. This fact fits my theory that he was gradually loosening up and preparing for his autobiographical volumes, which would release the primitive elements in him and stimulate his interest in murder and warfare.

Index